YORK CASTLE PRISON

YORK CASTLE PRISON

THE HISTORY OF YORKSHIRE'S COUNTY GAOL

GARETH VERNEY

PEN & SWORD
TRUE CRIME

An imprint of
Pen & Sword Books Ltd
Yorkshire - Philadelphia

First published in Great Britain in 2026 by
Pen & Sword True Crime
An imprint of
Pen & Sword Books Ltd
Yorkshire - Philadelphia

ISBN: 978 1 03619 805 3
ePub ISBN: 978 1 03619 806 0
PDF ISBN: 978 1 03619 807 7

A CIP catalogue record for this book is available from the British Library.

Typeset in INDIA by IMPEC eSolutions
Printed and bound in England by CPI Group (UK) Ltd, Croydon, CRO 4YY

The Publisher's authorised representative in the EU for product safety is Authorised Rep Compliance Ltd., Ground Floor, 71 Lower Baggot Street, Dublin D02 P593, Ireland.
www.arccompliance.com

For a complete list of Pen & Sword titles please contact

PEN & SWORD BOOKS LIMITED
47 Church Street, Barnsley, South Yorkshire, S70 2AS, England
E-mail: enquiries@pen-and-sword.co.uk
Website: www.pen-and-sword.co.uk

or

PEN AND SWORD BOOKS
1950 Lawrence Rd, Havertown, PA 19083, USA
E-mail: uspen-and-sword@casematepublishers.com
Website: www.penandswordbooks.com

MIX
Paper | Supporting responsible forestry
FSC® C013604
FSC www.fsc.org

Contents

Introduction

Each morning, then, at five o'clock,
The adamantine doors unlock;
Bolts, bars, and portals crash and thunder;
The gates of iron burst asunder;
Hinges that creak, and keys that jingle,
With clattering chains, in concert mingle.

This is how the poet James Montgomery described waking up in York Castle Prison in 1795. Those who visit the site of York Castle today may gain insight into life within the prison through displays at York Castle Museum. Perhaps they have attended a trial in progress at York Crown Court or even been unfortunate enough to be on the wrong side of the law in court. However, for many, the idea of the site being a prison is a shock, given the grandeur of the buildings that still stand and the openness of the surrounding area. It is, therefore, no surprise that it is hard for many to even imagine the site as a prison, let alone understand its evolution or what life might have been like for prisoners and staff who lived and worked there. However, this level of detail will be of particular interest to those discovering the prison through the Castle Museum, who would like to know more, as well as to those with a keen interest in the local history of York or those who have discovered a 'black sheep' in their family that was once incarcerated here.

The history of York Castle is fascinating, from Roman burials, through its medieval heyday as a fortress, and even into its modern heritage focus. However, it is the site's history as the county gaol for Yorkshire that is perhaps its most evocative legacy. Yet the county gaol itself is understudied, despite one existing in every county in England. Often reduced to a location in someone's story, the county gaols are usually mere footnotes in history. Yet they have fascinating histories themselves. Growing and functioning over centuries with thousands of men, women and children coming through their walls for serious crimes, for debt, or for political reasons. They were some of the most important buildings in their respective counties and a centre for administrative functions. Often originally situated in castles, such as York, Lincoln, Lancaster, Norwich or Oxford castles, which were themselves dominating and oppressive buildings, the importance of the county gaol on people's lives should not be overlooked. Yet, with the modernisation of the justice system and the facilities that contained them, the functions of county gaols became dispersed by the late nineteenth and early twentieth centuries, relegated to the footnotes of history that we often see.

What made county gaols so important to their respective counties? They were essentially extensions of royal power into the heart of every county in England. Here, it was the king's justice that would be carried out. Most notably, it would be felons who would be brought to a county gaol for trial. Those who would face a death sentence if they were found guilty. It is these prisoners that are often the most well-remembered visitors to the county gaol. The most populous part of a county gaol, however, would be reserved for debtors, those who owed money through borrowing, gambling, having business interests go wrong, etc. However, a county gaol would also see the king's justice carried out on those who committed treason, as well as political prisoners and prisoners of war. But a county gaol was not just about prisoners; it also included court facilities to try these criminals. These courts would also serve as centres of administration for counties, where monarchs were proclaimed on behalf of the county or elections were held to elect MPs to Parliament. These were the most significant buildings in their counties. However, with them now relegated to footnotes in history, how do we go about studying somewhere like York Castle?

By examining the disparate archives that contain records of the prison, newspapers from the time, and first-hand accounts, such as those of James Montgomery, we can piece together a picture of what life would have been like for prisoners here. We can get an insight into the system of county gaols that operated throughout England until the 1900s. Studying York Castle provides the perfect opportunity to examine the evolution of the county gaol over several centuries. How they evolved and changed, and why they were at the forefront of the justice system for so long. Hopefully, the reader will find the stories within this text enlightening on what a county gaol was like and how it fitted into the broader British justice system.

To create a comprehensive account of York Castle Prison, we will examine two key areas: the buildings that comprised the prison and the conditions found within it.

We will discover that the changes to the buildings at York Castle often reflected significant shifts in prison conditions and their use. This lets the reader imagine and understand what the prisoners would have seen at York Castle. Additionally, the site's history allows the reader to see the changes in the use of York Castle throughout the ages, from when the prison was a small part of the castle through to when it dominated the site, ultimately leading to the destruction of most of the original castle.

Prisons have never been intended to be a pleasant experience, and the further back you go, the worse it appears to have been. We must approach several themes to give an idea of life within these sites. Firstly, we need to examine the position of York Castle Prison and county gaols within the prison systems of Great Britain. Secondly, how changing laws, in turn, changed the lives and fates of prisoners. Finally, we need to examine the conditions of the prison and what life was like inside its oppressive walls. In doing this, we must also remember the lives of those men and women who ran the prison and how their lives intersected with those of the incarcerated, shaping the identity of York Castle Prison. Altogether, this should bring together a picture of what someone would go through when they entered the walls of York Castle, for whatever reason that might be.

Ultimately, with any project of this scale, biases inevitably creep into the work, whether consciously or not. The population of prisons throughout history was predominantly male, and as such, many of the more famous, well-publicised and well-recorded stories are also inherently male dominated. During the Victorian period, approximately 17 per cent of the incarcerated population was women.[1] However, most of these were short custodial sentences at local prisons, so the number of stories to choose from is limited. That is not to say that women are not well represented in the stories covered here; in fact, there are a lot, but the majority are, by necessity, men. Similarly, LGBTQ+ histories only tend to raise their head when it comes to punishment and execution when these characteristics were considered crimes and, as such, are vastly under-represented here, as are records of ethnic minorities, or at least ethnicities are rarely noted if they are present. Research is needed in these areas, but it falls outside the scope of this book's aims.

As the county gaol for Yorkshire, York Castle Prison was the venue for trials of those who committed the most serious crimes. With this in mind, the reader should expect many of the crimes listed here to be serious, violent and sometimes unsettling. As such, there is also a bias towards execution being the punishment delivered for many of the crimes talked about here. The majority of those held at York Castle Prison had different fates, predominantly being debtors or having their death sentence commuted to something like transportation. However, the most serious crimes often prove to be the most interesting for the reader and the best-recorded offences, especially in newspaper archives.

Having navigated through the disparate source material, the endless newspaper archives and stories of life within York Castle Prison that have been left to us to compile this book, it is hoped that, by the end of this book, the reader will have a thorough understanding of how York Castle developed into a prison, the system that shaped it and the experiences of those incarcerated within. Ultimately, it will be clear that the site of York Castle is significant, not just for Yorkshire but for the nation.

Chapter 1

The Site of York Castle Prison, 1068–1705

Walls of Wood

To understand the history and development of York Castle Prison, we need to start by looking at its origins as part of York Castle. Many county gaols and assize courts were placed within royal castles, which tended to be located in important cities within their respective counties. The castle was already a sign of authority and something to be feared. In addition, the defences that kept an enemy out would also prove helpful for keeping prisoners inside.

Before getting into details, it is important to acknowledge the limitations of understanding the prison during its earliest period. These issues come from the disparate sources we must work with. On the one hand, York Castle and the prison contained within were important enough to be mentioned by many sources from the period. On the other hand, we are not given detailed descriptions, so the exact layout of the buildings is still an educated guess. Instead, we are left to make our best interpretations from small snippets of evidence. With these limitations in mind, what exactly do we know?

There has been activity on this site for nearly 2,000 years. Archaeological evidence suggests that it was a Roman cemetery. After the sixth century, the site became a cemetery again, but it was likely also used for housing at times.[1] However, after the Norman Conquest the site acquired the functionality that has come to define its historical significance.

The castle originates in 1069, through the Norman Conquest and the Normans' attempt to establish a base of control in the north. Yet the castle as it was built is not the huge stone construction we know today. This early castle was constructed, like many others, from wood. It may have been covered in lime plaster, like at Old Sarum, making it white/grey in colour, but no direct evidence of this has ever been found. The wooden construction made the castle quick to build, a necessity for controlling a recently conquered population.

The design was a typical Norman motte and bailey castle. The castle's main keep, the most crucial part of the castle, was built on a mound or

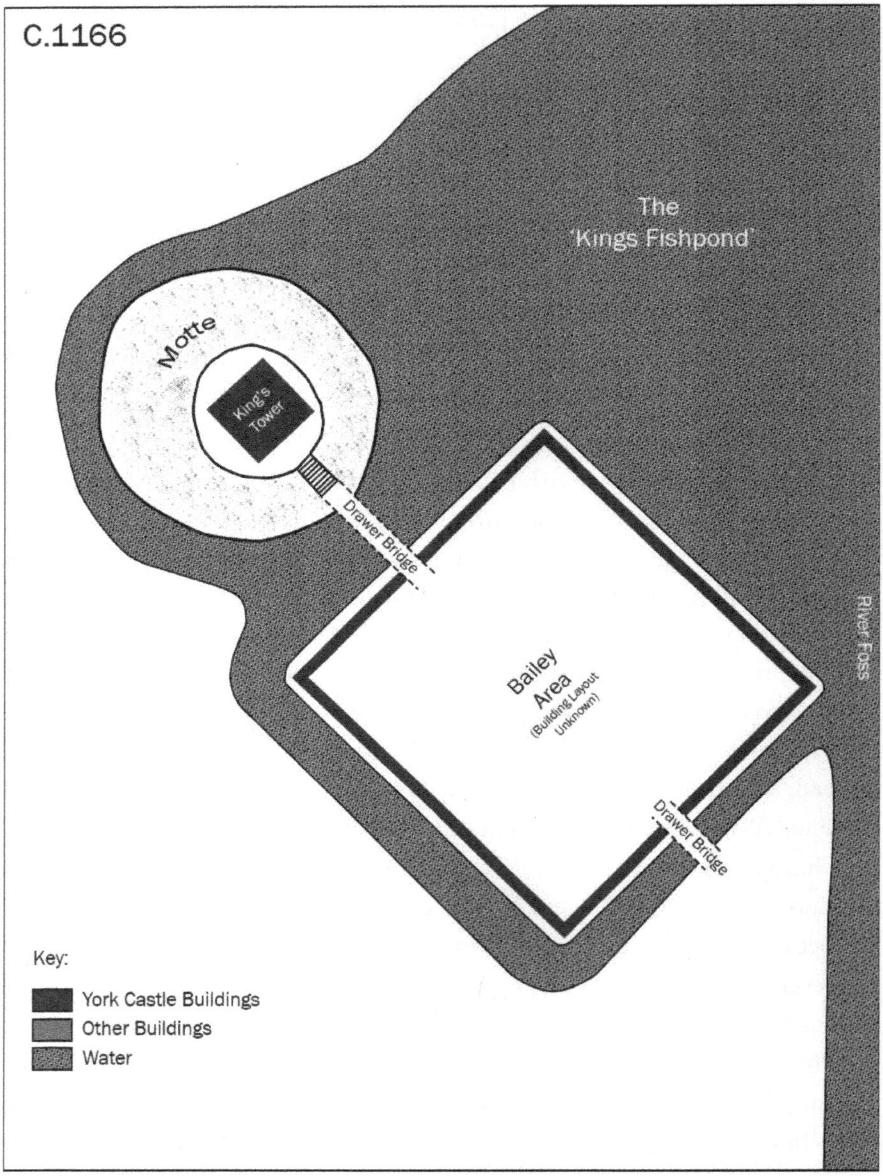

A plan of York Castle in its earliest days. Note how little we know for certain during this period of the castle's existence.[2] It is unfortunate that so much of the archeology of the castle would be destroyed by the future prison buildings.

'motte' surrounded by water. The only access to the keep would have been across a drawbridge from the lower 'bailey' area. The keep was, therefore, essentially impregnable unless accessed across the drawbridge. The bailey area was also surrounded by water, with access coming from a drawbridge at the south end. The bailey area housed the main buildings that made up the castle's functionality. This would have included a hall, kitchen, stables and workshops.[3] At some point, other functions would include a chapel and the county mint. Importantly, the first prison buildings would also have been constructed in this bailey area.

The castle's location was strategically chosen, with the River Ouse on one side and the River Foss on the other. The confluence of these two rivers formed a major part of the castle's defence. In addition, the Foss was dammed to flood about 150 acres of land and create an area referred to in the *Doomsday Book* as '*Stagnum Regis*' or the 'King's Pool'.[4] This water, in turn, filled the moat of York Castle. This ensured that to capture the keep, you had to fight into the bailey area across a river, and once you were inside, you would start again to capture the keep.

York was not the only major city to receive a Norman castle to help control the local population. Places like Warwick, Nottingham, Lincoln, Huntingdon and Cambridge also received new castles at this time.[5] It is also worth noting that this was not the only castle built by the Normans in York. Slightly earlier, in 1068, another castle was built across the River Ouse at a site now known as Baile Hill.[6] The modern name references the Norman design of the castle, the motte and bailey style. Baile Hill would soon fall into disuse, leaving the area of York Castle as the administrative centre for the city.

During its first few years, York Castle would play an important part in the Harrying of the North. As the North rebelled against William the Conqueror, the new king swiftly made harsh judgments on the areas he saw as disloyal to him. The castles, an important symbol of William's rule, soon became targets of those who opposed him. It was not long until York Castle fell to the local rebels with the help of the Danes in September 1069.[7] Many soldiers, as well as the guardian of the Castle, were killed.[8] William I himself led an army from Nottingham to York to deal with the rebellion. The Danes, who had helped secure York Castle, were paid off and returned home. Soon, the remaining rebels dispersed and fled. William laid waste to many towns, villages, and cities, including York, to reassert his control over the area. Norman lords were established to ensure the North remained loyal to William.[9] Often described in modern language as a genocide, it is estimated that up to 100,000 people lost their lives during William's suppression of the Northern Rebellion.[10] Even nearly twenty years later, in the *Doomsday Book* of 1086, much of Yorkshire is described as 'wasted'.[11] This was an economic blow from which the North has never truly recovered.

The aim of this early period was one of control. During the time of the Norman Conquest, Yorkshire was part of Northumbria, by far the largest county in Britain, recorded in the *Doomsday Book* as stretching from coast to coast. As such, the castle was designed to be both strong and impressive. As one early nineteenth-century commentator states, the two castles in York were 'made so strong in order to keep the citizens and Northumbrians in awe'.[12]

Then, in 1166, the assize of Clarendon was held. This was effectively the start of a system of justice in England that exists to this day. It introduced the jury system to England, establishing a grand jury in each district. Importantly, Clause 7 said that the sheriff of each county was to erect a county gaol, the cost of which would be covered by the Crown.[13] By 1216, all but five counties in England had established a county gaol.[14] Eighteen county gaols were created almost immediately in 1166; most would be in existing castles, as these were ready-built secure structures. This first batch of new county gaols included one at York Castle.[15] The exact location of the gaol within the bailey area is unknown. We also don't know if this was a newly constructed or repurposed building. Wherever the structure was, 1166 can be considered the start of York Castle being an official prison/gaol. Since Yorkshire was now the largest county in England, it is interesting to note that the county sheriff constructed two county gaols; the other was located at Tickhill Castle, south of Doncaster.[16] However, this second gaol appears not to have been maintained for long and was probably no longer used for this purpose when Tickhill Castle was given to the future King John in 1189.

It was during this period, at the beginning of the assize courts, that York Castle played its most important role as a court. It was not just the county assize sessions being held here; during the reign of Henry II, the Pleas of the Forest were held at the castle, as was another unspecified court over which the king himself presided.[17]

On 16 March 1190, one of the most significant events in the history of York Castle occurred. After the Jewish community in York was attacked in an attempt by barons determined to liquidate their debts, the Jews sought protection from the county sheriff. These families were given refuge in the keep and some other buildings within York Castle.[18] However, the mob that pursued them did not give up. The castle was besieged, and eventually, the royal constable of York Castle abandoned his protection of the Jews.[19] As a result, some of the Jews were captured and put to death. For those who remained, fear of falling into the hands of the mob led to a horrific ending. Those that remained in the keep killed each other in 'an act of mass self-destruction' before setting the tower on fire, killing those that remained and burning the keep to the ground.[20] It is estimated that, in total, 150 men and women lost their lives that day.[21] This series of events left a stain on York's history that is still remembered today.

It would not be long before the keep was rebuilt. However, in 1903, during work to underpin what is left of the keep, charred remains were found 13 feet below the current top of the mound, suggesting that the mound was likely enlarged after the Jewish massacre.[22] This would also be consistent with the smaller mound that remains at the Baile Hill site, which had been abandoned by this time and consequently was never enlarged. While the massacre left a stain on York's reputation, it did not stop the monarchy from using the tower, and as early as 1200, the newly-crowned King John stayed in the keep while in York.[23]

This was the first of many visits King John would make to York Castle, and as a result, money would continue to be spent keeping York Castle to the highest standards. In 1205, £2 12s 3d was spent repairing the gaol. In 1210, King John, once again visiting, paid for repairs to a house and a bridge in the castle and irons for Irish prisoners who were in 'durance vile' or long-term imprisonment at York Castle.[24] We also have a reference from 1237, which talks about establishing a women's prison within York Castle.[25] This building is also associated with the prison chapel, also constructed in 1237.[26] These were likely part of the same building, with the chapel above the newly-built female prison.

Walls of Stone

By the early 1200s, the wooden walls were no longer enough for a royal castle. In fact, during the winter of 1228, possibly while King Henry III was staying in York (likely at York Castle), a storm blew the castle's keep down.[27] It appears

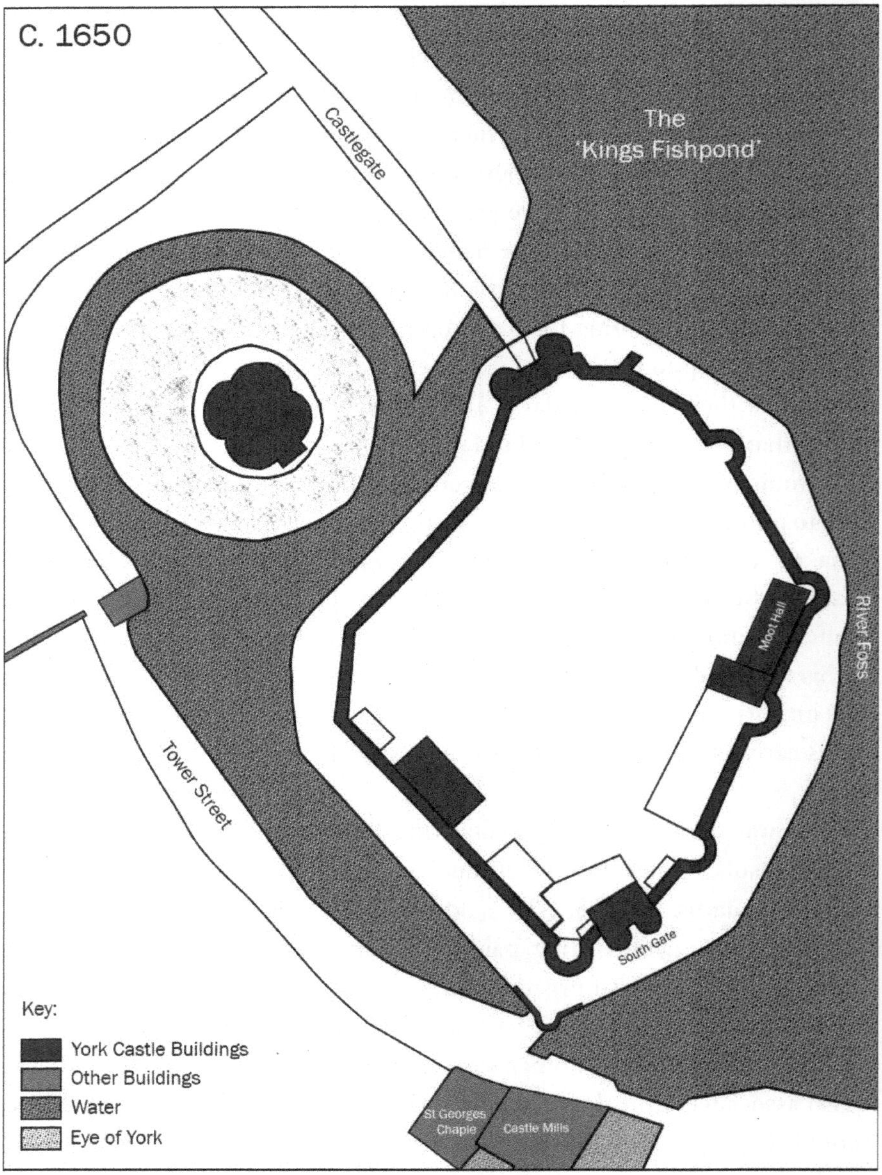

A plan of the site of York Castle during the mid-1600s. Although we have more information about the site, many of the building locations cannot be accurately placed.[28]

to have been quickly rebuilt, and Henry III also spent money on repairing the gaol once again in 1238.[29]

Stronger, more modern stone constructions were needed to replace the wooden walls of the castle. The first part that was rebuilt in stone was, of course, the keep. This process began in 1245–1246, once again under the reign of Henry III. However, it was thirteen years until the work was completed in 1258–1259; this would cost £2,000.[30] It has been suggested that the design was probably by Henry de Rynes.[31] This belief comes from the tower's unusual design: a quadrate stone keep with distinct lobes and features forming a clover leaf shape. Similar keeps are at Ambléný (Aisne) and Étampes (Essonne) in France.[32] The rebuilding of York Castle was just one part of a massive castle rebuilding programme undertaken by Henry III, which also included the construction of York's stone city walls, a feature that remains iconic to the City of York to this day.

The walls of the bailey area would not be reconstructed from stone until the reign of Edward I.[33] The exact years of construction are unknown, but Edward I was quarrying stone from just outside of Tadcaster in 1281, which might be related to this construction.[34] However, many of the buildings inside the bailey would likely have been made of wooden construction for many years, although specific, important buildings could well have been reconstructed in stone.

Along with the walls, a stone gatehouse was erected in the southern part of the castle. This was built of two rounded towers with an arched gate between them. Records exist of this being used as late as 1597.[35] Today, the foundations of these towers can still be seen. A watergate, or sallyport, led from the river near the southern gate, and another entrance, constructed on the northern part of the bailey, was known as the Castlegate postern gate. Even in 1597, the Castlegate gate was known as the 'lower or lesser gate'.[36] However, later in its history, Castlegate would become the main entrance to the prison at York Castle.

Unfortunately, no detailed information is available regarding the exact locations of buildings within the bailey area. While we can place buildings such as the exchequer, gaol, or king's hall inside the bailey area, later works destroyed much of the archaeology.

While the reconstruction of the castle in stone was essential, these modifications did not come cheap. The cost exceeded £2,450. We know that this cost covered the redevelopment of Clifford's Tower: 'the bailey walls, towers, gates, bridges, two halls, a chapel, a kitchen'.[37] More importantly, we know that a prison was constructed at this time; this was presumably a stone replacement for the original county gaol. However, these might not have been the first stone buildings in the castle. The women's prison, built between 1237 and 1241, would likely have been a stone building. It had the chapel above it, and neither the prison nor the chapel appears to have been rebuilt by Henry III; presumably, this relatively new building was already up to modern standards.

During this period in the history of York Castle, it also achieved its highest national importance. The first war of Scottish independence, led by Robert the Bruce, was an essential focus of King Edward II. Edward II spent a lot of time in York. As a result, many crucial functions, like the exchequer, were moved to York Castle in 1319, and they were not moved back to London until 1323. This made York the effective capital of England for significant periods. York Castle was at the centre of this, carrying out the administrative functions of England. It was in effect from York Castle that England was being run. In August 1327, King Edward III ordered the exchequer to be brought back to York Castle while the king was fighting the Scots; it would remain there until at least early 1328, when peace was brokered.

Abandonment to the County

Over the next centuries, the story of York Castle became one of feast or famine. While England was at war with the Scots, the castle was maintained, described as 'the bulwark which checked their further advance into the heart of England'.[38] However, during times of peace, it was allowed to fall into disrepair, and it is unlikely that any major changes happened to York Castle after the late fourteenth century.[39] By 1358, two 'great cracks from the foundations to the summit' had appeared in the keep, and repairs were again needed.[40]

This is why, despite the important early history of the castle at York, it is rarely talked about as one of the great castles of England. It was neglected and left to ruin for several centuries after its heyday. This has left little record of what happened on the site around the castle between 1362 and 1596. The castle now had two main functions: as a military garrison and, secondly, as the county gaol for Yorkshire. However, at this time, the castle also briefly achieved the peak of its judicial power. King Richard II was a regular visitor to the castle at York, and in 1392, the Court of the King's Bench, the highest criminal court in England, was held in the courtyard at the castle.[41]

The one detail we get from the time is where the assize courts are being held within York Castle. In 1360, the castle's 'little hall' was being used, although the location of this building was lost. The castle soon started to fall apart due to a lack of investment. By 1446, the courts had moved to the 'King's Great Hall' or 'Motehall'.[42] This hall was described as a 'timber plaster erection' and required repair in 1451–1452. It was in this building that the assizes courts for Yorkshire would be held until 1777.[43] This is probably the first building from which we can derive its location with any certainty.

There was also an attempt to rebuild the castle in 1484. Richard III, who had spent many years effectively running the north from York during the reign of his brother Edward IV, partly demolished the castle to rebuild it. However, his death in 1485 meant that these works were never completed. York was left with a partly demolished castle that was not fit for the military defence it was designed for. By 1535, the castle was described as 'in ruins'.[44]

In 1596, the gaoler of York Castle, the man running the county gaol, was Robert Redhead. Little is known about the man, but he had clear intentions regarding the castle. He talks about demolishing parts of the castle, including one wall of the bailey (likely next to the watergate or sallyport), the bridge over the motte, and parts of the keep.[45] Interestingly, we get the first historical reference to the keep's modern name from this destruction: Clifford's Tower. The name's origins are unclear, but it possibly refers to the Clifford family, who claimed to be the castle's hereditary constables. The earliest record is of Henry Clifford, the sheriff of Yorkshire in 1522.[46] This could explain why the first reference to the name is not until the end of the same century. Previously, it had been referred to as the 'Kings Tower' or the 'Great Tower'.[47] Eventually, after protests from the citizens and petitions from the city council to the lord chancellor and the lord treasurer, Redhead was stopped from his destruction of the castle. However, the top few courses of stone are still missing from Clifford's Tower to this day. It was said that York would have no 'other buildinge for showe of this cittye sarve of but onlye the minster and churche steples if the said towre shold be pulled downe'. In 1608, £243 would be collected to repair the bridge and hall at the castle.[48]

During the late sixteenth century, we get more detailed descriptions of the prison buildings. Located near the southern gate,

> it seems to have consisted of two wings, several stories high, joined no doubt by the keeper's house. The two wings looked onto the yard and the Moot Hall, where the Assizes for the county were held.[49]

The location of this prison would be similar to the debtors' prison building built in 1705. One wing of the prison building is described as housing felons awaiting trial, and the other housing Catholic recusants like Margaret Clitherow. We also get some details about the inside; the rooms were 'little', and there were references to a kitchen and parlour. 'There were plenty of chimneys, but no doubt fuel, like all other necessities, cost the prisoners dear …'[50] In addition, there is a mention that the prisoners were free to have 'money, clothing and bedding sent in'.[51] Based on what the prison would be like when it was rebuilt in 1705, this description of where the recusants were held sounds closer to the debtors' accommodation than the felons' holding area. This would also explain why the recusants found York Castle such a good home or a 'catholic retreat'.[52] They had more freedom to practise their religion inside the prison than outside. However, this was not one homogenous group as the recusants were divided into groups of 'priests, schoolmasters and the learnder sort; gentlemen; inferior persons, "to it, men"; women', and they were not allowed to mix.[53] Despite this, the recusants found a way to group together, and we know that mass was given and confessions heard within the prison 'sometimes through holes in the wall or the floorboards', giving us an idea that the building was in disrepair.[54]

Civil War Rebuild

In 1641, Charles I abolished the Council of the North, which had been based at the abbot's house (now King's Manor) at St Mary's Abbey and dated back to Richard III in 1484 and was re-established by Henry VIII after the Reformation.[55] Rather than this being the end of York's importance, it was the start of a brief renaissance for the site. King Charles I made York his capital during the First English Civil War, and refortified the Castle in preparation for a potential siege. In 1642, Henry Clifford, the 5th Earl of Cumberland, garrisoned the castle. The main change to the site was the rebuilding of the keep. Moulding with the royal arms of Charles I and below that, Henry Clifford can still be seen today, marking these renovations. Eventually, the siege of York began in 1644. The keep was regularly hit by cannon fire during the eleven-week siege of the city, and fired upon the parliamentarian forces assembled on Heslington Hill.[56] On 2 July 1644, York surrendered. Once the city had fallen to Parliament, and in the wake of the battle of Marston Moor, the castle would be left indefensible like so many castles around England. It can only be wondered what any prisoners held at the castle at this time felt, being regularly fired upon.

This was not quite the end of York Castle as a military site, although that was now not too far off. When Oliver Cromwell visited York in 1650, a gun salute was fired from the tower to greet him. But this would come just before many of the cannon and some 300 muskets were transferred to Hull or London by 1652.[57] In 1662, forty men were stationed under the command of Major Scott to keep Clifford's Tower as a magazine. It was described in 1680 as being 'sufficiently strong having some cannon, two culverins, and a sacker or two on the platform, with a continual garrison therein for its defence'.[58]

Court House and Jury House Buildings

By 1649, steps were taken to 'consider how the Castle of York and Clifford's Tower may be made so independent of one of the other, that the prisoners may be kept safe in the Castle'.[59] At this point, the site can be considered as two separate, independent structures, at least for now. The tower on the motte was the military structure, and the bailey area was now dedicated to the prison.

However, with damaged walls and buildings being neglected, problems would soon appear. In 1653, there was an escape from the 'low gaol' due to a weakness in the walls of the building.[60] In the wake of these escapes and given the run-down nature of the whole site, some renovations were in order. In 1667–1668, the grand jury house on the west side of the bailey was re-fronted for £133 6s 8d.[61] The name suggests that the building was for use by the jury or, more broadly, by the court. In 1670, the 'common hall', specifically the 'crown side', was repaired; this was the castle's great hall or moot hall. This work continued in 1674–1675 when the common hall was rebuilt for £650.[62] Further expansion to the Nisi Prius, or civil side, of this building would occur in 1684–1685.[63]

The End of the Castle

By the late 1600s, the castle itself was beginning to disappear. The south gate was now disused and blocked up by 1682,[64] leaving the only entry into the bailey area through the Castlegate postern gate. As we will see, by 1735 the impressive original south entrance to the castle had been demolished.[65]

However, the true end of the castle came very abruptly and violently. On 23 April 1684, St George's Day, a gun salute had been fired from the top of Clifford's Tower. This was not an unusual event. However, that night at around 10.00 pm, a huge explosion came from the magazine of Clifford's Tower. A loud explosion was heard throughout the city as the explosion completely cleared the inside of the tower. The walls were made from stone, but the fire 'consumed to ashes all the interior thereof'.[66] Luckily, no one was killed by the explosion apart from one man hit by a flying piece of timber.[67] Much has been said about this having been sabotage, with toasts in the city 'to the demolition of the Minced Pie', as it was unaffectionately known,[68] and it is suspicious that 'the gunner had got out all his goods before it was discovered'.[69] The explosion resulted in the tower being damaged beyond economic repair. From this point, we can consider York Castle to be York Castle Prison, as it no longer held a permanent military presence after 1690. The tower would soon become separate from the rest of the castle and under separate ownership. In 1699, it passed to the Sowray family, and then, from 1727, three generations of Samuel Wards owned it.[70] It would not be until the 1800s that ownership of the site would be reunited under prison authorities.

Chapter 2

Life in York Castle Prison, 1068–1705

The Early British Justice System

To understand York Castle Prison and life within its walls, we need to begin with a much broader approach. We must examine the system of crime and punishment in England between the twelfth century and the beginning of the eighteenth century in a broader context, just as we did with the site. To do this, we must look at how criminals were caught, the court system that sentenced these criminals, and the different categories of crimes that someone might commit to end up at York Castle Prison. Understanding this will give us a basis for understanding the changes to the system that we will see later in the development of York Castle Prison.

People sometimes struggle to understand how criminals would have been caught before the police force existed in the nineteenth century. The reality is an almost overcompensation of maintaining law and order by having every man in England be part of it. The most important people concerned with catching criminals would have been the sheriff, the constable, the watchmen, and the thief-takers.

However, we will start at the lowest part of the medieval criminal justice system, the frankpledge. This required every 'villein' (a tenant farmer under the feudal system) between the ages of 12 and 60 to become a member of a 'tithing'.[1] At the age of 12, they would take the bible and pledge,

> I will be a lawful man and bear loyalty to our lord the king and his heirs, and to my lord and his heirs, and I will be justiciable to my chief tithing-man, so help me God and the saints.[2]

The system meant that if anyone in the tithing broke the law, it was the responsibility of the others to report them. The chief tithing man was then expected to report these events at the manorial court. However, these lower parts of the justice system slowly disappeared, and by the Elizabethan period, the manorial court was in terminal decline, with most crimes going through the local constable.[3]

The constables were most concerned with collecting county rates; however, they were also obligated to pursue felonies that might be reported, but they were not detectives. This is why witnesses played such an important role in trials up until the early nineteenth century. The constables would move prisoners where needed and take them to court, but earlier on, this was a part-time, often unpaid role.[4] The result was inconsistencies between excellent constables and those uninterested in the role.

The constable could also issue an order of 'hue and cry' (a hunt for a criminal), where if a crime was committed, and the culprit's identity was known, then 'hue and cry' would be used to find the criminal. Everyone nearby would view the crime scene and help catch those responsible.[5] If the criminal was caught, they would be delivered to the local constable to be formally taken to gaol.

By the early modern period, many crimes were taken straight to the constable. Later, the role of the constable would be split into the high constable and the parish or petty constable· By the seventeenth century, the role of petty constable was effectively the lowest in the country. Many other more archaic parts of the justice system, like the frankpledge or manorial courts, had disappeared. In the North Riding, the pledge for a constable was as follows:

> You shall … well and truly present all mannour of bloodsheddes, assaltes and affreys and outcryes there … done and committed against the kings Ma[jes]ties peace: all manner of writes, warrantee and preceptes to you lawfully directed you shall truly execute: the Kings Ma[jes]ties peace in your own person you shall conserve and keepe as much as in you lyeth: and in all things that apperteyne to your office you shall well and truly behave yourselfe.[6]

The problem was that constables were not always around. This made nighttime especially dangerous and a haven for many criminals. Watchmen were responsible for ensuring the safety of towns and cities during the evening and night. They would stop suspicious people or even follow and 'watch' someone they thought did not have a good reason to be out at night. They could be successful at catching criminals if they caught them in the act or while they still had stolen goods on them.

It should be remembered that despite these officials being responsible for administering justice, not all criminals were brought to trial by the authorities. Many prosecutions were private, with charges brought about by the victims or the families of victims. This was an expensive process, often out of the reach of the poorest in society, but if you had the money, it was often the best way to ensure a trial would take place and the offender would face justice. But what happens if you don't know how to apprehend a criminal? Those who wanted to catch a criminal but did not understand how to do it could pay a thief-taker to do the work for them. These men would investigate the crime, find who committed it and bring them to justice for you – if you could afford them. They lived off the rewards offered for apprehending criminals and returning stolen goods.

Most criminals were brought to gaols to await trial through this combination of constables, watchmen and thief-takers.

Now the criminal has been caught, they need to go to court and have someone judge if they are, in fact, guilty of the crime they are accused of. The constable would direct crimes to the hundreds court; in York, a northern town, this was known as a wapentake. This term is derived from the Danelaw version of the hundred court and appears in the *Doomsday Book*. The bailiff was the person who oversaw the wapentake. Essentially serving under the sheriff, especially later in the period, the bailiff would serve writs and carry out arrests.[7] The bailiffs' job was to hold the monthly petty (or high constable) sessions and give an appropriate punishment. The most common punishment at wapentake was fines, but it could also involve public humiliation, like the use of pillories.[8] The petty sessions would later become the preserve of the local magistrates who would hear cases and decide upon an appropriate punishment or send the criminal to the quarter sessions or the assize sessions.

By the thirteenth century, another level emerged, with keepers of the peace appointed; in 1361, they would be renamed justices of the peace.[9] They presided over the quarter sessions, held every three months, dealing with less serious crimes than at the assize courts at York Castle. The justices were mainly drawn from local elites, as this was not a paid role. This role was crucial at a local level. Initially, justices of the peace would deal with 'trespasses', which we might think of today as misdemeanours; occasionally, they would also judge some felonies. This meant that by 1388, the justices of the peace had the power to arrest people, imprison them, fine them, and in some cases, even hang them.[10] However, this power starts to wane by the 1500s. Around 1590, it became uncommon for the quarter sessions to hand out capital sentences. Instead, these cases would move up even further to the assize sessions. However, it is worth noting that the last capital sentence handed out by a quarter session in the North Riding was in 1654,[11] although this was very much an exception, even at that time.

From 1576, justices of the peace would also take on the role of building houses of correction. These were local prisons where someone could be held for a short time if they were found guilty of minor offences, i.e. misdemeanours. After 1600, many of those convicted at the quarter sessions would end up at one of these new houses of correction.[12] The late sixteenth century also saw the

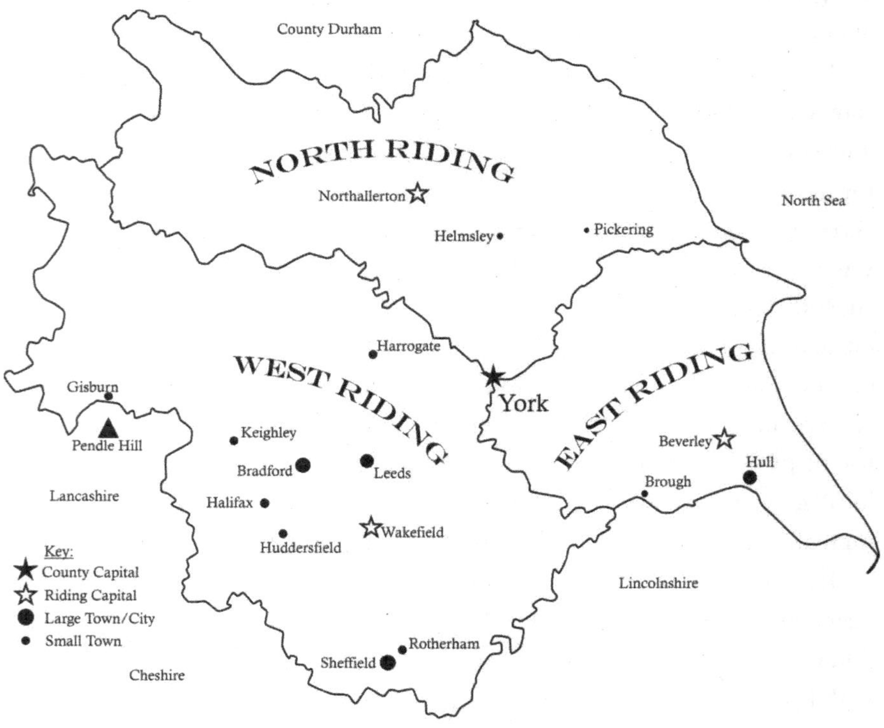

A map of the three Ridings of Yorkshire. Also shown are places associated with criminals tried at York Castle.

number of cases being dealt with at the quarter sessions increase. As a result, the petty sessions were set up monthly, during which the justice of the peace (later the magistrate) would act, without trial by jury, to judge small crimes.

Finally, we come to York Castle's role in the justice system as the county gaol for Yorkshire and home to the Yorkshire Assize sessions. However, this is a good time to learn some of the geography that might determine whether you would be brought to York Castle Prison to await trial at the assizes or even brought to York Castle Prison as a debtor to be imprisoned until your debt is repaid.

Historically, Yorkshire was the largest county in England (5,961 square miles).[13] Split into three Ridings, North Riding, East Riding and West Riding, with York itself, a county borough from 1396. Petty sessions were held in each town/city, but if a jury was required, the trial would be sent to the quarter sessions. Each Riding had its own quarter session, usually held in the riding's capital – Northallerton for North Riding, Beverley for East Riding and Wakefield for West Riding, although these locations did move around occasionally, and there are records of quarter sessions being held elsewhere. However, these were crimes we would consider misdemeanours today. Any crimes considered felonies, or occasionally treason, would see those awaiting trial being moved to the county gaol, in this case, York Castle Prison, to await their trial at the assize sessions. The assize courts, like those at York Castle, were responsible for enforcing royal law, i.e. 'common law' at a more local level. This system, comprising petty sessions, quarter sessions and assize sessions, would form the basis of the criminal justice system from the early modern period until the 1970s.

The question remains of how exactly the assize court came into existence. After years of turmoil in England during King Stephen's reign, Henry II inherited the crown. However, with a large area to rule, not just England but Normandy, Aquitaine, and Anjou in France, Henry needed to establish a system that allowed his kingdom to be ruled even when he was not there.[14] This was important as Henry II was outside of England for roughly two-thirds of his thirty-five-year reign.[15] For royal justice, this was enacted at the assize of Clarendon in 1166: 'An attempt by Henry II to bring all the laws of England into one unified and recognised framework'.[16] This had two significant impacts. It broadly meant that all crimes in England should be investigated by the Crown, regardless of any local jurisdictions held by the local Lords.[17] Initially, this justice was done by a commission of royal judges travelling around the country on a large circuit known as the General Eyre.[18] Twelve local men were to make the judgment. Murder, robbery, theft, and ten years later, arson, forgery and counterfeiting became the preserve of the assizes and royal justice.[19] The second important part of the assize of Clarendon was that it determined that there should be a prison in every county.[20] As we have already seen, the sheriff of York immediately created a county gaol at York Castle Prison.

Being sent for trial at the assize sessions could mean a long and costly stay in the gaol at York Castle Prison. This was because of how the judges worked. York was part of the Northern circuit, usually starting at the Yorkshire Assizes at York Castle. After this, it would see the judges travel through places like Wakefield, Thirsk, Beverley, Richmond, Rippon, Knaresborough, Doncaster, Leeds, Hull, Sheffield, Halifax, Durham (a county gaol), Newcastle, Morpeth, Carlisle, Lancaster (a county gaol), Manchester and Liverpool amongst others. By 1330, six circuits had been established and remained almost the same until the mid-nineteenth century. Each circuit had two judges and was ridden twice yearly, once in winter and again in summer. Here, the judges dealt with any serious crimes that had occurred since their previous sitting.

The judges were 'good discreet men, who were not 'of the place',[21] i.e. they were of a certain social standing, but importantly, they would not know anyone to be brought before them. Around the late sixteenth century, the assize courts established a monopoly on trials that could result in the death sentence if a defendant was found guilty.[22]

One author has described the assize system as 'a remarkably neat means of enforcing royal law in the localities'.[23] It was not perfect, but it did the job well enough to make it a tolerable system. The assizes' power increased from their creation in 1166 throughout the medieval and early modern periods. By the late 1600s, they alone held the power of life and death over the subjects of England. This increasing power of the assizes became one of the driving factors in rebuilding York Castle in the 1660s. Felonies tried at the Assize included murder, rape, robbery, arson, causing death by witchcraft, grand larceny (theft of goods worth more than 12d), highway robbery, buggery (in this case meaning an unnatural sexual act, normally with an animal) and sodomy.[24] All felonies were punishable by death if found guilty. During the medieval period, a third of accused men were executed, and the rest were released. There were very few alternatives available to the judges.[25]

It is also important to know that there were some exceptions to the system of twice-yearly circuits. York Castle would occasionally see these 'special sessions', most notably with the Jacobites in the 1700s and the Luddites and Peterloo rioters in the early nineteenth century. Special sessions could be held to try specific, high-profile cases if required. These special sessions, while rare, would cause great excitement around the county gaol, with many interested parties wanting to attend court to see the trials of these high-profile cases. This could cause problems, so special sessions would usually also bring in extra security, sometimes even the military, to control the prisoners and the public.

Finally, we should remember that up until the 1700s, the assize court system was not just the preserve of trials, bringing a modern feeling of justice. Some notable examples of what we might consider to be 'medieval punishment' are still present in the system.

Alternative trials, known as 'trial by ordeal', also existed. This allowed guilt to be determined by the outcome of the ordeal and also came into the legal system as part of the assize of Clarendon. There were three different types of trial: cold water, hot water and hot iron. The idea was that God would not allow an innocent person to suffer and so would take away the pain of an individual, allowing them to complete these trials. Trial by iron involved walking a certain distance holding a red-hot iron, and trial by hot water involved picking up something like a stone from the bottom of a cauldron of boiling water. These would both produce serious injuries, and doctors were used to view how the wounds were healing. If they were healing well, the person was innocent; if infection set in, they were guilty. However, it is trial by cold water that is most often recalled. This usually involved either tying someone up so they could not swim or placing them in water. If they floated, they were guilty. They were innocent if they sank (and were subsequently rescued). This is often associated with witches, but was used for many crimes. This later evolved into punishment by submersion on a ducking stool, although those who were frail or subjected to this in cold weather could sometimes die from the complications and shock of the ordeal. York's ducking stool was in the 'Castle ditch', just outside York Castle.[26] These types of ordeal were uncommon, but York Castle would have witnessed these events on infrequent occasions.

In addition, we need to consider the use of torture at York Castle. In theory, in 1219, torture was replaced with trial by jury, but that is not to say it was no longer used.[27] There was no actual law for it or against it. However, in 1628, it was ruled outside the law.[28] This change to the law did not stop some forms torture from still being used at the assizes. Most importantly, *Peine forte et dure* (strong and hard punishment) was used for those who refused to plead at their trial. This involved the person being laid on the ground with a board on top of them and weights added, crushing the unfortunate victim. The original version of *Peine forte et dure* involved a three-day process where the victim would be pressed on the first day and then allowed to plead. The second day would be the same as the first, and then on the third day, if they have not pleaded either guilty or not guilty, the weight would be continuously added until the person died. Most commonly, those set to endure this punishment suffered because it was the only way to stop the Crown from seizing their property, which would happen if the felon was found guilty and executed. While this was not technically execution, the result could often end with the death of the defendant. Pressing would not be abolished until 1772, when no plea was determined to be an automatic guilty verdict.[29] It would not be until 1827 that no plea would be treated as not guilty, and a trial would occur.

Other Courts

York Castle was Yorkshire's county gaol and home of the assizes for Yorkshire, so this is where the focus of this text will be placed; however, two other courts are worth noting for the reader: the Church Courts and the Royal Courts.

The highest court in England was the Royal Court. The Royal Court was made up of three courts: the Court of the Exchequer, for dealing with the Crown's financial deals; the Court of Common Pleas, generally for debt, theft and fraud cases, but also acts as a court of appeal; and the Court of the King's Bench, which heard criminal cases and appeals from other courts. The King's Bench was the only one of the three that had criminal jurisdiction. The purpose of the Royal Court was to uphold 'common law'. 'Common law' was the law that took precedence throughout England and had its roots in older Anglo-Saxon laws, although this had been rewritten and revised many times after the Norman Conquest. 'Common law' applied to the whole country and took precedence over any local by-laws that might contradict it.

The judges of the King's Bench and Court of Common Pleas were the ones who would travel around the six circuits, hearing cases twice per year at the assize sessions.

Later, between 1540 and 1640, there was also the Court of the Star Chamber, being the King's council sitting as a court on the monarch's behalf. This mainly involved breaches of the king's peace, i.e. riots, assaults, fraud, forgery and perjury. However, this court had little impact on what happened at York Castle Prison.

While we have established an understanding of the court system, it is important to realise that this was not the only justice system in England. There was also a separate system of the Ecclesiastical or Church Court. This enforced canon law, the law of the church. This would deal with things like 'payment of tithes, sexual misconduct, the validity of marriages, wills, heresy and witchcraft'.[30] This was not uncommon, one source suggesting that over a third of York were arraigned for sexual offences (i.e. affairs, children out of wedlock, etc).[31]

While this is interesting, it is not this part of church law that is relevant to us looking at assize history. One aspect of church law allowed for the 'Benefit of the Clergy'. This allowed those who were part of the clergy to be tried in a church court rather than at the petty, quarter and assize sessions. The church courts would generally hand out fines or lesser punishments. The question is, how do you show that you are part of the clergy? The answer was simple – you had to read a specific passage from the Bible:

> Have mercy upon me oh God, according to thy loving kindness: according unto the multitude of thy tender mercies blot out my transgressions.
>
> Psalm 51, Verse 1

This passage became known as the 'neck verse' because of its ability to save someone from hanging. If you were facing a death sentence, you could claim you were a clergyman by reciting the above verse; therefore, you were not liable to be executed under common law. Originally to be cited in Latin, it was expected that only the clergy or the extremely well-educated would be able to read it. As you can imagine, this system was abused, with many people avoiding execution by remembering the verse and pretending to read it in court. It is because of loopholes like the benefit of the clergy that only 24 per cent of those indicted of serious crimes are executed.[32] As you can imagine, situations like this caused tensions with the Royal Courts.

While the church courts were often seen as an easy way out of trouble, their power should not be underestimated. In addition to creating assize courts at the assize of Clarendon, King Henry II also tried to bring those who committed crimes within the church under Crown rule. But Henry's former friend Thomas Becket, the Archbishop of Canterbury, saw this as a step too far. Becket's refusal to allow royal prerogative over the church was a catalyst for the rift that ended Becket's life and almost brought down Henry himself.

Your Day in Court

The system of petty sessions, quarter sessions and assize sessions would remain largely unchanged until the 1820s, and even then, the reforms would mainly focus on policing. Lesser crimes and criminal offences would be tried locally at the monthly petty sessions or quarter sessions every three months, usually held at Epiphany, Easter, Midsummer and Michaelmas.[33] For felonies, which could potentially lead to execution if found guilty, the magistrates would refer the case to a higher court like the assize court at York Castle. Here, those accused of serious crimes would await trial, which could take several months. At this time, an indictment would be drawn up for the court, stating what the person had been accused of and what evidence/witnesses there might be.

Your indictment would be read to the grand jury, who would decide if this was a 'true bill', where you would stand trial. If there was insufficient evidence, it would be declared 'ignoramus', and you would be released. If a true bill was not found, the person could be released; however, it should be remembered that for many, this vindication only came after a long and expensive time in gaol awaiting their day in court. If you have a true bill found against you, a petty jury will hear your trial. Although this trial was likely to be brief, even by the 1500s, it is unlikely to have lasted more than ten to twenty minutes. This also left juries with little time to consider the finer nuances of each case.

There were still several deterrents to prosecution. While cost was not always an issue, time could be a problem, especially if you come to an assize court and your trial is several days into the session. The amount you might lose from not working for several days might outweigh any trial outcome. The potential of a capital crime could also put people off prosecuting. Your family might persuade you that this is not the right course of action, especially if the culprit is also a family member. A lack of prosecution should also be noted from women. Many women who might have been sexually assaulted would be reluctant to seek prosecution because of the embarrassment of the situation.[34]

Even after spending months at York Castle Prison, on their day in court the accused could be hearing the case against them for the first time, with no time to prepare a defence, especially in the conditions inside a gaol like York Castle Prison, where trials were over quickly. Trials usually took a confrontational style between the prosecutor and the defendant. Often, defence would be no more than a denial of the offence and the presentation of character witnesses to attest to the person's good character.[35] It is easy to see that miscarriages of justice were likely quite common without the rigorous modern standards of prosecuting a criminal case. It would not be until the nineteenth century that lawyers started to act on behalf of a defendant. They were not allowed to sum up their case until 1836, and it would not be until 1898 that a defendant could be sworn in and give evidence on their own behalf.[36]

The system was often against those appearing as defendants. Higher-class men dominated both the judges and juries. This gave an inevitable bias against the lower-class criminals and women on trial. However, there was one thing that an accused could potentially do to help themselves on their day in court. They had the right to challenge the jury selection if they felt it was biased. If they had committed a felony, they could challenge twenty jurors; if they were facing a charge of petty treason, this could be up to thirty-five.[37]

Women and the Law

By this point, many readers will be thinking about what has been missing from this discussion on medieval and early modern courts. So far, there has been very little mention of women. All the major players, from the chief tithing man, the lord, the constable, the sheriff and the clergy, are all male. Women had no role in applying the law at this point. Women's experiences of the law at this time came when they fell on the wrong side of it. This was usually through the murder of their husband (if he died in their arms), the loss of an unborn child or if they were the victims of rape. A woman's role in criminal justice was minimal. Even reporting crimes was complicated for women. The

Magna Carta explains that 'no one shall be arrested or imprisoned on the appeal of a woman for the death of any person except her husband'.[38] Even this, the most widely known document of the time, shows us that women had no power even to report a murder. Women had no power in courts and could not bring cases to court.[39] Even a rape claim was unlikely to be successful!

If all this sounds terrible and misogynistic, it is because it was, yet we should also remember that there were cases where this could work in the favour of the woman. For example, if accused of a crime alongside her husband, the woman would often get away with the offence; after all, in law, she was bound to obey her husband.[40] It must be his fault if she was led astray! Women were less likely to face prosecution for violent crimes. It was not thought that a woman was 'capable of beating a man'; this meant that unless the victim died or the victim of the assault was another woman, it was highly unlikely that many women would find themselves in court.[41]

There was also no benefit of the clergy for women, but they did have the next best thing. If a woman was either pregnant at the time of trial or became pregnant while in gaol (often because of easily persuaded or highly abusive turnkeys and gaolers), they could 'plead the belly'. It was not moral to hang an expectant mother, as the unborn child was innocent. Therefore, a reprieve would usually be given until the child's first birthday, by which time the woman would hopefully be lost in the legal system or pardoned.

The impact of these perceptions and workarounds on women in the law should not be underappreciated. Because of these reasons, while York Castle Prison had enough women coming through to justify building a female prison in 1237, things were very different regarding the trial. For example, over 85 per cent of those indicted for theft were men because of these loopholes.[42]

Capital Punishment

It is important to remember that York Castle Prison was not a prison for punishment at this point, while some prisoners were held there for long periods: these were the exception, not the rule. Imprisonment as a form of punishment was not used at this time because of the prevalence of capital punishment.[43] This is why it is more accurate to describe York Castle Prison as a gaol at this time, somewhere you came to await something, most likely a trial.

For those found guilty of a felony at trial, the outcome would often be a punishment of death. The most common execution method would be hanging. In York, this was generally in one of two places, most commonly at the Knavesmire, now York Racecourse, where the 'three-legged mare' was constructed in 1379 after a meeting at York Castle.[44] This would become known as York Tyburn, sometimes referred to as Micklegate Without. Its location is still marked to this day. The second gallows in York was known as Walmgate Without and was located near Green Dykes Lane. This set of gallows was less commonly used and ceased being used completely after the execution of Leonard Gaskil and Peter Rook in 1676. It was also sometimes referred to as St Leonards, Green Dykes. There were also other forms of execution carried out in these two locations. Women might be burned for petty treason, but this was extremely rare; even witches were usually hanged in England. On some occasions, men who were convicted of treason might be hanged, drawn and quartered at these same locations. Beheading, often thought of as common in medieval England, was usually reserved for nobility as a quicker death.

After execution, there was a bit of a grey area as to what happened to the bodies. Execution cemeteries did exist.[45] However, it is not known if or where this was in York, and many churches hold the bodies of executed criminals, such as St Mary's Church on Castlegate in York, where the highwayman John Nevison was buried. Likely, no specific restrictions existed on where those who had been executed were to be buried. There were groups out there, such as the Knights Hospitaller, who would claim the bodies of those executed. However, it is likely that those who had a family to claim the body would not suffer this fate.

Other Punishment

Of course, not everyone found guilty was executed. At certain times of war, which was common during the Plantagenet era, you could be lucky and be put into military service instead of a death sentence. However, depending on your fighting skills, this may only delay the inevitable.

To reduce the number of executions happening, particularly with so many occurring in the aftermath of the English Civil War, a new punishment was introduced in the form of transportation. This was not a new idea. Banishment had been an alternative punishment for centuries, and transportation was a logical extension of this concept. The idea was not new when it emerged under Oliver Cromwell's rule. Transportation was first passed in the Elizabethan Act

1597 'for the punishment of Rogues, vagabonds, and Sturdy Beggars – to be banished out of this realm and all other Dominions thereof'.[46] These criminals were mainly taken to places like Virginia, Jamaica and Barbados.[47] However, in the aftermath of the English Civil War, through Acts of Parliament in 1664 and 1666, transportation was brought into force for the first time in a manner later generations would recognise. Those found guilty would be sold to a shipping company, which would move them to their destination and then sell them into indentured servitude for the duration of their sentence.

However, there were problems with this system. Those companies providing the ships wanted to maximise their profit and could be picky when it came to the prisoners that they wanted to move; those that were not physically strong, or indeed women, would not fetch as much money and were often not taken.[48] Fixed prices by the government for prisoners made it very difficult to make a profit at all. Some successful ship owners benefited from the system, but by the time we got to the Glorious Revolution of 1688, the practice of transportation had effectively been abandoned.[49] It would not be until 1717 that the system would be brought back.

Other punishments were also available to judges, even for those convicted of crimes that could carry the death penalty. Corporal punishment in the form of public whipping could be used. Public humiliation in the stocks or pillory was also common. Many first-time offenders would be branded, usually on the hand, with a letter that represented their crime, for example, RT for a rogue or thief or M for manslaughter/murder. You would presume that this last one would be an automatic death sentence, but branding might be applied in cases where the evidence was unclear. If the person reappeared in court for the same crime, their guilt was almost automatically accepted because of their brand. Branding was sometimes also used for those who had previously claimed benefit of the clergy. You could only claim benefit of the clergy once; any second offence, and you would be tried at the assizes like everyone else. The location of this brand changed over time, but included the chest, most commonly the palm of the hand and, in some cases, on the face or forehead. Branding would not be officially abolished in Britain until 1822.[50]

We have set out the basics of the English justice system up to the late 1600s, but not everyone who came through York Castle Prison was accused of a felony. There are two groups we should not forget: those who committed treason and those held for a debt.

Treason

There was one crime that could come through the trials at York Castle that falls outside of the category of felony. This was treason! 'To become a traitor is to turn your back on those who trusted you. To betray and to violate your allegiance to a person, institution, or group.'[51] More serious than piracy or murder, treason would carry the ultimate punishment. The origins of treason in a modern sense date back to the Treason Act 1352. The concept of treason existed in some form before 1352, most widely popularised with the story of William Wallace in 1305. In fact, at York Castle in 1291, Welsh prisoner Rees Amereduk was sentenced to be 'drawn for the sedition and shall be hanged for the homicides, arsons, robberies and larcenies and demolitions of castles'.[52] However, this form of treason, while not arbitrary, was primarily defined by individual monarchs to deal swiftly and brutally with situations at the time. The 1352 Act formally defined treason, locking it into British law and public consciousness. While added to or changed many times over the centuries, the Treason Act 1352 is still on the statutes of Britain today.[53] The broad definition of treason included attempts to kill the king, the queen or their children, violating the queen, the king's eldest daughter or the wife of the heir to the throne, levying war against the king and counterfeiting either the coinage of the realm or the king's seal. No specific method of execution was defined, but some form of hanging, drawing and quartering was already a common punishment for treason. This would involve the guilty party being drawn to the place of execution, hung by the neck but cut down while still alive, having their bowels removed and burned in front of them, their head removed, and the body cut into four quarters. This was the core of the punishment; however, over time, some elements were changed, moved or added depending on the case's specific circumstances.

Along with the definition of what would later become 'high' treason, the 1352 Act also added the crime of 'petty' treason. This was the murder of someone who it was deemed had an allegiance owed to them. These included servants killing their masters, clergymen killing a religious superior, or the murder of a man by their wife.[54] This final one would rear its head several times during the prison's history at York Castle. For these women found guilty of treason, the punishment would not be hanging, drawing and quartering. Instead, they would be sentenced to death by burning.

Debtors

It is worth noting that others were held at York Castle Prison, not just the felons. At times, there were prisoners of war held here, and many were held because of their religious beliefs, but one group needs to be looked at further: the debtors. Debtors would make up the largest group of people held at York Castle Prison. It was technically York Castle Gaol for the felons as they were not being held as part of their punishment; the debtors were held in York Castle as a debtors' prison, giving it its often-used designation of York Castle Prison. Imprisoning someone for owing a debt would go on to define the site of York Castle in the eighteenth century, but its origins go much further back. There would have been debtors to the Crown held at York Castle intermittently since its original construction. These would have mainly been those that defrauded the Crown or made false claims for payment. However, in 1352, this would also change. From this point on, common creditors were in the same position as the Crown, giving any creditor 'the power of imprisoning his debtor's body until the debt in dispute should have been settled'.[55] Smaller amounts could be dealt with locally, and there was a debtors' prison on Ouse Bridge in York for this purpose. Factors that could determine how you were dealt with as a debtor include the scale of the debt, the presumed extent of your credit or your character.[56] Those who owed too much often ended up at the county gaol until their debt was cleared.

Debt could cause problems for any class of person. It was common for those deemed to be from 'respectable society' to overreach what they could afford to keep up appearances. Debt was also a crime that was heavily biased towards male prisoners. Men were generally responsible for their household finances at this time, so they were inevitably the ones who got sent to debtors' prisons. However, for the families of these men who had no other way to support themselves, the wives and even children could also end up having to come to prison until the debt was repaid.

Even innocent felons could get caught up in a debtors' prison. Gaolers could charge various fees to felons while they were imprisoned. After their trial, even being innocent did not guarantee a prisoner's freedom. Those who owed money to the gaoler could find themselves staying until that debt was repaid.

Charity or bequests were used to help those who could not hope to pay back their debts. However, it is unlikely that this was common enough to make a difference for most debtors.

Life in York Castle Prison

The local sheriff was responsible for maintaining the county courts and gaols. However, the sheriff's role decreased through the early modern period; by the seventeenth century, the position was more ceremonial rather than one that carried any significant judicial power. This was largely because of the rise of the importance of justices of the peace and the quarter sessions.

The system was, however, far from perfect and was open to massive abuse and corruption. An example of this was in 1366 when the sheriff of Yorkshire, Thomas Musgrave, was accused of 'malicious arrest, wrongful imprisonment, extortion, and the entrapment of an innocent man through the employment of a packed jury'.[57] He had arrested a servant of one of his enemies, tortured him, forced confessions out of him for serious crimes and then forced him to accuse his master, allowing Musgrave to be able to arrest his enemies.

The creation of county gaols and the responsibility for running them and keeping prisoners until their trial may ultimately fall on the county sheriff. However, the day-to-day running of the gaol was given to the gaoler. The gaoler would answer to the sheriff. As such, it was the sheriff's prerogative to find someone they trusted who would maintain the prison/gaol buildings and bring in as much income as possible from the prisoners during their stay. However, the Crown would start to ignore this and place its own men into the position of gaoler, bypassing the sheriff. By 1339, York Castle had a royal-appointed gaoler.[58] This practice continued into the fifteenth century.[59] This was not without its problems, not only for the sheriff, who had to rely on someone they did not know, but even the Crown could end up with someone they didn't know. In 1362, the gaoler at York Castle was appointed for life.[60] He 'alienated' his office in favour of another, i.e. he didn't want the role, so he paid someone else to do it. This person then did the same again, leaving York Castle being run by the employee of the employee of the person who was supposed to be doing the job. The practice of royal appointments was forbidden by a statute of 1504, but this did not last long, and by 1541, it was again common at York Castle, a process that would be maintained until after the English Civil War.[61] Ultimately, this was a hefty job with a lot for a gaoler to do; as such, we have records of an under-gaoler being appointed at York Castle from 1441 to help with the burden.[62]

Early gaolers were paid servants of the sheriff, unlike those we will meet later in the eighteenth century. In the late 1220s, the remuneration of a gaoler for his time is given as 7d per week.[63] This was not a great wage, and the gaoler was expected to make up for his poor pay by getting money from prisoners for the time they spent at York Castle.

It is hard to underestimate the gaoler's control over the prisoners. A poorly paid man who holds absolute control over the lives of prisoners, some of whom would have been lawless or violent, is not a job many people would want. It is unlikely this job would ever appeal to someone of good character. The brutality these gaolers could show is well recorded at many county gaols throughout England. One example of this at York Castle is in 1274, where the gaoler apparently 'tied a prisoner naked to a post and kept him starving'.[64] Sadly, the context of this incident is missing from the records, but it illustrates the brutality that a gaoler could show to a prisoner he either disliked or one who would not pay his way in prison.

This brings us to the critical point that your stay in gaol is not free. Your accommodation, food and many other items must be paid for. It would have been difficult for many prisoners to pay their way while in prison. As such, in earlier periods, gaolers would usually put prisoners under duress to try and get them to 'turn approver', to give the names of others involved in their crimes who were not already in gaol. These men, who were brought in, could bring in the 'normal fees and lodging charges or bribes for release'.[65] For York Castle, it is unsurprising to find that the same gaoler of 1274 carried this practice out.[66] This practice was so common among the county gaols that an Act was passed in 1327 to stop it. Although this was less than successful, in 1388 a gaoler at York Castle was again accused of this behaviour.[67]

Of course, more generally, torture could be used to coerce or punish those in prison. Whether in the hope of getting a confession or finding the innocence of someone, torture is a topic often associated with medieval and early modern prisons. While this was not common in England, and specifically placing this within the walls of York Castle is almost impossible, it is worth mentioning some of the more common methods as they fit into some stories of people who were held at York Castle. The reason that torture was so important was because of the quirks of the legal system requiring either two eyewitnesses or a confession for a conviction. With witnesses being difficult to find, there was a need to help with the process of confession.

The rack, designed to extract a confession by pulling on the limbs, stretching and tearing the tendons, and sometimes resulting in dislocation of the limbs, is probably the most popular image of medieval torture. Some authors argue that the first rack in England was placed in the Tower of London in 1447.[68] However, there is a reference to the rack being used, on the authorisation of King Edward II, on the Knights Templars held at York Castle in 1310. With no description of the device, it could be argued that this was not necessarily the rack we easily imagine today, it is difficult to interpret the word in any other way. Whether it is, or is not, what most people imagine as the rack, it does suggest that this type of torture was used earlier than is often thought and could well have been more widespread than we often believe in England.

As the county gaol for Yorkshire, prisoners were brought to York Castle throughout the year in the gaol deliveries. These were special convoys that visited the local gaols and collected anyone accused of a felony who needed to go to the main county gaol. These deliveries would bring an influx of new prisoners into the gaol. What they would find on arrival was not pleasant:

> As the prison for the whole of Northumbria, not a few brave Englishmen have been led through its gates to an ignominious death. Martyrs for conscience sake have died broken-hearted within its dark dungeons; and scores of poor manacled prisoners have succumbed to pestilence, starvation, and brutal official ill-treatment in its cells.[69]

As we have already hinted, the first part that needs to be acknowledged is the financial cost of spending time somewhere like York Castle. One author describes the cost that comes from spending time in prison at this time as involving

> A constant drain of money to the gaoler for rent, fuel, laundry, food and cooking, or for the privilege of providing their own commons, fees for fetters, and bribes for their removal. The gaoler, having paid for the patent of his office, was obliged to recover the outlays best he could, and his hand was ever stretched out for bribes to turn a blind eye on forbidden activities.[70]

This is a theme that, as we will see, will continue in English prisons into the nineteenth century.

Since York Castle was not a government facility, the gaoler had the prerogative to earn money from the prisoners while they were there. Being imprisoned could be quite expensive, even if you were innocent. For example, it was common for prisoners to be put into irons upon entering the gaol. Those who had some money behind them could pay for either lighter-weight irons or to have them removed completely.[71]

This is a cost that you will never get back, regardless of the outcome of the eventual trial. Of course, if you had the money, the conditions of your stay could be better, and with the benefit of the clergy, it would be unlikely that you would face the same ending after a trial anyway. These unequal costs combined with the disease we will see later is why one author describes York Castle as a 'Den of Iniquity and Horror' where only those with an iron constitution might survive.[72]

It is also worth noting that these costs didn't just apply to felons. Debtors and other prisoners would also be expected to pay for their stay at York Castle. An interesting example of costs for the felons imprisoned at York Castle comes in the reign of Edward I, when:

> whoever is imprisoned at York shall, on going in, pay a penny for a cord, although he may be a true man; and so, if he be found guilty the gaoler shall find for him a rope, and if he be set free he loses his penny.[73]

Yet even with these prisons being controlled by dominating gaolers who put their wealth before the health and wellbeing of the prisoners, this could, on some occasions, be used to the advantage of the prisoners. In 1388, William Holgate was a gaoler who was known not just for extorting money from the prisoners but for withholding alms, the charity that was paid to help support those who could not afford the cost of prison. However, he could be a friend to others and is known to have helped prisoners escape from York Castle – for a reasonable fee.[74]

Some small charities could also help prisoners through their time at York Castle. From 1289, St Leonards, on the other side of the city near St Mary's Abbey, regularly delivered half a rye loaf to each prisoner weekly,[75] although it appears that this was a situation unique to York. It is also unknown how long this went on, but the dissolution of the monasteries around 1536 would have permanently ended this charity. Another example might be posthumous benevolence, where someone leaves money in their will to help prisoners pay their fees or occasionally secure the release of debtors. In 1430, a will stated that 'bread, ale, beef, and mutton were to be found for the prisoners of three York prisons'.[76] Members of the church could also donate money to help prisoners. In 1351, a Yorkshire parson left 2½ marks to be distributed among the prisoners of three prisons in York.[77] Much of this charity would likely have been spent on food to ward off starvation.

Illness

Like all the others, the earliest prison buildings on the site would have been wooden. This would mean a cold and damp winter, with sickness commonplace. Conditions inside county gaols were not very good at the best of times, but by the Elizabethan period, it was becoming dire. Due to years of neglect, the decay of the infrastructure at York Castle was becoming apparent. There are records referring to 'the decay of the structure of the Gaol and the unpleasant nature of life within it'.[78]

The death and disease within these structures becomes easy to imagine. Gaol fever (mainly typhus, but sometimes dysentery) was rampant; therefore, even surviving to their trial was unlikely for some. There is an infamous example at Oxford Assizes in 1577, where sick prisoners infected the Judges and Jury members alike, with a large death toll as a result.[79] York Castle was no stranger to the disease. A man died from 'pestilence' here in 1391.[80] There was also a serious epidemic at the castle in 1528.[81] Given the conditions throughout this time period, as well as several major outbreaks of plague in the country, there were likely many more occasions where many died from disease at York Castle.

These conditions were not helped by the increased number of prisoners being held at York Castle. By the 1570s, Catholic recusants, those who openly continued to defy the Church of England and practise their faith, both male and female, began to fill up the gaol at York Castle. These conditions were exacerbated even more by the additional burden of people being held here for petty offences that would typically fall outside of the remit of a county court. It is for this reason that in 1636 Robert Ryther, keeper of the castle (a title many gaolers would use through the centuries), described how 'many who are in gaol for petty offences are likely to starve, while others are very unruly; all which might be helped by erecting a house of correction'.[82] It is hard to argue against awful conditions when the gaoler himself complains about them.

Despite these terrible conditions, it should be remembered that those held at any prison were not without recourse regarding aspects of their confinement. We will often see the use of petitions over the centuries. These were essentially complaint letters that would be taken and read to the justices of the peace, hoping they would step in and help resolve the situation. These were quite versatile documents that covered such eventualities as complaints about the conditions in the gaol, complaints about the overbearing gaolers' attitudes, and withholding of payments due to the prisoners. All the prisoners had to do was to have the petition drawn up and gather as many signatures as possible from people who supported their case. The more signatures, the better, but many signatures were not a guarantee of success. The hope was that the justices would see the injustice written in these petitions and force the gaoler and turnkeys to comply. However, the petition could also be used to commute sentences of death on prisoners; sometimes, these would include the signatures of victims who did not agree with the death penalty.

Just because we see such poor conditions as common at York Castle, it should not be overlooked that some areas did improve over time, if only marginally. It is reasonable to presume that when the castle walls become stone, one of the first buildings to be reconstructed would be the prison, if for no other reason than security. This would have brought at least a temporary improvement in conditions for the felons. King Henry III, who started reconstructing the castle in stone, provided some support for the upkeep of the gaol. This included payment of gaolers and 'making and repair of iron collars and fetters worn by prisoners'.[83]

When York Castle was beseiged during periods of war with Scotland, it appears the prison was also invested in. After all, some prisoners would be held here because of these conflicts. Over the centuries, prisoners of war from Scotland, Wales and Ireland were held at York Castle. In 1295, Welsh prisoners were given 4d per day as sustenance while imprisoned at York Castle.[84] Because these prisoners were being held effectively on behalf of the Crown, they were treated differently from those imprisoned for felonies. In fact, because of the Welsh War in 1295, the ordinary assizes were halted. This left many in the gaol dying of hunger, and many more constantly in danger of death because of the unusually long time that they spent in the gaol at York Castle.

Chapter 3

The Site of York Castle Prison, 1705–1777

The Prison

At the beginning of the eighteenth century, the buildings that made up York Castle were suffering from 'neglect and decay'.[1] While York Castle was not abandoned, less and less was happening. The defensive capabilities were virtually non-existent after the end of the Civil War, and the keep was irreparably damaged in the explosion of 1684. The primary function of the buildings on the site was now their role as a prison. The site effectively changed from York Castle into York Castle Prison.

A 1699 Act of Parliament allowed justices of the peace to build and extend county gaols. For Yorkshire, this resulted in a 3d tax being levied across the three Ridings of Yorkshire to raise enough money to build a new county gaol on the site of York Castle.[2] Most of the former castle within the bailey area was cleared to make way for the new, state-of-the-art prison building Only two buildings from the original castle were standing left, the moot hall (the court building) and jury house, both of which had only been reconstructed in the 1660s.

Construction of the new prison building at York Castle began in 1701, but this was going to be an expensive project, with the total cost of the building being £8,000.[3] Some relief on the taxpayer was afforded, however, when a petition was sent to the Treasury as follows:

> Petition of the Knights, Citizens, and Burgesses serving in Parliament for the City of York, and others, the Justices of the peace of that county, to the King, praying for a warrant to make use of the ruinous wall, &c., of the King's Manor house at York, to build the gaol.[4]

This petition refers to the ruins of St Mary's Abbey, the large amount of stone that still existed on the site, and the ruinous parts of York Castle itself.[5] This request was granted, allowing the construction of what we know today as the debtors' prison building.

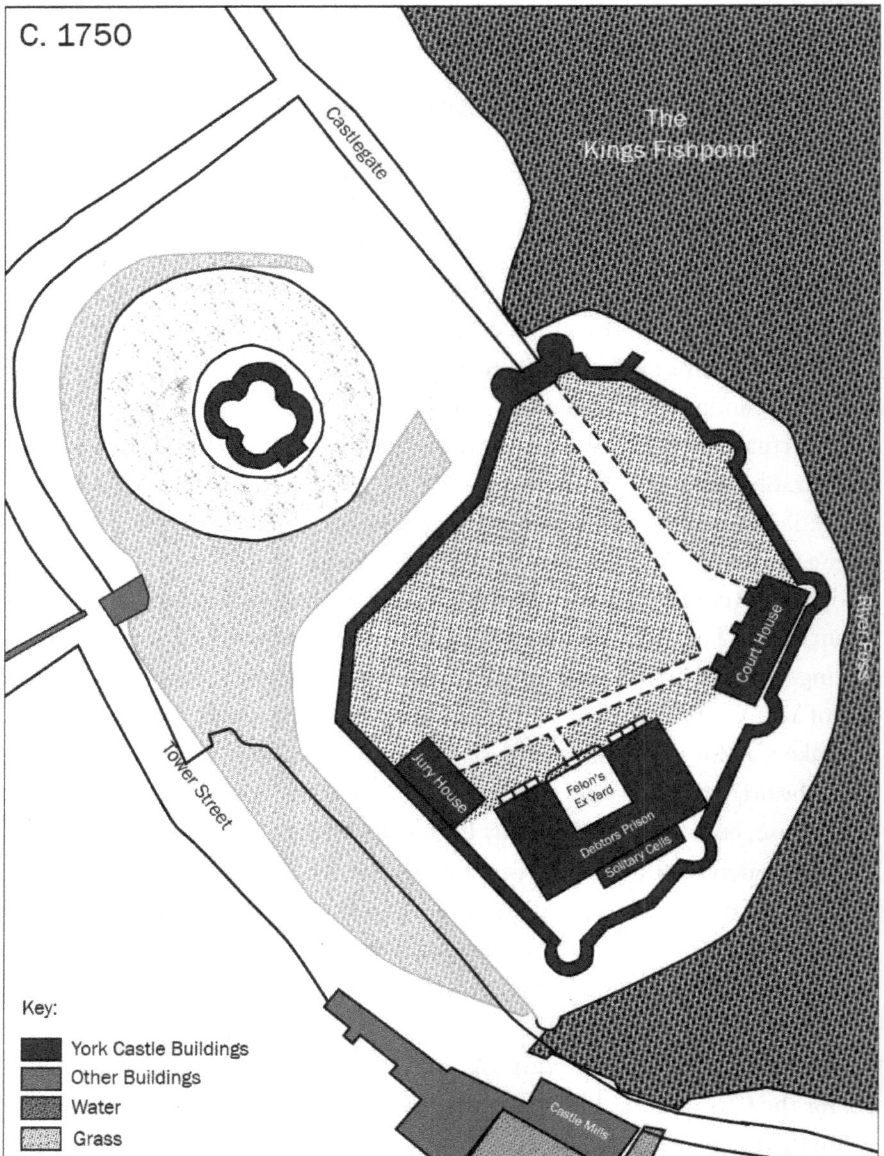

A plan of the site around 1750. N.B. The location of the western moat is shown, although this gradually silted up and was finally removed around 1731.[6]

The new building was completed in 1705. The architectural choices of the architect William Wakefield[7] make this the only baroque-style prison ever constructed. This gave York a unique and rather grandiose prison building, something unique at the time. It has been suggested that after the construction of the debtors' prison, only York Minster was more significant in York.[8] Why was such a grandiose building needed? We can attribute this to civic pride, as it seeks to draw attention away from the now ruinous Clifford's Tower. On the other hand, some authors have suggested that the design acted as an 'instigator of virtue',[9] helping to reform the prisoners through their grand surroundings. The façade of the building can also be considered exactly that – a façade, concealing the terrible conditions inside and giving a false impression of grandeur and rationality to those observing. Some of this grandeur was also due to the ambitions of the architect William Wakefield, who wanted to showcase his talent when creating the building. As a result of this excessive design, the debtors' prison would remain the largest purpose-built prison in England until Newgate Prison in London was rebuilt in the early 1770s.

Around the early 1730s, Daniel Defoe, the author of *Robinson Crusoe* and *Moll Flanders* visited York Castle on a trip around the country, describing it as:

> A Prison the most stately and complete of any in the whole Kingdom, if not Europe … the Castle Yard is larger than the Areas of the fleet or Kings Bench in London, and the situation is so high, pleasant, and airy, that 'tis surprising that prisoners should remove themselves by *Habeas Corpus* to either of those prisons, unless it be with a view of purchasing the liberty of the Rules, because here they are never permitted to go without the walls. Strangers, who visit the inside of it, seldom depart without making a trifling Purchase of some of the small Manufactures the Prisoners work up for Subsistence.[10]

The Fleet and King's Bench were debtors' prisons in London, where Defoe had spent some time as a debtor. This makes his praise more significant, coming from someone who has experienced a debtors' prison firsthand. This description also refers to the ability of wealthier debtors to purchase the freedom to stay just outside these prisons in London, due to their constant overcrowding, something York's new debtors' prison was designed to prevent.

At this point, from the experience of someone who had spent time in debtors' prisons, York Castle was the best that could exist.

The front façade of the building, with its grand arches above each wing as well as the entire ground floor, was constructed of stone, mainly recovered from St Mary's Abbey and the castle. Behind this façade, the two upper floors were constructed of brick to reduce costs. This part of the building was not easily visible from outside the prison, so it is understandable why they didn't go to the expense of using stone.

In addition to the baroque architecture, there were other interesting design aspects. The most significant was that many of the windows on the ground floor, as shown in pictures from that time, were not real; they were merely superficial features on the outside of the building, not extending through to the inside. The prison reformer John Howard alluded to this, and other authors have also suggested that this was a trend for prisons at the time.[11] This meant that the felons' apartments, covering the ground floor of the building, had no natural light entering them. This seemingly strange decision was not uncommon, as a window tax had been introduced in England in 1696, which required buildings with more than six windows to pay a levy. The fewer actual windows on your building, the cheaper this levy would be.

When it comes to understanding what was happening inside the new debtors' prison building, it is easiest to imagine it split into three parts: the rear of the building and the two wings on each side. To differentiate these wings, it is easiest to use the terms east wing and west wing. The rear part of the building was itself split by its architecture. The two upper floors housed the debtors and would have had largely the same floor plan on both floors. The ground floor was occupied by the felons, either awaiting trial or awaiting their sentence. But what was happening in each area?

The east wing was 'occupied by debtors and the governor, with rooms for the under gaoler.' The gaolers and under-gaolers' offices were located on the first floor with a staircase leading up to them from the front of the building. The ground floor of this side housed spaces for the turnkeys, kitchens, and space for the governor's parlour. In the west wing, on the ground floor, were 'chambers and cells wherein the felons were imprisoned …'[12] The prison chapel was also housed in the west wing, accessed once again by stairs outside the building.[13] This took up both the first and second floors of the west wing of the building and must have been an impressive sight.

The chapel was described as 'handsome and beautiful ... with Altar handsomely railed in, and the Pavement black and white marble, a decent Pulpit and all the Furniture of it answerable'.[14] Interestingly, when the prison reformer John Howard visited most prisons in England in the 1770s, chapels were rare in these institutions. This made York Castle quite unusual at the time.

John Howard also gives us one of the best descriptions of the debtors' prison building during the 1770s:

> IN THE SPACIOUS AREA is a noble prison for debtors, which does honour to the county. You ascend by a fine flight of stone steps to a floor on which eleven rooms, full sixteen feet square, near twelve feet high. Above them is the same number of rooms: one or two of these, for the common-side Debtors. The rooms are airy and healthy. On the ground floor are the Gaolers apartments &c.
>
> The Felons court-yard is down five steps: it is too small, and has no water: the pump is just on the outside of the palisades. The day-room for men is only twenty-six feet by eight: in it are three cells: in another place nine cells: and three in another. The cells are in general about seven feet and a half by six feet and a half, and eight feet and a half high; close and dark; having only either a hole over the door about four inches by eight, or some perforations in the door of about an inch in diameter: not any of them to the open air, but into passages or entries. In most of these cells three prisoners are locked up at night; in winter for fourteen to sixteen hours: straw on the stone floors; no bedsteads. There are four condemned rooms about seven feet square. ... A sewer in one of the passages often makes these parts of the Gaol very offensive: and I cannot say they are clean. Indeed a clean prison is scarcely seen, where the Water is to be brought in by Gaoler's servants. The next house to the Castle-gate, and others in the neighbourhood, have river-water laid in at moderate expense.
>
> Women-felons are kept quite separate: they have two court-yards, but no water: you go down four steps to their two rooms, a day and a night room. Their condemned room is in another part of the Gaol: near it is a room to confine Debtors who do not behave well.

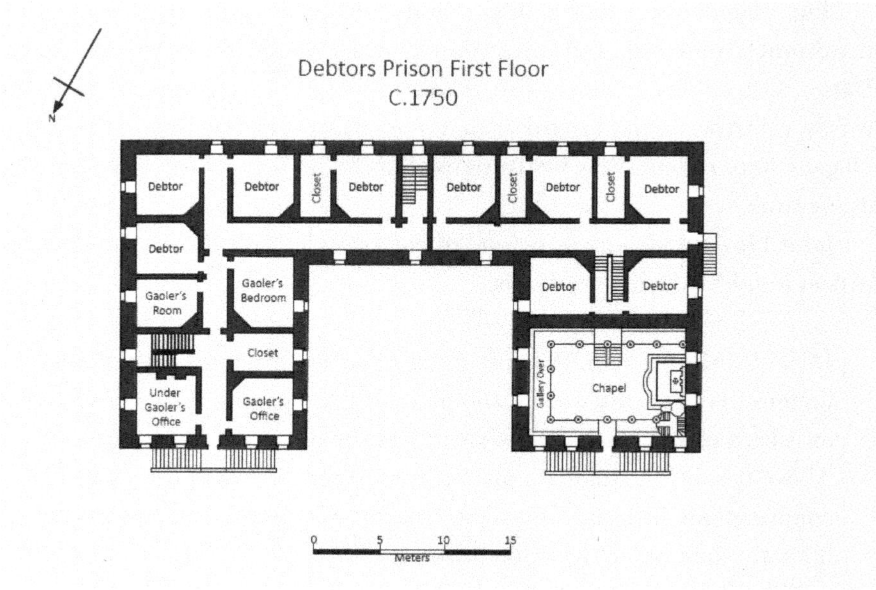

A plan of the first floor of the debtors' prison around 1750 showing the chapel and layout of the debtors' apartments.[15] It is worth noting that sources are unclear if the stairs in the center at the back were added later or not. This could have been another closet at this period.

The Infirmary near the gate is only one middle-sized room. When Prisoners of one sex are there, those of the other are excluded. A sick man was kept out for that reason when I was there.

At Assize some prisoners appear in court on their trial in the County-Clothing.

The County pays one John Sherwood £10 a year to inspect and weigh the bread and deliver it to the prisoner. He constantly attends for this purpose on Tuesday and Friday.

Transports convicted at Quarter Sessions have, besides the bread allowance, one shilling per week. Those cast at Assize have the King's Allowance of 2s 6d. a week.

There is a grand Shire-Hall in the castle yard almost finished. I hope the Gentlemen of this great county will not stop there; but proceed to build a proper Prison for Felons; in which Boys may be separate from Old Offenders, and the other Inconveniences of the present Gaol avoided.[16]

We can pull out a few interesting things from Howard's description of York Castle Prison.

The debtors' accommodation is described as spacious, measuring 16 feet by 16 feet and 12 feet high. These large rooms can still be seen today in the galleries and offices of York Castle Museum. These large rooms still have an angled corner where the fireplace would have been. The layout of the debtors' floors reflected their functionality:

> Each Floor is divided into four zones: the chapel; the first class debtors with servant quarters; the second class debtors; and the Governor's office and apartments. Each zone had its own staircase access between the two floors and its own separate identity ...[17]

The terminology used by this author in terms of first class, second class and the use of the term 'governor' as opposed to gaoler appears to be later than the dates suggested; however, the distinct, separate areas of the building are likely to have been consistent throughout the history of the debtors' prison.

Not mentioned by Howard was the debtors' exercise yard, a rather spacious yard at the back of the debtors' prison, surrounded by the now reconstructed castle wall. This exercise area was accessed via a staircase located on the first floor. The debtors also had access to what is now known as the Eye of York in front of the debtors' prison building. However, this access would have been restricted during the assize sessions. It is important to remember that the debtors' accommodation, being far more spacious overall, was a much nicer place to spend time than the felons' cells. Debtors were a different class of criminal, and the accommodation reflected this, with one author describing it as 'in keeping with the country house aesthetic, a relative home from home'.[18]

By contrast, Howard's picture of the felons' cells is very bleak. However, Howard's description does not provide the complete picture of the period we are examining; instead, it is a snapshot of the time Howard visited. Initially, the small sleeping cells visible on the plans did not exist. The original ground floor consisted of large rooms, as shown on a 1732 plan.

It was not until 1732, when twenty-one felons escaped from York Castle Prison, that things changed. As the turnkey was coming to lock the door to those prisoners awaiting transportation, they rushed the turnkey, overpowering him, and fleeing through the fence in the central courtyard and escaping. Although some seventeen of these prisoners were recaptured, it prompted significant changes to how the felons' cells were structured. The large rooms were broken up into smaller 7.5 feet by 6.5 feet sleeping cells. The idea was that it was easier for the turnkeys to manage smaller numbers of prisoners at a time. It is this prison layout, with smaller cells, that Dick Turpin would have been familiar with just seven years later.

This original layout of the building is also why Howard mentions four condemned cells. The original condemned cell is broken up into four sleeping cells. It is important that Howard also mentions the lack of ventilation in these cells. He mentions some perforations in the cell doors and small ventilation holes between the sleeping cells, but even these were possibly not put into the prison until after the suffocation of nine prisoners in October 1737.[19]

The felons' cells were separated into several smaller areas following the plan of the original large rooms. Until the late eighteenth century, all these areas of the felons' cells were only accessible from the central felons' courtyard, between the two wings of the building, sometimes called the

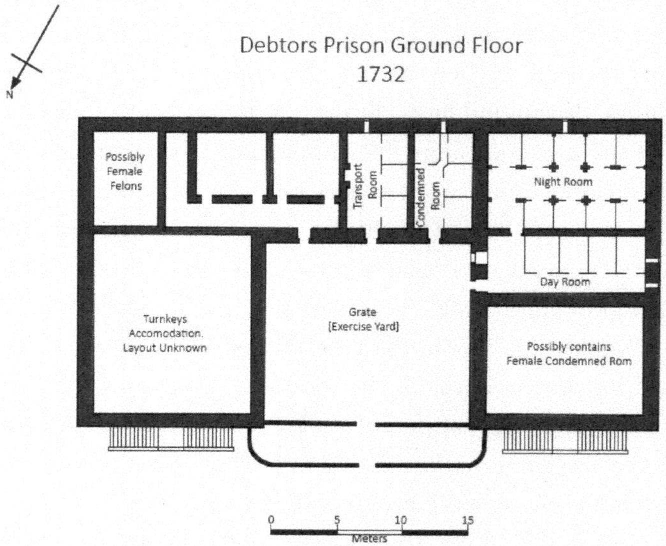

A plan of the ground floor 'felons apartments' based on the 1732 partial plan at Wakefield archive. Some of the layout is unknown; these areas should be regarded as a 'best guess'.[20]

'Low Grates'.[21] Located between the two wings of the prison, this small exercise yard had a railing running across to enclose the open end, allowing the debtors and the public to observe the felons. This area was used for any interactions between the felons and the public. Poor debtors were allowed to beg at this grate; this meant mixing with the felons, so you had to be quite desperate. We also know that butchers would come to the low grates on a Sunday and sell their unsold, poor-quality cuts of meat to prisoners.

> About four butchers come with bits and pieces of meat … On a Sunday morning, in front of the low grates, they spread a cloth on the flags, and the men felons bargain as hard as they can, for poor meat, the refuse of Saturday's York market. The window soles in the passage are used for showing meat to the debtors. I have never seen but one good piece offered by those people … An old woman goes to the flesh market for the unfortunate women felons.[22]

A second fence was added after the 1732 escape attempt, but the exercise yard itself was small, just as Howard describes it. The function of some areas leading from the courtyard is easily determined from the 1732 plan. You would have seen five doors from inside the exercise yard with the fence and the Eye of the Ridings behind you. Directly in front would have been a door that leads to the area for those awaiting transportation. This area would have been something else before 1718, but it appears to have been for transportees for most of the rest of the eighteenth century. To the right of this door is the door to the condemned cell for those awaiting execution. Along the right-hand wall, the first door, near the condemned cell, leads to an area for those awaiting trial. This was the largest area of the felons' cells. This, however, is as much as the 1732 plan reveals to us.

Understanding the other parts of the felons' cells requires some detective work. The easiest question would be asking what we are missing. The simple answer here is where the women would have been held. Once again, Howard helps us understand where the women were kept with four pieces of information:

1. They were separated from the men;
2. They had access to two courtyards;

3. The area had day and night rooms;
4. The female condemned cell is in another part of the prison near a cell for 'debtors who do not behave well'.[23]

These are important clues and suggest that the female felons occupied both parts of the felons' cells we are trying to understand, one as a condemned cell and one as a female prison. However, we do get another clue in 1778. A letter written by William Preston provides information about a change in the location of female prisoners from 1778.

> What is now the women's prison to be for atrocious offenders, two of the rooms at the West end of the Castle to be made for the Women's prison with a yard in the space adjoining the south end of the new Court ...[24]

This indicates that female prisoners were relocated to the west wing of the debtors' prison, suggesting they had previously been housed in the eastern part of the felons' cells. We also know that at some point, the east section becomes the condemned cell for male felons, replacing the more central room we have previously discussed. This is likely the room for 'atrocious offenders'. However, there is not enough detail in either description to make us confident that we can place the female felons with any certainty before 1778. While the eastern part is likely, the western two rooms are a large space for the female condemned cell and a room for poorly behaving debtors. Consequently, something else would have also been happening here. The description provided to us by Howard also closely matches the changes listed in 1778, not the location in the eastern part of the felons' cells. There was no access to two courtyards from the eastern location. However, it should be noted that the exact layout of the eastern section at this time is also unknown. The description from Howard suggests that this move may have already begun before 1778, at least to some extent. The best we can do before this period is to suggest that the female felons were likely held somewhere in the eastern portion of the felons' cells until the mid to late 1770s, when they were moved to the front of the western wing of the debtors' prison building.

Later Changes

Overall, the building of this new prison can be considered a success. We have already seen that the author Daniel Defoe describes York Castle Prison as: 'a Prison the most stately and complete of any in the whole Kingdom, if not in Europe'.[25] Another author, Tobias Smollett, says that York Castle Prison is 'the best, in all respects, I ever saw at home or abroad'.[26] This is not to say that there were no problems, particularly with the building's maintenance. Repairs were needed frequently during its early years, with maintenance of the clock and repairs to the 'causey-ways at the Castle of Yorke' being pushed forward in 1723.[27]

There were also some small additions to the building, most notably in 1716, when a clock was added to the top of the debtors' prison building. This clock can still be seen today. Built by John Terry of York, it originally had a single hand, although an additional hand was added in 1854 along with a new escapement.[28] It is unclear when this extra hand disappeared, reverting to the single hand it now has. It is also interesting to note that the brass plates of the clock record the original installation in 1716, as well as details of modifications by George Blakeborough in 1854 and G.J. Newey in 1902.[29]

The Castle

The construction of this brand-new building may have been the most significant change to the site during the eighteenth century, but there were also some changes to what remained of the castle itself during this period. In 1708, the south entrance, referred to as the 'towers' was taken down.[30] The south entrance had been blocked since at least 1682 and was no longer usable anyway. In 1731, the 'Wet Ditch on the west side of the river Foss' was drained,[31] removing the last remaining part of the castle's former moat, and allowing for a road to be constructed in its place. Additionally, in 1732, a coach house was constructed on the site for the High Sheriff.[32] Finally, in 1735, the north gate, leading onto Castlegate, was rebuilt.

Chapter 4

Life in York Castle Prison, 1705–1777

Running the Prison

Life for those unfortunate enough to find themselves incarcerated within the walls of York Castle Prison was primarily defined by the men who ran it. It is important to remember that these institutions were still always run by men at this time. This was the same for all gaols throughout England. We have already established that these were generally not the best of men, but rather, that their personalities would define the stay of any prisoner in the eighteenth century.

It was the sheriff's responsibility to run the county gaol, but they would offload this responsibility to a gaoler who would deal with the day-to-day running of the gaol. It could be quite expensive to run a county gaol. In 1717, we know that the rent on York Castle, paid by the gaoler, for the use of the buildings was around 300 pounds per year.[1] This value does not account for various other factors, such as the cost of staff to operate the prison, maintenance and additional expenses that may be incurred in its operation. In 1717 alone, the cost of repairing the roof of one of the buildings was estimated at £47.[2] If a debtor escaped, the gaoler was essentially on the hook for that debt. If prisoners escaped, the gaoler would have to pay for the recapture of the prisoner. One such example at York Castle comes from the gaoler, Richard Woodhouse. He was the gaoler in charge of York Castle Prison in 1732 when twenty-one prisoners escaped. In the records that survive, he describes himself as being left with 'great difficulties to make payments to his Creditors' because of the cost of recapturing the prisoners.[3] Additionally, the ground-floor felons' apartments had to be modified to prevent a repeat of the incident, which would have further exacerbated this expense. Over the course of two years, seventeen of the escapees would be recaptured, costing Richard Woodhouse £150 in expenses.[4] It is perhaps unsurprising that of the seventeen men that were recaptured, ten would be executed, and the other seven transported because of their escape.[5] This was not the first time Richard Woodhouse had to petition for money to keep his finances afloat. In 1730, he petitioned to collect the costs of prisoners he had been forced to release without them having paid the usual release fee. This included twenty soldiers who had been held at York Castle Prison for desertion and subsequently released.[6] Once again, this cost Richard Woodhouse money; after all, he had put them up while they were at the castle, so why should he not get compensated for this? We don't know if his request was successful, but he likely ended up out of pocket again.

The burden of recouping these costs to the gaoler fell upon the prisoners. Money meant everything to those unfortunate enough to be incarcerated in a Georgian prison. For the poorest, it could be a death sentence, but for those who had money, they could afford a more comfortable lifestyle, including the ability to pay for day release.[7] With poor quality food, many prisoners had to rely on the generosity of their families to survive.

The gaoler had no annual salary. The only way a gaoler could afford to run a prison was to profit from gaol fees, as well as the food and liquor brought into the prison. This system for getting additional money from prisoners was common throughout England and became known as 'garnish'. All prisoners paid 3s 4d on arrival; the gaoler also received ten guineas per transport.[8] Often, even larger fees would have been extracted upon discharge from prison.[9] At York Castle Prison, one of the most extreme forms of 'garnish' was a charge of 6s 8d to the gaoler plus 2s to the turnkeys if the prisoner was found not guilty.[10] Even the innocent were extorted inside the gaol, and the inability to pay could see you moved with the debtors. This could become even more expensive after 1729, when a prisoner charged with several offences had to pay for each individually.[11]

Of course, there were other ways to make money as a gaoler or turnkey, and the turnkey Thomas Ward (who would later become gaoler himself) ran a side business 'to show the Gentry & others the Castle, for which he got upwards of sixty pounds per annum to his own use …'.[12]

York Castle Prison is just one example of a Georgian prison's inadequate facilities for housing prisoners. The gaolers having to spend their own money running the prison meant that they had to rely on the justices to provide food, irons, medical attention, or even accommodation for children left in prison.

Food

Food and drink came at a cost to prisoners. The county allowance provided a small amount of bread each week, but this had its problems. For those that relied on the county allowance, the lack of provisions sometimes got so bad that those with nothing else to live on 'are almost starved'.[13] Luckily, the petition that contained this remark was successful, and the allowance doubled at York Castle Prison. However, sometimes, this was too late, and in 1728, it was recorded that some prisoners on the county allowance would not make it: 'several of the said prisoners have been dead very lately and no less than four in the last week ...'[14]

This could become even worse if you were acquitted at trial or sentenced to branding or whipping. If you could not pay the release fee to the gaoler and turnkeys, you would continue to be held in York Castle Prison. However, your county allowance is also reduced, putting these prisoners in a greater danger of starvation.[15]

Even for those who could afford to buy food and drink, the prison staff could make this a terrible experience. We have a record in 1709 of an 'ambitious and insulting Gaoler' Mr Chippendale, Mr Pearson, the under gaoler and the turnkey Thomas Ward, stopping prisoners from acquiring their own beer and wine.[16] Instead, they charged them double the price of the items, making a tidy profit for themselves. Even if a prisoner acquired a certificate of poverty, allowing him to receive charity, the under-gaoler and turnkey wanted their share before anything was handed out.[17]

Irons

Sometimes, the lack of provisions was more concerning for the prison's security than for the prisoners' welfare. In 1720, Thomas Ward, now gaoler of York Castle Prison, complained that there were so many prisoners being held that he

> hath not Irons Shackles or Bolts sufficient to load them with attending to the Crimes they are severally commit for but is forced very often to Borrow the same from the Gaoler of Ouze bridge & att other times link two or 3 prisoners together ...[18]

It says a lot about the treatment of prisoners when they are linked together because there is a lack of irons sufficient for them to each have their own. This exacerbates an already difficult situation for the prisoners.

Medical Treatment

In 1728, we are told that of the 140 prisoners at York Castle Prison:

> [Many were in] The miserable state they are under in case of Sickness lameness accidental or otherwise. There being no person appointed to give proper Medicin's or attendance for want of which great numbers have of late died of fever and other distempers and mortifications occasion'd by the settling of humours into their limbs. And in that miserable stinking condition have been in danger of infecting the whole Gaol.[19]

This was a petition from prisoners begging for medical intervention to save their lives. Once again, the expense that this would usually incur was one that the gaoler would not want to pay. Therefore, it was down to the prisoners to petition the justices of the peace for medical care to be provided.

Children

Sometimes, parents who were transported or otherwise punished might end up leaving their child inside York Castle Prison. Sometimes, the staff looked out for these children, and Richard Woodhouse would house one child in his own home.[20] In 1718, gaoler Thomas Ward got an apprenticeship for a 12-year-old boy named Thomas Burgan, who had been left behind when his mother was released from York Castle Prison.[21] However, this was likely Thomas Ward's own child with Mary Burgan, a condemned prisoner, so in this instance, his kindness was self-beneficial. This was important as keeping children in the prison was another cost that the gaoler had to find, inevitably, once again, from the prisoners. In 1728, Richard Woodhouse submitted a list of costs, which included some small building costs but also the upkeep of two children and a midwife for the birth of a third. The total cost was £16, with the majority of this amount covering the cost of the children.

If we look at everything we have seen from a modern perspective, this appears to be an ineffective way to run a prison. However, there was also no real pushback to help influence prisons to change; the public opinion was that a prison's 'purpose was to restrict the movement of prisoners and to produce a stream of revenue for prison officials'.[22]

This lack of oversight meant that the character of each prison in England was unique, determined mainly by the personalities of those in charge. With such enormous burdens for the gaoler to bear, it is perhaps unsurprising that until reforms started to come into effect in the late 1700s, many of the gaolers were overbearing, creating a standard of life for prisoners that was subhuman at best.

Edward Hinchcliffe appears to have been a decent gaoler. He would end up in York's debtors' prison on Ouse Bridge after he helped a pregnant prisoner obtain bail. In 1711, he was fined £25 for 'not keeping a sifisant Womens Gaole'.[23] While this makes him sound like a decent gentleman, helping a woman get out of the horrible conditions of York Castle Prison at the expense of his own freedom, Hinchcliffe was certainly not without his own terrible acts within the prison. A few years earlier, in 1707/1708, he was brought before the quarter sessions at Wetherby for his treatment of Thomas Sympson, where Hinchcliffe:

> then Gaolor there caused to be put such heavy irons without joints on the said Thomas Sympson so that he was not able to stand or so much as turn himselfe without help, and threatened him that he the said Sympson should lye and rott upon the stone floor he then laid on unless he would signe & sealeth bond or warrant of Attorney to confess a judgment for thirty pounds and also give the said Gaolor his house.[24]

The example of Hinchcliffe highlights the dichotomy of an evil gaoler but also reveals his genuine human side. He was willing to do the right thing to help someone when he felt that their incarceration was morally wrong, but equally, he had a huge rent on the building to pay and would make sure that he was able to pay his own bill, even if that came at great expense to the inmates of York Castle Prison.

Another example of how a gaoler could be brutal, causing a horrific environment for prisoners, is Thomas Griffiths. He was involved in several serious incidents during his tenure at York Castle Prison. He was a gaoler at the prison and directly involved in the death of at least one prisoner, William Petyt. William was a debtor who got on the wrong side of those running the prison; he was beaten up by those in charge, including Thomas Griffiths himself, and thrown into the felons' cells on the ground floor of the debtors' prison, only to succumb to his wounds a few days later. Despite this incident and subsequent enquiries, Griffiths was still gaoler in 1746 when the Jacobites were brought to York Castle Prison. It was the arrival of this large group of prisoners and the soldiers who accompanied them as guards that was to be Thomas' downfall. He did not get along with the soldiers and tried to enforce his control over them. This friction led to the removal of Thomas Griffiths from his position as gaoler. For most people, dismissal would end their association with the buildings, but this was not the case for Thomas. Over the next few years, he made poor investments in local properties and was subsequently returned to York Castle Prison. However, this time, it was as a debtor. He would spend his final days in the establishment that he had once terrorised, dying in the debtors' prison in 1751. He was buried only a few hundred metres away in the churchyard of St Mary's.[25]

The story of Griffiths brings home just how horrible the wrong gaoler could make a prison in the 1700s. Along with other men like Hinchcliffe, Chippendale, Woodhouse or Ward, it appears that most of these gaolers knew how to use their power. However, the stories of all these men reveal how close they came to ending up in a debtors' prison themselves, a fate that both Hinchcliffe and Griffiths faced. While the eventual end could never justify these brutal regimes, perhaps it does give us some understanding as to why gaolers felt the need to terrorise and extort their prisoners.

The enormous cost of running a prison also meant that looking after the prisoners was of relatively little concern; the fact remains that they were treated very laxly, being allowed to get away with much while in prison. The prison reformer John Howard explains that 'Gaming' was a particular problem within prisons.[26] This was a mix of gambling and general sports, where they could be played. When talking about county gaols, like York Castle Prison, he notes that 'one can seldom go in without seeing prisoners at play'.[27] This was because there was no discipline system within a place like York Castle Prison. Those held here were essentially left to their own devices, with the gaoler and turnkeys only there to ensure that prisoners stayed there.

So, how would a prisoner obtain the money to pay for their stay and, hopefully, their release afterwards? Those who had money would not have had a problem. Those with friends and family who could support them would also have had no real issues paying for their stay. For others, as we will also see with debtors, some could make small items to sell. In fact, during a visit to York Castle Prison, the author Daniel Defoe mentions that 'Strangers, who visit the Inside of it, seldom Depart without making a trifling Purchase of some of the small Manufactures the Prisoners work up for Subsistence'.[28] There was also a small amount of charity towards the prisoners. The reformer John Howard listed some of these charities. For example, the 'honourable and ancient City of York' gave 2s 6d per week in bread. Alternatively, Dr Phineas Hodgeson paid 2s weekly to 'all that hear the sermons'; the prisoners were paid to attend church services.[29] There were other small charities, but with the cost of prison, these would barely help a person survive. Ultimately, it was a simple system; if you could afford it, your life would be as good as it could be, given the circumstances. For those who couldn't afford their stay, where the next meal came from was a greater concern than the prospect of trial.

Changes to the Law

Like the previous few centuries, the justice system of the eighteenth century was not static. However, to understand the broader attitudes toward crime and punishment during the eighteenth century, it is necessary to go back a few years to the Glorious Revolution of 1688. The events surrounding this would set the tone for the eighteenth century. For the country, it marked the beginning of the end of the Stuart Monarchy, with the foundations laid for the Georgian era that began in 1714. Politically, it gave rise to the Jacobites, who attempted to restore James II and his descendants in 1689, 1715, and finally in 1745. Economically, it gave rise to new forms of wealth, increased the money and 'portable property' around, and essentially brought financial capitalism to the country, giving England increased wealth and prosperity.[30] It also saw a proportional increase in people's aspirations; everyone wanted to be part of the new wealth and were no longer content making a meagre existence off the land. Consequently, we also see a rise in new forms of wealth, giving rise to new forms of crime, with harsh penalties handed out to those who transgressed against this new wealth in their 'rage for "luxury"'.[31] It was the right of the new wealthy classes to protect their wealth, and so, as a result, punishment became ever more severe. In 1688, there were approximately fifty crimes in Britain that carried the death penalty, and many of these were often evaded due to the benefit of the clergy for the offences. After 1688, more and more crimes were added to the felonies list, i.e. those that could carry the death penalty, with the number increasing to 160 by 1765, with another 65 added between 1765 and 1815, taking the total to a staggering 225 crimes on the British statutes that the death penalty could punish.[32] In addition, the ability to claim the benefit of the clergy was gradually reduced, initially with the introduction of the Provisions Act 1706, which restricted its use.[33] The result was that capital crimes now had a greater chance of being tried in court.[34] Many of these crimes were to protect the new wealth, with crimes like stealing sheep or pickpocketing more than 1 shilling becoming eligible for capital punishment.[35] These new crimes were pushed for by specialist lobby groups seeking to protect their own interests.[36] Britain would be set to be ruled by what would become known as 'The Bloody Code'. The bloody code itself was a culmination of several pieces of legislation. The most important were: the Riot Act 1715, Black Act 1722, and the Murder Act 1751.

Riot Act 1715

Designed to deal with the Jacobites, the Riot Act 1715 made it a non-clergiable felony to have more than twelve people assembled and to not dissipate within an hour of the Riot Act being read out by a magistrate or for the twelve people to prevent the reading of the Riot Act or commit any property damage before it was read.[37] There appear to be few cases of this being used in Yorkshire, although rioting was a bigger problem in London, most notably the Gordon Riots of 1780. Although repealed in 1973, it was an important piece of legislation. To this day, the phrase 'to read the riot act' is still used in common sayings when someone is reprimanded or warned of consequences.

Black Act 1722

The second, and perhaps the most significant, legislation for the 'Bloody Code' was the Waltham Black Act 1722. Following the collapse of the 'South Sea Bubble' in 1720, an economic downturn led to increased social tensions, prompting the wealthy to seek protection for their assets. The 'Black Act', named after the custom of poachers blacking their faces when committing crimes, would form the backbone of Britain's ever-increasing reliance on capital punishment. In total, fifty offences were added to Britain's capital crimes under this act alone. This was supplemented in 1724, 1725 and 1729 acts to add all types of forgery to the list of felonies.[38] One of the predominant themes of the Black Act was its focus on economic crimes.

Murder Act 1751

The Murder Act 1751 'for the better preventing the horrid crime of murder' mandated the dissection of the bodies of executed murderers, both men and women. For those executed in York, this dissection would usually take place at York County Hospital.[39] Still, it was also common for bodies to be taken somewhere local to the crime for dissection. Dissection was considered abhorrent to most people; with the Christian significance of the body for resurrection, this could be seen as a fate that carried on after death. As a result, executed prisoners were some of the few bodies that surgeons could get their hands on to learn about the human body and practise their methods. The Murder Act also established that prisoners should be executed the 'next day but one after their sentence of death has been passed … and, further, that the prisoner should be fed on bread and water only, after being sentenced.'[40]

The 1751 Act was designed to ensure that punishment was proportional to the crime. As a result, for some crimes like brutal murders, robbing mail coaches, or highway robbery, punishment could be taken even further. Considered to be even worse than being dissected after execution, the Act made provisions for gibbeting. Gibbeting was the act of publicly displaying the body of someone, often close to the place of their crime, to act as a deterrent to people in the future. It also meant that there would be no grave for the executed. As one judge put it, they would be 'suspended betwixt heaven and earth, as unworthy of either'.[41] With their body displayed in a purpose-built cage and left to rot in public view, gibbeting was a final humiliation that would carry on long after their death. For one murderer tried at York Castle Prison, Frank Fearn, who was so brutal in his crime that the victim was only identified by the clothes that he wore, this was indeed a long process. Executed in 1782, his body remained gibbeted until Christmas Day 1797, when the bones finally fell away from their chains. The post where Fearn's body had been displayed was finally taken down in 1807, some twenty-five years after his execution.[42]

The bloody code reveals that eighteenth-century law prioritised retribution against criminals and the deterrent effect of harsh sentences, rather than a more modern approach to offender rehabilitation. This is not to say that everyone was compelled to support the criminal system of the day. Just like today, arguments were made for the most extreme sides and throughout the spectrum of possible punishment. For example, when it came to the death penalty, some argued that the system was too soft,[43] even suggesting that everyone convicted of a capital crime should be executed every time, with no reprieves. The reality was that only around half of the people convicted of a capital crime were executed, dropping to a third in the later eighteenth century.[44] An example of this in York can be shown in the newspapers of the day:

> Last Friday, the Assizes for this County ended on the Crown Side, when Richard Varley, for Robbery on the Highway; Joseph Wilson, for Horse-stealing; William Burnet and Joseph Field, for Sheep-stealing; Richard Holdsworth, for Burglary; and Elisabeth Webster, for stealing in a Dwelling House above the Value of 40s. all reciev'd Sentence of Death. Before the Judges left the City they were pleased to reprieve Joseph Wilson, William Burnet, Joseph Field, and Elizabeth Webster.[45]

For those who were reprieved, instead of execution, they would receive secondary punishments, such as transportation, whipping, fining or even detention in the local house of correction for a period of between six months and four years.[46] Those most likely to be reprieved include those who were married with a family and men of good 'character' who could find a respected 'pillar of the community' to vouch for them.[47] Those who were loners or didn't have the right connections had a far greater chance that the sentence would be carried out. But it should be remembered that even with the relatively low number of executions in the eighteenth century, there were people who argued for the abolition of the death penalty as it was not a deterrent, primarily because not everyone was executed.[48] To some people, a 50 per cent chance was good enough odds to warrant risking committing a felony. This played into the primary purpose of execution in the eighteenth century: social control. Enforcing the rigid social structure necessitated the death penalty to enforce it, but pardons and reprieves played their part in showing the mercy of the ruling elite.[49] Strangely enough, while the number of capital crimes in Britain significantly increased through the eighteenth century, the actual number of executions throughout the country decreased, with less than 200 people per year being executed in England and Wales by the end of the eighteenth century.[50]

Life Inside York Castle Prison

Life within any prison in England during the eighteenth century depended a lot on your background. A prisoner would have to pay for their food and accommodation to a private guardian. That meant that if you were wealthy, you could afford a better life in prison, perhaps a room to yourself and a better quality of food bought from the gaoler. If you did not have money, imprisonment was very closely akin to being held in a dungeon. Cold, dark and damp, with a bed on the floor and little more than bread and water for food.[51] Even at York Castle Prison, where the main idea of the architecture of the building was to separate the debtor from the common criminal, your status in life could easily create a more blurred boundary between the two. Wealthy criminals might be able to afford better accommodation with the debtors, and the poorest debtors might find themselves incarcerated with the criminals if they were out of favour with the gaoler. John Howard mentions a room in the felons' cells specifically for 'Debtors who do not behave well'.[52] However, don't imagine that just because you are paying for your accommodation as a felon, your accommodation will be of an acceptable standard. Everything is relative here and we have a particularly visceral complaint about the conditions here in 1746 while the Jacobite prisoners are being held at York Castle Prison. We are told by Thomas Herring, the archbishop of York that 'when the turnkey opens the cells in the morning, the steam and stench is intolerable and scarce credible'.[53]

Debtors' Prisons

This brings us to the purpose of a debtors' prison. We have briefly examined this for the medieval period, but now we will discuss it in more detail. The concept of imprisoning someone who owes money, goods or services for debt seems quite alien to modern society. Still, until 1869, this was a relatively common punishment that could affect all parts of society. Debtors formed by far the largest group of prisoners in Britain between the sixteenth and eighteenth centuries.[54] As we have already seen, the origins of imprisonment for debt go back to 1178, when it was used for debtors to the Crown; this was extended to all debtors in 1352.[55] It was common for people from all walks of life to end up in a debtors' prison. It is estimated that at its height, some 40,000 debtors were arrested annually in England and Wales.[56]

The newly built debtors' prison building was essentially two buildings in one. The ground floor where the felons were held was dark, damp and full of human suffering. For the debtors on the two upper floors, the situation was very different. A debtor was a distinct class of prisoner and not regarded as a criminal in the sense we understand today. As such, conditions for the debtors would be much better if you could afford the price of staying there. One of the more colourful ways that a debtors' prison has been described is as 'like a somewhat noisy tavern'.[57] It should be remembered that it was not just the debtors themselves who were affected by their imprisonment. Families outside could be left struggling to eat and may have found themselves in the workhouse if the main breadwinner could not find a relatively quick release. It was, therefore, not uncommon for wives and children of debtors to accompany them into prison.[58]

If debtors were not criminals, how would someone find themselves in a debtors' prison? Eighteenth-century economics relied heavily on a credit system. Persuading someone to undertake a venture with the hope of a profitable return was commonplace, as was securing small loans. The lender (the creditor) would lend money under agreed conditions, and if those conditions were not met, then legal processes would come into play.

The process itself is broken down into two parts. The 'mesne' starts when a creditor starts legal action for an unpaid debt.[59] This gave time for negotiations to take place with the debtor's friends and family to acquire payment. If this fails, the process moves on to the second part, the trial. The result of being found in breach of your agreement was the creditor's choice to either have the debtor imprisoned, such as at York Castle Prison, or to seize up to half of the debtor's property. Imprisonment was the preferred option as this meant that the full amount could be recovered in the future. The only problem was that this option required the debtor to be able to pay their debt while in prison. This made it rare for a debtor to secure release from a debtors' prison without the help of friends and family. As a result of this inability to pay, it was not uncommon for debtors to spend years in prison trying to obtain their release. At York, we know of Mary Moss, a debtor released in 1843 after spending twenty-four years and seven days there.[60] However, this later example was not the longest. That record possibly belongs to Millicent Rasby, who died at York Castle Prison in 1761. She is described as 'an old gentlewoman, who had been confined in the castle 38 years for debt; buried her 2nd November'.[61]

With the cost of being a debtor so high, how could anyone ever make enough money in a debtors' prison to survive, let alone secure their release? A debtors' prison was broken into two parts: a 'master's side' for those who could afford to stay, and a 'common side' for those who could not. In theory, most people should be able to afford to have enough money to survive while in a debtors' prison. The creditor was supposed to provide the prisoner with a small amount of money to provide bread and water. However, this was often not provided and had to be paid back alongside the original debt anyway.[62] Interestingly, when the prison reformer John Howard visited many prisons in England in 1774 and 1776, he singled out four prisons, including York Castle Prison, where no debt relief was being given to any debtor.[63] Without this money, other options had to be explored. For many, the help of friends and family was the most effective way to secure a release. For others, they might be able to live quite well by exploiting the system. For these individuals, entering prison was preferable to forfeiting half of their property. While in prison, they could still negotiate with their creditors and, to a certain extent, continue economic activity outside of the prison.[64] This higher class of debtor meant that prisons like York Castle Prison would also have had to provide grander accommodation for these people.[65] For other debtors, they may still have a trade that they can carry out within the prison.[66] However, for some of those debtors who could afford the 'master side' but not pay off their debts, the only choice was to spend the rest of their lives in the debtors' prison. Debts were not inheritable in the eighteenth century, so by sacrificing their lives, they could protect those that they loved from further claims from creditors. This may be what happened to poor Millicent Rasby.

The question that comes to mind is what happened to those prisoners who could not pay. For these, it was a trip to the 'common side', left to survive however they could, generally through begging. There were other ways out for some of the poorest debtors; obtaining a release through 'decay' and 'wearing' was one option for those too ill or old to be held in prison.[67] There are also instances of bequeathments to the prison to help secure the release of the poorest prisoners. One was Mrs Mary Lawson of Micklegate, who left £100 in her Will to 'discharge a certain number of poor prisoners, whose debt did not exceed £20 each'. A total of thirty-two debtors were released from York Castle Prison due to her generosity.[68] Of course, not everyone was lucky enough to benefit from this, and in all debtors' prisons, begging for charity to help them was common. Some prisons had designated areas for this, like 'the grate' at Farringdon Street (London) or a similar idea at the Marshalsea in London.[69] At York, this appears to have been begging at the fence of the felons' yard, known as the 'lower grate'. The result of this begging might be to help some of the prisoners avoid starvation at least. The lengths someone might go to help pay their debt or make their life in prison more comfortable cannot be underestimated. In 1771, John Hutchinson stole a watch worth £3 from William Martin while begging for charity at the gaol fence. He was sentenced to seven years' transportation. A sentence he received with 'greatest joy'.[70]

Overall, it is worth remembering that for most prisoners, life as a debtor was not particularly harsh. For example, at York, until 1835, better-off debtors 'were allowed to roam with the deer over the castle green all day'.[71] Being a debtor at York Castle Prison was a very different experience from being a felon.

Three Ways Out of York Castle Prison

So what about the felons? After all, York Castle Prison was the county gaol. Once someone is imprisoned in a gaol, their options for what happens next are extremely limited. To understand this, we need to understand the eighteenth-century legal system. There were four broad categories of crimes within British law: high treason, petty treason, felonies and misdemeanours.[72]

Misdemeanours were generally less serious crimes, usually dealt with by fines, humiliation in the stocks and pillory, or corporal punishment such as whipping or branding. As such, these crimes were typically dealt with at the local level, tried in the petty sessions and quarter sessions. You would have to commit a more serious crime to get to York Castle Prison. As we have already seen, high treason was a crime against the monarch or the realm, and this could include not just significant uprisings or the murder of royalty, but also forgery or the coining of money. Petty treason was treason against someone of a higher social status. This included the murder of someone 'to whom allegiance was owed'.[73] This could include the murder of a master by their servant, a servant stealing their master's seal or some other crime against someone of a higher status. The most common form of petty treason was the murder of a husband by his wife. A very sexist distinction: a husband murdering his wife was simply murder – a felony, but a woman killing their husband was classed as treason. Finally, while definitions changed over time, felony referred to more serious crimes such as murder, rape, larceny, robbery and burglary.[74] Importantly, in the eighteenth century, a felony was also a crime that carried a potential death sentence if convicted. Ultimately, it is a felony that covers most prisoners who awaited trial at York Castle Prison.

The punishments for high treason, petty treason and felonies were harsh, meaning that if you were brought to York Castle Prison, most of the time, there were just three ways that you would leave again. Of course, you first had to survive in prison until your trial. This could prove to be more difficult than you would hope. Imprisonment itself could be as good as a death sentence for some unfortunate prisoners. Whether you were innocent or not did not matter; disease did not choose. As John Howard noted after visiting many prisons in the UK, 'Many who went in healthy, are in a few months changed to emaciated dejected objects'. An eighteenth-century prison was almost the perfect breeding ground for diseases. Cold, damp and filthy conditions, as well as overcrowding with people from all over the county of Yorkshire, helped diseases like 'Gaol Fever', usually typhus, spread while also weakening the prisoners' immune response. One historian of York Castle Prison records that 'Criminal prisoners died at about the rate of four a year; chief diseases – dropsy, fever, insanity, consumption, decay'.[75]

'Gaol fever' or typhus was a particular plague in prisons throughout Europe, with outbreaks often occurring around the times that new prisoners were brought to the prison in large numbers for the assize courts. Typhus gives flu-like symptoms about two weeks after you catch it, with a rash developing about five to nine days after that. It is a bacterial disease carried by fleas and lice, which tells you a lot about the conditions in York Castle Prison and prisons throughout the country. As the reformer, John Howard, would note, 'in 1773 and 1774, I was fully convinced that more were destroyed by it [gaol fever], than were put to death by all the public executions in the kingdom'.[76] It was not just the prisoners who had to fear gaol fever; the prison staff, judges and jurors could catch typhus, spreading outbreaks to the outside world. Of course, disease is only one potential hazard. On 27 October 1739, nine men suffocated to death in one of the felons' apartments at York Castle Prison,[77] although in this case the deaths were caused by smoke inhalation from a fire, which one of the prisoners started in an ill-conceived attempt to escape.[78] Why was the prison system allowed to become this horrible petri dish of death and disease? As one author puts it: 'the same culture that supported the Bloody Code stood by the idea that prison should be unpleasant to deter crime.'[79]

If you survive long enough to have a trial, there were realistically only three possibilities on how you would leave York Castle Prison. Firstly, you may be released through either a true bill not being found against you or because you are found not guilty. This covers about half of the people who came through the felons' cells at York Castle Prison. Secondly, you might be found guilty but not warranting a death sentence; for these people, a secondary punishment of transportation would usually follow. In this case, after you were sentenced, you would be moved from the section for prisoners awaiting trial into the area for those awaiting transportation, where you would stay until the next ships were ready to take you to serve your sentence. Finally, for some, they would only leave York Castle Prison one last time on their way to be executed.

Transportation Act 1718

Not every sentence of death was carried out, and it was not uncommon for prisoners to find themselves reprieved and incarcerated in a house of correction, forced to join the military or, in some cases, asked to act as executioners to save their own lives.[80] It was not just those on trial who wanted to avoid the death penalty. Judges and juries often played a role in either dismissing cases before trial or mitigating crimes to lesser offences, thereby avoiding capital sentences.[81] Transportation itself served two purposes: it showed the king's mercy, limiting the number of executions that took place, and, in theory, kept public order.[82]

As we have already seen, the origins of transportation began during the rule of Oliver Cromwell, when those considered 'dangerous to the social order' (i.e. Irish Catholics for Cromwell, and Jacobites after 1688) were sent to North America.[83] However, opposition from those in America and conflicts with merchants, who would transport the convicted to sell them as indentured servants at the other end, ultimately prevented this from working. As a result, the merchants were only interested in the fittest and most able bodied of these people. Eventually, the use of transportation in its original form declined rapidly after the Glorious Revolution of 1688.[84]

This changed with the Transportation Act 1718. This Act allowed those convicted of clergiable offences to receive a sentence of seven years' transportation, and those convicted of a non-clergiable offence to receive a sentence of fourteen years. Those who had been sentenced to death but reprieved could be sentenced to life. Many of the 'old' capital crimes, i.e. murder or highway robbery, would still have the sentence carried out to the full extent of the law, but laws introduced after 1688 would often be commuted to transportation instead.[85] This should not give the impression that secondary punishment was not used between 1688 and 1718. Evidence shows an increase in the use of houses of correction as a secondary punishment between 1706 and 1718.[86] However, it would be in the early nineteenth century that the idea of imprisonment as a punishment truly came to fruition in the form of early penitentiaries.

To make the system of transportation work this time, the merchants would now get £3 per person and possibly make up to £10 (£8 or £9 for women transportees) more when they sold the convicts at the other end, making it a more viable business proposition. Once the convict's sentence had ended, they could either stay on as settlers or return home to England – if they could afford it after paying the required legal fees for their release.

If anyone was caught returning before their sentence ended, they would face more significant punishment. Seven years of transportation would become fourteen, and a sentence of fourteen years of transportation or transportation for life would often become a death sentence.[87] One example of this is Thomas Spence, who was sentenced to transportation. In 1732, he was sentenced to death at Assize sessions after returning before his time was completed.[88]

The system had some teething problems, like the one that left forty transportees in one cell at York, threatening to escape if they were not transported soon.[89] This bravado is understandable, as some of these unfortunate men had spent up to seven years in that cell. The tragedy for these men is that their sentence would not start until they made landfall at the other end, meaning that they would be spending at least another seven years as indentured servants to pay for their crimes.

Transportation was not always popular with the general public. Some argued that the punishment, being out of sight of everyday folk, did not act as a deterrent. With the prospect of a better life, some suggested that criminals would commit minor, clerical offences to get themselves transported.[90] Presumably, this was the case, as we have seen, with the debtor John Hutchinson and his theft of a £3 watch, which resulted in his transportation.

However, transportation was going to face a significant problem. With the American Revolution in 1776, Britain no longer had a place to send its prisoners.

Execution

Of course, there were many felons and those convicted of treason who were not lucky enough to be reprieved and transported. For these few hundred people, their final journey would begin at York Castle Prison and proceed through the streets of York, heading down Tadcaster Road, eventually ending at Micklegate Without. This was now the only execution site in York. The end would usually be hanging by the neck from the 'three-legged mare', a permanent fixture at the location. But for some, the punishment would be very different. Four women would be strangled and then burned, having been found guilty of petty treason. Men who were convicted of treason would be hanged, drawn and quartered there. During the eighteenth century, the Jacobites would suffer this fate. However, on Monday, 1 May 1758, Robert Cole would become the last person to be hanged, drawn and quartered in York, for his part in the 'Wensleydale riots'.[91]

Women and Children in Prison

Some statistics suggest that in the late seventeenth century, as many as 45 per cent of those tried at the Old Bailey in London were women.[92] Additionally, women were more likely to be imprisoned in the eighteenth and nineteenth centuries than they are today. The system was biased against women because all the judges and jurors were men. However, it should also be noted that these judges and juries were drawn from the higher social classes, whereas many of the accused were from the lower social classes. The importance of class in society through the eighteenth and nineteenth centuries meant that this was also a bias against most male offenders. For women, this bias worked both ways. Sometimes, men could be partisan against women. However, women were seen as the fairer sex, and as a result, many juries were unwilling to apply the death penalty. However, it should be noted that the rate of execution of both men and women at this time was about a fifth of those tried for capital crimes.[93]

Women overwhelmingly committed some crimes. Prostitution is one, but the act of infanticide, child murder, was almost solely carried out by women.[94] The most serious crimes that would see women end up at York Castle Prison were the 'staple' crimes of killing, often abusive, husbands or lovers, who abandoned them.[95] Poisoning was the preferred form of murder amongst women, either due to the distance of not having to look into your victim's eyes or by the opportunity afforded by traditionally being the one who prepared the food. Poisoning was one of the most feared forms of murder, and for this reason, poisoning carried a de facto sentence of death if convicted.[96] Interestingly, one of the crimes most heavily associated with women over the sixteenth and seventeenth centuries, witchcraft, would no longer be a capital crime after 1736. Instead, they were associated more with crimes of deception.[97]

The conditions within the prison were not great for women, with exploitation by the male staff and prisoners being a serious threat during the eighteenth century. Many women would become pregnant while in prison. Sometimes, this would be beneficial to the prisoner. A common way a woman might avoid the gallows was by becoming pregnant. Any execution would be put off until after the child was born, and this often led to sympathies for the condemned, given the temporal dissonance from the crime.[98] For example, in York, there was the case of Mary Burgan, which we have already come across. One of the earlier prisoners from this period, in 1705/1706, Mary Burgan, was sentenced to death for murdering an illegitimate baby. She was, however, not executed. She became pregnant again and gave birth to her son, Thomas Burgan. Mary Burgan was pardoned in 1710, but when she left, she left one important thing behind: her son, Thomas. This sounds like a horrid thing to do, but the young Thomas Burgan was probably the illegitimate son of turnkey Thomas Ward. He stood a better chance at life in prison with his father than with his mother, Mary, as a convicted felon. Thomas had grown up living with the gaol staff, and in 1718, Thomas Ward, now gaoler of York Castle Prison, acquired funds to get Thomas Burgan an apprenticeship.[99] While this turn of events was beneficial for Mary Burgan, sparing her life, it should also be remembered that 'pleading the belly' and becoming pregnant in gaol was sometimes the result of abuse while in prison. However, their gender could also serve as a survival strategy for women. A relationship with the turnkey could offer a woman some protection or privilege within the gaol while she was there.

As we have seen, women in prison also lead to children being in prison. There were two main ways that this could happen. Firstly, either the child was born in prison, or the mother was nursing when she was sent to prison. This was intended to be limited to the first twelve months, after which children would be sent to relatives or, later, to the workhouse; however, this did not always occur.[100] This happened in York, most famously with Thomas Burgan. Secondly, children could find themselves imprisoned for a crime they committed. There was no separate juvenile system during the eighteenth century or even during most of the nineteenth century. Regardless of age, anyone committing a crime was subject to the same laws and, therefore, the same punishments as adults. This could include transportation or even execution!

Chapter 5

The Site of York Castle Prison, 1777–1835

The Prison

By the time we reach the end of the eighteenth century, York Castle Prison had once again begun to suffer from its ageing infrastructure. The debtors' prison might have been built earlier in the century and, therefore, still in reasonable condition. However, the jury house and courthouse, the last remaining buildings of the original castle, were refurbished in the 1660s. They were showing their age and needed to be replaced with something more modern and in keeping with the prison's important role in civic affairs. Planned as far back as 1765, building work commenced in 1773, and the new Assize court building was completed in 1777.[1] This was not a direct replacement for the old courthouse, as the new courthouse was built on the site where the old jury house once stood. This allowed the old court to continue functioning while the new building was being constructed. Designed by the renowned architect John Carr, this new courthouse proved to be a significant upgrade from the previous court facilities on the site.

It was a grand, state-of-the-art building with two large courtrooms for trials. York historian William Hargrove's writings about York confirm that the two courtrooms were being used for different purposes. The southern was the crown court, and the northern was the *nisi prius* or civil court. Each courtroom was thirty feet square with a dome at the top 'supported by twelve Corinthian columns'.[2] Hargrove also tells us that there are rooms for grand and petit juries.

After the construction of the new courthouse was complete, a new prison building was placed directly opposite where the old 'moot hall' courthouse once stood. The new prison was designed to mirror the new courthouse. These two new buildings, alongside the debtors' building, created a U-shaped enclosure around the Eye of the Ridings, which can still be seen today. The second prison building, referred to today as the female prison building, was

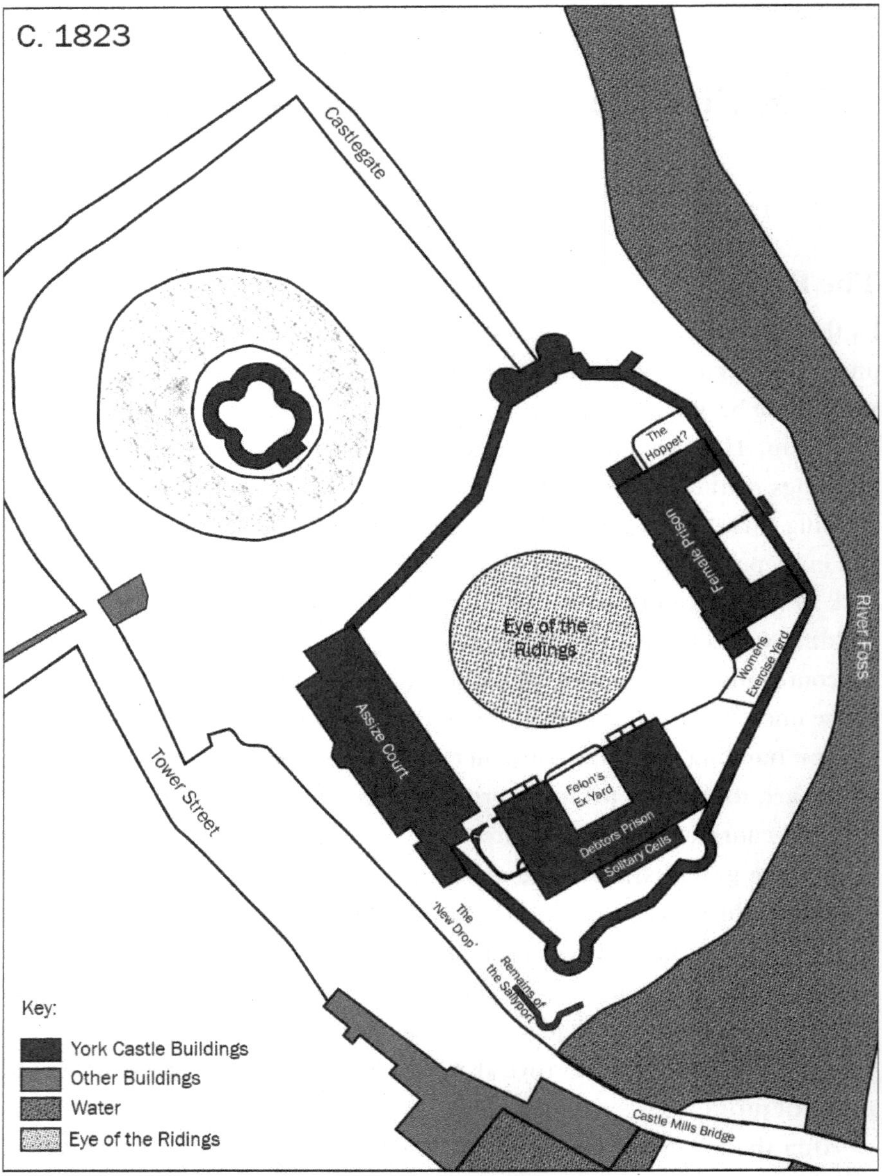

The site of York Castle around 1823, showing the new buildings and the newly created Eye of the Ridings.[3]

built in 1780. When it was completed, like the debtors' prison before, it was a grand sight. 'the approach to it is by a flight of five stone steps; leading to four Iconic pillars, supporting a portico'.[4] At completion, the female prison was primarily 'to supply several accommodations, which were thought requisite by the county magistrates',[5] just like the jury house building had previously done. However, as its name suggests, the female prisoners would eventually also be relocated to this building.

As completed, the two buildings differed slightly from what we see today. The female prison was notably narrower when viewed from the front. Additions to the female prison building were made in 1802/1803, with extensions added behind these new sections in 1819, restoring the building to its original rectangular shape.

The modifications to the female prison in 1802/1803 'contained offices for the clerk of assize; apartments used for depositing records, and other purposes'; it also appears that it was around this point in time that its designation as the 'female prison' came about when 'portions of it were appropriated to misdemeanants and female felons'.[6] These modifications

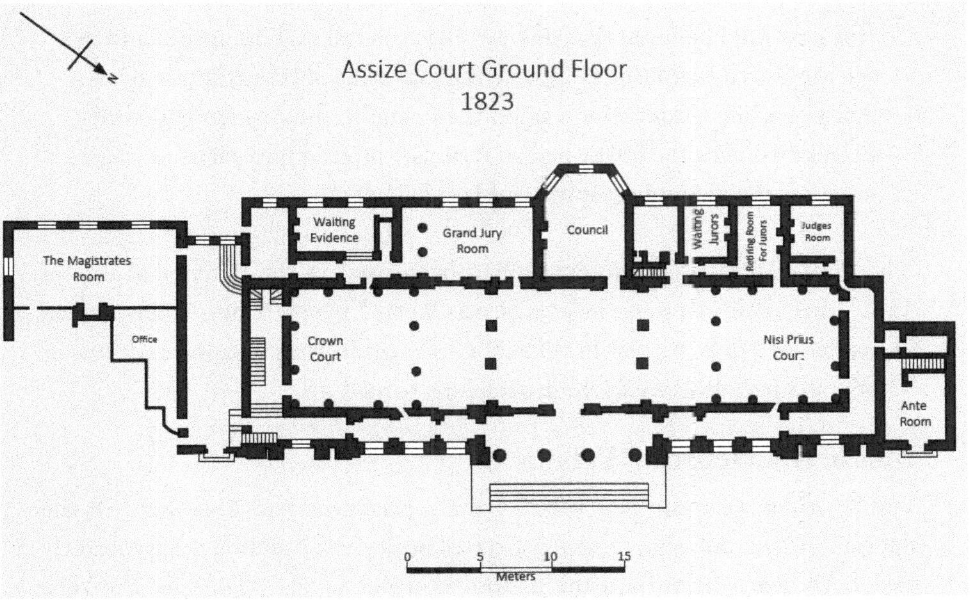

A plan of the assize court around 1823. This layout appears to have remained very similar until additions to the court in the late 1800s.[7]

made the mirroring of the two newest buildings almost perfect. Interestingly, in these modifications, the design of the outside of the buildings, being close mirror images, took precedence over the internal function of the female prison. Today, you can see that the floors of the female prison building intersect the large windows at each end about three-quarters of the way up.

The cost of these buildings was never going to come cheap. Once again, the question was how the county would pay for these buildings. Similar to how funds for the debtors' prison had already been raised in 1705, rates were levied on the county to cover the costs of these new additions to the site.[8]

A curious side note to the construction of the new prison building is that it marked the end of one of the more unusual events in the history of York Castle Prison. On 8 July 1780, a human skeleton was discovered while clearing some overgrown areas behind the old courthouse: 'They found a human skeleton laid about a yard distant from the wall, with legbones enclosed with double irons'.[9] While the exact identity of this skeleton will never be known, it was firmly believed at the time that it was the remains of William Thompson, who disappeared, and was thought to have escaped from York Castle Prison. In 1820, Hargrove asserted that:

> It is now fully believed that this was the skeleton of Thompson, and in attempting to escape, he had got to the top of the old courthouse, by the assistance of a ladder which stood there, and in the descent had either been killed with the fall or had so seriously injured himself as to linger out a protracted and most miserable existence.[10]

The disappearance of Thompson had been used in the defence of one of York Castle Prison's most infamous prisoners, Eugene Aram. Aram argued in his defence that the victim, Daniel Clark, could have disappeared, just as Thompson had. In the end, both skeletons turned up.

Inside the Debtors' Prison

Unlike when we examined where female prisoners had been held in the debtors' prison, locating female prisoners in the new building is significantly easier. We learn from both the prison reformer James Nield and the York historian William Hargrove that the women are housed in the southern portion of the new prison building. However, we also know that this section was not added until 1802/1803.

So, where were the women held until this point? We have already previously touched upon this topic and the location that we got in a letter in 1878:

> What is now the women's prison to be for atrocious offenders, two of the rooms at the West end of the Castle to be made for the Women's prison with a yard in the space adjoining the south end of the new Court...[11]

Women were relocated to the front of the western portion of the felons' cells in the debtors' prison building, with the old female cells forming the new condemned cell and a few miscellaneous cells. The women felons occupied this location from around 1778 until the construction of the new wings of what would become known as the 'female' prison building in 1803. The other interesting part of this letter is the construction of 'a yard in the space adjoining the south end of the new Court'. This small exercise yard, which could be one of the two courtyards mentioned by John Howard, would become known as Half-Moon Court due to its unusual shape. It adjoined two rooms in the front of the western part of the debtors' prison and would later serve as the exercise yard for prisoners awaiting transportation. Some of the best-surviving graffiti at York Castle Prison is located in this area. Sadly, if any female felons left graffiti, it no longer survives.

With the women occupying two rooms and the condemned cells being relocated, it is likely that this was also when the corridor running the length of the felons' cells was cut through the former cells, creating the layout of the felons' apartments that we still see today. The smaller of the two rooms now occupied by the female prisoners had a door that was the only way to access the rear west portion of the felons' cells; this door is likely to have been blocked up to separate men from women, necessitating the corridor.

While it can be assumed that until the female prisoners were moved into the new building after 1803, much of the debtors' prison would have functioned similarly to how it had during the previous seventy plus years. Inside, we have a good idea of what happened after 1803, once again from William Hargrove and the prison reformer James Nield. Nield describes the prison during his visit in 1809. He tells us first about the debtors and their ascent to their apartments from their courtyard. He mentions this courtyard is about an acre in size, which suggests that he refers to the castle yard enclosing the Eye of the Ridings, with steps up to the first-floor entrance located just behind the recently constructed Half-Moon Court. There were eight rooms for the debtors on this floor during Nields' visit. Nield also mentions that the common-side debtors occupy twelve rooms on the top floor. This is the whole floor at the top of the building. This suggests that not only was the common side numerous, but it also hints that the wealthier debtors were now in the newly built prison building. Nield describes the debtor's rooms as 'airy and Wholesome' but tells us that the prison has a problem with debtors having a view into the felons' exercise yard as well as the solitary cells at the back of the debtors' prison. He explains that this has become problematic when 'Dangerous implements have been conveyed to very improper hands, and the regularity and orderly conduct of the Gaol frequently disturbed'.[12]

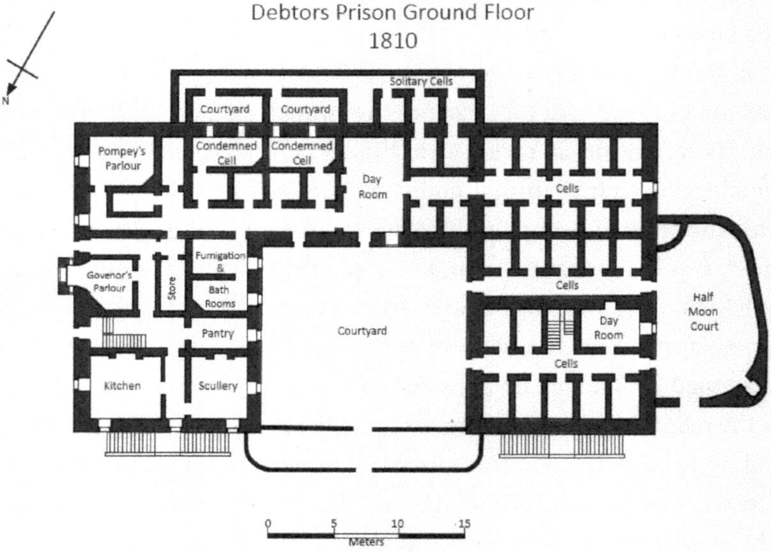

A plan of the debtors' prison ground floor around 1810. N.B. In addition to 'pompey's Parlour', two other condemned cells were established ah the back of the building at some point after 1810, but before the 1820's. Their locations are shown here despite being later changes.[13]

In addition to discussing the debtors at York Castle Prison, Nield also describes the conditions in the felons' cells. From this, it is apparent that things have changed a lot down there. The small sleeping cells are still roughly where they were, but now the main entrance into the felons' cells is from the exercise yard into the central day room that had previously housed those awaiting transportation. The corridor, which now runs the whole length of the felons' cells, is easily accessed from this entrance room. The cells are described as having 'oaken floors' being 'well[-]ventilated and dry'.[14] This is much better accommodation than when the debtors' prison was first built. Hargrove elaborates a few years later, in 1820, that by this point, 'Every cell in this building, is provided by the county, with an iron bedstead, a flock bed, and rugs; on each of which beds, two felons generally sleep'.[15]

This raised the question of where the transportees move to. According to an 1810 plan, we know that Half-Moon Court was used as an exercise yard for those awaiting transportation, suggesting that they now occupied the front of the west wing, where the women had been held between 1778 and 1802. Nield describes the day room in this area as capable of housing fifteen young offenders.[16] Two areas had access to Half-Moon Court; one would likely house the transportees, and the other would house young offenders. The area at the front of the west wing would probably be the area for juveniles. It has a dayroom; if we take two per cell as a standard, there are enough cells for fourteen people. This leaves the corridor with five cells further back in the west wing for the transportees. It is also likely that the distinction between these two areas may not have been as clear as this, depending on how many needed to be held in these areas. Hargrove also notes that those sentenced to transportation from the local quarter sessions are also being held at York Castle Prison, awaiting their sentence.[17] This could have made this area very crowded at times.

We also know that the condemned cell had moved; it was now situated at the back of the east end of the building, in the area we have already speculated was used to house the female inmates earlier in the history of the debtors' prison. It has acquired the nickname of 'Pompey Parlour'.[18] However, the origins of this name are unclear. We do have a great description of it, and standing in the space today, we can still get a sense of the room as a condemned cell:

> The cell is arched over, has a boarded floor, a fire place, no fender, fire irons, or shovel; the coals laid on the floor, near the hearth, the edge of

> which is raised two or three inches; a good fir; the thickness of the wall, and the smallness of the window under it, render necessary a lighted candle to read by; there are two holes about two inches wide each, and twelve long on each side of the cell, which is absolutely necessary, as the persons are seldom let out, but to chapel or death.[19]

Additional details include that the cell has a single window as well as a table and chair.[20] Other than that, the cell is mainly devoid of any distinguishing features. William Hargrove elaborates on the condemned cell ten years later, stating that by 1820, there were three condemned cells within the felons' apartments.[21] One of them, only used as a condemned cell, is 'Pompey's parlour'. The other two condemned cells appear to have only come into existence after Nield's visit, possibly because of the Luddites, where more space would have been needed to house the fourteen men who were condemned. These separate condemned cells are also shown in 1828 when father and son William and John Dyon were recorded as being held in separate condemned cells, suggesting that it was now common practice to separate condemned criminals before their executions.

The front of the east wing of the debtors' building is still the gaolers' apartments. This area would provide everything the gaoler and staff needed without requiring them to enter the main prison. Interestingly, a door now appears to provide access to the felons' cells. Above this still sits the gaolers' office, with Hargrove giving us a description as follows:

> The entrance is by a double flight of stone steps, on the top of which is a door that leads into a passage. The first door in this passage, on the right, opens into the governor's sitting room, and the under-jailer occupies the room on the left. In this latter room is a large closet or recess, in which the deadly weapons, heavy chains, &c. of the most notorious offenders are exhibited.[22]

The existence of these instruments is backed up by the biographer of James Montgomery, who revisited York Castle Prison in 1828. He states that

> Montgomery, who had no taste for horrors of any description, turned with repugnance from a collection of instruments of murder, and of legal torture.[23]

This could likely have been used to scare new prisoners, hoping they would behave themselves in prison. Many of these items would no longer have been allowed to be used, but the thought might be enough to deter some people. It is also possible that this collection housed what have long been argued to be Dick Turpin's shackles. However, there is no evidence to support the authenticity of this claim.

Over in the west wing, on the first floor, Hargrove provides a detailed description of the prison's chapel. He describes it as being 'calculated for religious worship, is so constructed, that each prisoner knows his proper seat'. He provides a detailed description of the regimented seating arrangement for those using the chapel, which appears to have been copied directly from Nield's description:

> The Women sit upon forms in the area, in front of the pulpit: The convicts, Felons for trial, and misdemeanours, are placed on seats close to the wall and nearly encircle the chapel. The gallery is occupied by the Keeper's seat, in which are debtors and occasional Visitors. All are in view of the Minister. A pew is set apart, Opposite the Keeper's seat, for those under sentence of death.[24]

The final section of the debtor's prison mentioned is behind the building, where solitary cells were added for prisoners being punished.

Inside The Female Prison Building

Moving into the female prison building, it can be thought of as three separate buildings. The south wing's ground floor accommodated female felons, with six sleeping cells and a day room. The same number of cells was also on the second floor. The courtyard just south of the building allowed female felons to exercise.[25]

The top floor of the south wing is where the prison infirmary was now located. It is described as having two 'infirmary rooms; one of which has a warm and cold bath, an adjoining dressing room, and patent water-closets'.[26] Most interestingly, this area also has access to the roof with a 5-foot-high railing, creating an area for 'convalescents to walk and take the air upon'.[27] It is also noted that in this wing, all the prisoners have 'wooden bedsteads, flock beds, blankets, and rugs'.[28] It appears that the female prisoners are being held in much better accommodation than the male prisoners in the felons' cells of the debtors' prison. The new building was of a modern standard, but the debtors' prison remained unchanged from its 1700s origins. However, by 1820, when Hargrove visited the castle, this was already in the process of changing. The wood beds would soon be replaced by iron ones that had already made their way into the felons' cells in the debtors' prison before 1820.

Additionally, the female condemned cell would have been relocated to this building with the women, but its exact location is not documented. Our best description tells us it is in 'an upper part of the new prison'.[29]

The central part of the building, the core that existed before 1802, had what Nield described as the 'chamber-story.' Nield described nine rooms, 14 feet by 12 feet, as being for 'the most respectable prisoners of this class'.[30] It is a much nicer environment in this area, as evidenced by the glazed sash windows and fireplaces, which differ significantly from the felons' area. This is likely where the poet and newspaper editor James Montgomery would have been housed while imprisoned at York Castle Prison. Sadly, we don't have any

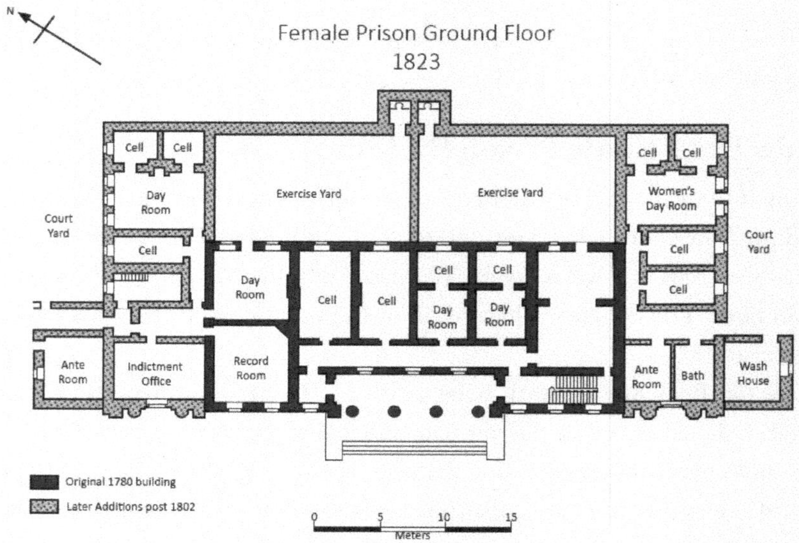

A plan of the female prison building showing the various changes through the first forty years of its life.[31]

detailed records of this central part of the building until the creation of a new chapel in its place in 1835.

We know about the north wing had eight sleeping cells and two dayrooms 'with fire-places, benches, tables, shelves, &c'; these gave access to two courtyards.[32] This area, as described by Hargrove, housed some of the court's functions.

> Considerable additions were made in 1803, under the direction of Mr Atkinson, the architect. The whole length now extends in length one hundred and fifty feet; and the wing next the porter's lodge, contains on the ground floor, offices for the clerk of assize, for depositing of records, &c.; behind which there is a day room … for prisoners charged with misdemeanours.[33]

This reference to misdemeanours was supported in 1819 when John Gurney and Elizabeth Fry described the female prison building as housing misdemeanants.[34] This suggests that this wing of the building performed a similar role to the house of correction, dealing with more minor, local crimes. It may also have held those awaiting an appeal at the *nisi prius* court.

The Hoppet

One of the most curious references from this period regarding York Castle Prison is the mention of the burial of two Luddites in 1813. We are told that the Luddites Joseph Crowther and Nathan Hoyle are 'interred in the hoppet at the back of the Castle'. There is not much to go on here, but there is enough to attempt to put together a theory of where these burials were located and, therefore, where burials in general were happening within the prison.

Unfortunately, this is the only reference to the hoppet, and it never appears on any plans. However, the *Oxford English Dictionary* defines it as a handbasket for holding seeds, or 'An enclosure; a yard, paddock, or the like…'[35] In the context of a prison, this is most likely an exercise yard or courtyard within the prison.

Some plans depict a courtyard located north of the female prison, which existed in 1823 and likely earlier. This is never mentioned in any texts about the prison, so it could be a possible location for our hoppet. This might seem like a leap of faith, but in 1998, archaeological excavations unearthed five skeletons in this area. They were dated to have been buried between 1802 and

1826. One of the skeletons shows signs of dissection, possibly indicating that it could have been someone who was executed.[36]

Overall, there is no 'smoking gun' for the location of the hoppet. The fact that the dates for the known burials, the Luddite 'hoppet' reference, and the existence of this yard are all contemporary with each other suggests that from around 1802/3 up until the construction of the later buildings, this might have been the burial location for those executed in York, as well as some who died of natural causes within the prison.

The Castle

The progress of time was also taking its toll on what remained of the castle itself. The watergate (sallyport) and stone wall were demolished in 1805–1806.[37] In addition, a debate is taking place in York regarding the future of Clifford's Tower, with many suggesting that the tower should be demolished and the land used for a new addition to the prison.

Clifford's Tower was not part of the prison site anymore, and James Nield once again provides insight, mentioning that Samuel Wilks Waud owned Clifford's Tower. His house is just to the north of the Castlegate entrance to the bailey area, where part of the castle moat had once stood. It might appear strange that such a monument might be in private ownership, but after all, it was just land, and Samuel happened to be the owner. However, I'm sure that Clifford's Tower made an attractive garden ornament.

In addition, we know that what is now referred to as the Eye of York was created when the old castle yard was levelled in 1777, and paths were established. This levelling of the yard is why Hargrove refers to the doorway to the bridge between the bailey and the motte as being three feet above ground level.[38] Hargrove also tells us that it had been made a feature that could be enjoyed by the public visiting the site or even debtors exercising on the castle green:

> The arch of this doorway, on the inner side, next the tower, has lately been tastefully converted into an arbour, adorned with mantling ivy; and in front of it is a gravel walk, shaded by the luxuriant foliage of hanging trees and shrubs, and ornamented with two stone pedestals, each with a small figure placed upon it.[39]

By 1790, the distinct oval shape had been established and had become known as the 'Eye of the Ridings'.[40]

Chapter 6

Life in York Castle Prison, 1777–1835

Prison Reform

It has been argued that there were three significant stimuli in prison building towards the end of the seventeenth century and into the early nineteenth century. Firstly, the war with the American colonies took away the primary destination for transported prisoners. Secondly, there was an increase in prisoners of war during the Napoleonic Wars. Finally, there was the work of the prison reformers, private citizens who would visit gaols and prisons and report back what they witnessed.[1] The wars with America and France would have had a limited direct impact on a county gaol like York Castle Prison, mainly felt in the cessation of transportation to America. However, the work of the reformers brought significant changes. These reformers' efforts changed the prison system from the horrible Georgian gaols where so many people needlessly died, into the Victorian prison system, one that was closer to a prison/gaol that we might recognise today. This was not a quick process, but 1777–1835 saw some of the most significant pushes by reformers to change prisons.

While some prison reform efforts had been attempted earlier in the eighteenth century by James Oglethorpe, this initiative had a limited impact, primarily confined to London and specifically targeting debtors. It can be argued that the first significant reform of British prisons was initiated by John Howard. Howard visited a large majority of the prisons in Britain (and eventually many in Europe as well), and his records of what he saw at York are one of the best contemporary sources for what was happening in the buildings at the time. Howard's efforts to reform prisons in Bedfordshire, where he was appointed high sheriff in 1773, led him to visit other prisons. What Howard found was shocking. Many prisoners continued to be held, even after being found not guilty, due to the discharge fees imposed. At York, he notes that the fees were 6s 8d to the gaoler and 2s 0d to the turnkeys for the release of a prisoner if found not guilty.[2] This increases if found guilty but then reprieved or pardoned.

Food was often in short supply, especially in county gaols like York, with variable bread allowances between gaols.[3] Howard states that 'many criminals are half starved: such of them as at their commitment were in health, come out almost famished'.[4] Prisoners of war, by contrast, appear to have been kept quite well.[5] Generally, air quality was not much better than the food, with diseases like 'gaol fever and small pox often being rampant in the gaols'; Howard himself resorted to smelling vinegar when visiting prisons to try and protect himself.[6] However, York Castle Prison does appear to have some redeeming qualities at this time, with Howard noting that, for the debtors at least, 'The rooms are airy and healthy'.[7]

Gambling was also a big problem in England's prisons; cards, dice, skittles, Mississippi, Portobello, billiards, fives and tennis (yes, tennis!) are all listed by Howard as vices that persist, especially at county gaols.[8] Heavy irons 'which make their walking, and even lying down to sleep, difficult and painful' don't escape his condemnation either.[9] He notes that in some county gaols, even the women do not escape this punishment, although it is unknown if York Castle Prison was included.

Howard's most significant issue, however, was the gaolers' use of the prison to make money and exploit the prisoners in the process. He proposed that the gaoler should be salaried and the system of garnish abolished. After taking his findings to the House of Commons in 1774, two acts were passed; firstly, the Discharged Prisoners Act abolished discharge fees for those found not guilty. Secondly, the Health of Prisoners Act stipulated that all rooms should be 'scraped and whitewashed' at least once a year and that fresh air should be supplied through ventilators. Baths were to be installed in all prisons, and sick inmates were to have separate rooms. Finally, a physician was to be appointed.[10] Even with these successes, Howard would continue to visit prisons throughout Britain and Europe until he died in 1790.

However, Howard was not the only person working towards reforming the prison system. William Wilberforce, better known for his later work abolishing slavery in Britain, was also interested in prison reform. In 1786, just two years after his first election to Parliament, he brought a bill into the House of Commons to try to abolish burning as a penalty for women found guilty of petty treason.[11] Although this bill would not pass, it demonstrates that serious questions were being raised at the highest levels about the legal system. Similarly, one of William Wilberforce's greatest allies in the abolition of slavery, Sir Samuel Romilly, was also interested in reforming the British prison system and the legal system. Although many of these early reform ideas failed due to political resistance, some succeeded, most notably Romilly's success in 1814 in effectively abolishing hanging, drawing and quartering. However, the deceased's body would still be decapitated. Officially, the punishment of hanging, drawing and quartering was not fully withdrawn until 1870.

James Nield was the next major reformer to have left us with details about what they found at York Castle Prison. His interests were around debtors and how hard it could be for some to pay off their debt, as well as the harsh laws that had grown in the 1700s, giving Britain an excessive number of crimes that could carry the death penalty. His accounts of visiting York in 1802 and 1809 provide a snapshot of the prison. He notes several interesting points about York Castle Prison. He remarks on the ease of access of debtors to the felons' courtyard below, where 'Dangerous implements have been conveyed to very improper hands, and the regularity and orderly conduct of the Gaol frequently disturbed'; he even suggests 'sloping boards' to prevent 'so hazardous a communication'.[12] The poor quality of life for some debtors in York Castle Prison is criticised as such:

> The County furnishes neither bedsteads, bedding, nor even straw for debtors. The Debtor who has a room to himself, pays for bedding and furniture three-pence per day: If a single bed amongst other Debtors, it is two-pence a day; and if two sleep in a bed, one penny each.[13]

The felons' exercise yard, between the wings of the debtors' prison, is criticised for being 'defective in being too small'. However, the sleeping cells for the felons themselves are described as having 'lofty arched roofs, and boarded oaken floors, well-ventilated and dry'; the county even 'liberally supplies rugs for the prisoners' bedding …'[14] The prisoners' behaviour in the chapel was described as 'orderly and attentive'. It is clear from these descriptions that York Castle Prison had both positive and negative traits regarding how it was now being run.

In the female prison building, sleeping conditions are described as follows: 'All the prisoners in this wing have wooden bedsteads, flock-beds, blankets, and rugs'.[15] A much nicer-sounding environment suggests that while the female prison building was built to the latest prison standards, the debtors' prison was left as it was and not brought up to these same standards. Overall, York Castle Prison was praised by Nield, who said that the 'design and execution of this county gaol are highly commendable'.[16] Once again, York Castle Prison comes off far better than many prisons visited by Nield, just like it did from Howard. Nield's work, alongside that of other reformers like Jeremy Bentham, helped create parliamentary pressure for prison reform.

The final prominent reformer to visit York Castle Prison and leave us records of their visit is Elizabeth Fry, who, along with her brother John Gurney, visited York Castle Prison twice in 1819. Like so many Quakers, the family were interested in societal reform. For Gurney and Fry, that interest settled on the conditions for prisoners. In general, their focus centred around reforming prisoners rather than prisons being for the 'punishment of the guilty', allowing a sort of 'legal vengeance' to be prescribed.[17] This came in two parts: firstly, a police force 'by which crime may be easily and immediately detected', and the reform of prisoners through 'a system of order, inspection, industry, and excellent moral discipline'.[18] In addition, they recognise the importance of separating the experiences of the tried and untried prisoners, assuming that those who are innocent do not deserve to be treated in the horrid conditions that most gaols offered.[19] The other purpose of their visits was to identify what they considered the main problems affecting prisons in England, 'food, clothing, firing, sleeping, irons, cleanliness, inspection, superintendence, classification, instruction and employment'.[20]

For Elizabeth Fry, in particular, there was also an interest in the conditions of women's prisons, focusing on two key areas. Firstly, the firmly held belief that women should be supervised by female officers and matrons, preventing some of the abuses that befell female prisoners at the time. These suggestions would come into effect only a few years later.[21] Fry suggested that the position of matron should be a live-in position. She also believed that a matron supervising female prisoners:

> ought to be a person of respectable, orderly, and active, habits, … plain in her dress, … gentle, yet firm, in her demeanor [*sic*], … of sufficient education to enable her to superintend the instruction of the prisoners, … and although not *greatly* elevated above her charge, yet in a station of life so far superior to their own, as to command their respect and obedience.[22]

Secondly, Fry was interested in setting up prison visiting committees to bring them 'scripture, instruction and employment'.[23] These ideas would be further reinforced in Elizabeth Fry's book in 1827.[24] These committees established specific rules for female prisoners to follow in order to receive assistance from visitors. Committees were successfully established at Newgate in London, but they were also set up in other locations, notably at the city gaol and house of correction in York.[25] However, when Gurney and Fry's book was published in 1819, this did not apply to York Castle Prison.

The visit of Elizabeth Fry and her brother John Gurney to York Castle Prison left an impression on the prison; the county magistrates were particularly frustrated that their administration of York Castle Prison had been heavily criticised.[26] Gurney and Fry describe York as 'a medium picture of good and bad qualities'.[27] What criticisms did Fry offer against the prison? The list was concise:

> On the whole, although this prison has some excellencies and great capacity, its evils are very conspicuous. They are as follows: … Easy access of debtors and of the public to the felons; insufficient clothing, and scarcely sufficient food; heavy irons; want of cleanliness, want of further classification, want of inspection, want of instruction, want of employment … Were the prisoners employed, they would not be occupied, as has hitherto been the case, by various devices for effecting their escape. Their chains might be knocked off with safety. They would not cut their iron bedsteads to pieces, as they have done in their present state. They would have no time to corrupt one another or the public.[28]

This is a damning statement about York Castle Prison, later noting that a prisoner could easily be 'loaded with heavy irons, and perhaps has not a shirt on his back.'[29] However, none of these were issues unique to York Castle Prison; as you will note, many of these problems are directly from the list of issues that Gurney and Fry believed were prevalent in England. Many of these issues are similar to those reported by Howard and Nield previously. However, it is that first line about York Castle Prison's 'Excellencies and great capacity', which shows that on the whole, York Castle Prison was probably above average compared to other county gaols of the time.

We also get a nice glimpse into daily life from Fry and Gurney, who mention that at York Castle Prison, firing (i.e. having a fire) was available to all prisoners, although based on the buildings, this can be assumed to be most likely only in the day rooms. Soap was also provided, but no clothing.[30] Access to fire and soap were improvements that had come about since Howard and Nield visited. On an interesting side note, Fry and Gurney noted that pawning of clothing was prevalent in York Castle Prison, probably explaining the two men without shirts that are also noted – you can see why the ease of access to the felons was such a problem.[31] Like James Nield, Fry and Gurney also noted that 'laces, caps, garters, &c.' were made and sold on the Eye of the Ridings by debtors.[32] The felons, though, were without employment.

After 1815, prisoners no longer had to pay for their food; it was now paid for out of local rates. The Gaol Fees Abolition Act 1815 stopped, once and for all, any fees charged to prisoners on their entrance and discharge from prison. This is hinted at in York Castle Prison by Fry and Gurney: 'The prisoners are allowed one pound and a half of wheaten bread daily, and one shilling per week ...'[33] However,

> From the squalid appearance of some of the men, it seemed to us questionable whether the allowance of food was sufficient to maintain them in health: the apothecary of the prison, whom we saw, expressed an opinion that it was not.[34]

The impact of the work of all the reformers cannot be understated. Still, in the case of John Gurney and especially Elizabeth Fry, many of the reforms they sought became the basis of what we would later refer to as a Victorian prison system.

Of course, prison reform was not without its detractors who 'generally, assumed that prisoners deserved to suffer life-threatening prison conditions because their violations of the laws constituted implicit forfeitures of the law's protections'.[35] There were even arguments that for some poorer classes of prisoners, 'imprisonment might provide a welcome respite from the ultraviolent street culture to which they had become accustomed.'[36] Of those that were anti-reform, two stand out. Firstly, the former prime minister Henry

Addington, Viscount Sidmouth, who would oversee the Peterloo Massacre in Manchester, and secondly, Lord Ellenborough.

Lord Ellenborough's name would become synonymous with the first major law changes of the 1800s. The Malicious Shooting or Stabbing Act 1803 is often called Lord Ellenborough's Act. This Act had two major parts. Firstly, it had a huge impact on the law for abortion, which until this time was not defined in common law. Secondly, it made provisions around stabbing, cutting, shooting, or poisoning someone. Any attempt that takes place where physical harm is done would now be treated as though a murder had been successfully carried out. York Castle Prison would see only the second conviction under this law, which would take the life of 16-year-old Peter Atkinson. The 1803 Act can also be seen as the start of important legislation affecting county gaols like York Castle Prison.

Insolvent Debtors Act 1813

The next important piece of legislation affected those imprisoned for debt. No longer would a debtor, who would never be able to pay back their debt, be forced into the common side and forced to beg at the 'lower grate' alongside the felons. From 1813, debtors could apply to the courts to be released. After fourteen days in prison, the debtor could apply for insolvency if they could prove that their total assets were valued at less than £20. This release would not result in the debtor not paying back their debt altogether. Instead, an agreement could be reached with the creditor for the value of the debt from the debtor's property and any future earnings. This would mean that the debtor would be able to return to a normal life, while for the creditor, they had a significantly improved chance of getting their money back. However, this did not apply to everyone; those guilty of fraud would have to stay inside the debtors' prison, as would those who were classed as having a trade. These debtors would be covered under the bankruptcy acts.

According to later *Gaoler's Journals* from York Castle Prison, declaring insolvency or bankruptcy involved the debtor being taken, usually by the gaoler, to the insolvent sessions at Wakefield to have their case heard (although Northallerton, Doncaster and Huddersfield are also mentioned for bankrupts).[37]

Gaol Fees Abolition Act 1815

It was passed through Parliament in 1815 that any fees corresponding to prisoners held should be removed and, if necessary, paid through county rates. In addition, the gaolers should be paid a salary to stop them from needing these fees to survive. It can be argued that this bill is one of the most significant turning points in the prison system, transitioning from private, fee-based gaols to more centrally run facilities, specifically designed for their intended purpose, regardless of the prisoner's or victim's financial position. However, this might not have been an issue for York Castle Prison, as according to Nield, in 1809, gaoler William Staveley had a salary of £450.[38] According to Hargrove, by 1820, this had risen to £700.[39] We don't know precisely when or why York opted for a salaried gaoler so early, but this can be seen as a positive step for York Castle Prison. However, this new cost was not generally well-received by most prisons. These fees were now being paid out of the local rates; this was unpopular, and magistrates tried to keep costs down.[40] In effect, this was unsuccessful, and it would be down to the 1823 Act to re-establish many of the areas that had, in theory, already been put into law.

Gaol Act 1823

In 1822, Britain had a new home secretary named Robert Peel. Now, several years after the Napoleonic Wars, politicians could focus on domestic politics within Britain. For Robert Peel, this was finally the right time to push through criminal justice system reform. Things started small with the abolition of branding in 1822.[41] However, the following year, Peel began to fundamentally change the criminal justice system in Britain. The Gaol Act 1823 was designed to bring about the sweeping change to the prison system that had been sought since the time of John Howard. The aim of this Act was uniformity. Uniformity of health, religion, the class system (relating to prisons) and hard labour. Public views on prisons were changing; while they were still supposed to be places you don't want to end up in, there was also an idea that those unfortunate enough to visit them should not become 'worse members of society, or more hardened offenders'.[42] The visiting magistrates would be given more independence to oversee the prisons. These justices appointed staff who regularly inspected the prisons, and chaplain reports were submitted to the home secretary. The gaoler, chaplain and surgeon now had to maintain journals, recording the intricacies of their job. This gave accountability to those responsible for maintaining the journals. Female warders were also now required for female prisoners.

While these measures provide us with some valuable bureaucracy to flesh out the finer details of life in York Castle Prison, other authors have pointed out that, without the mechanisms to enforce these acts, the Gaol Act 1823 'had no teeth'.[43] Arguably, the most successful part of the Prison Act 1823 was that gaolers were no longer running prisons as a profitable business. Instead, they would receive a regular salary.[44] However, it should be argued that the importance of placing female staff in charge of female prisoners cannot be overstated.

For York Castle Prison specifically, the 1823 Act was significant because it established the framework that enabled the construction of the next phase of York Castle Prison.

Offences Against the Person Act 1828

Capital punishment has long been a controversial topic, with calls for its abolition dating back to the early eighteenth century.[45] The difference between those convicted and those hanged was quite substantial, with transportation serving as the de facto punishment in some cases, even when the sentence was death. For example, in 1824, of 1066 people sentenced to death in England, only forty were executed.[46] Despite this, it was not uncommon for juries to give verdicts that would reduce the value of goods stolen to take them out of range for a capital sentence.[47] With this background for secondary punishments and avoiding the death penalty, especially by juries, it was decided that capital punishment in the UK needed to be reformed. In 1828, the number of capital crimes was reduced from 225 to just 6: murder, attempted murder, high treason, piracy, rape and homosexuality. One notable crime is missing here: petty treason, which no longer existed within British law. From now on, those who previously fell under this category are now simply charged with murder.

1829: The Police Force

In 1829, the first police force was established in Britain, marking a significant shift from the previous system of constables and watchmen tasked with maintaining order throughout the country. Created once again by Robert Peel, hence their nicknames of 'Peelers' or 'Bobbies', the force represented a revolutionary change in how criminals were apprehended. There is no longer a need for private citizens to find and arrest individuals; dedicated and paid professionals now handle this task. However, the main aim of the police was to prevent crime. Many more minor 'street' crimes, such as public order offences or illegal street selling, were quickly arrested by this new, more visible police force. What we would later class as Victorian ideals went hand in hand with the increase in dealing with drunks, vagrants and prostitutes.[48] However, the idea of a police force was not universally popular, as it was seen as a French import, and feelings against the French were still strong after the Napoleonic Wars.[49] However, the establishment of a paid and dedicated police force was a significant step in reforming the criminal system. It changed how people could end up in a county gaol like York Castle Prison.

However, it was not an overnight change; the Municipal Corporations Act 1835 brought this new form of policing to the provincial boroughs, although it would not be compulsory until the County and Borough Police Act 1856.[50] Even with the new police force, not all crimes would be prosecuted.

An interesting side note for York is that York Minster had established its own police force a few months prior to this in response to a massive fire that was the result of arson. The culprit, Jonathan Martin, would go on trial at the courthouse in York Castle. However, this force was – and still is – specific to York Minster and its immediate vicinity.

Anatomy Act 1832

This period's last major piece of legislation changed the now-defunct Murder Act 1752. The spate of body snatchers trying to make money from dead bodies and sometimes even murder, epitomised by the case of Burke and Hare in Edinburgh, meant that other sources of bodies needed to be found and made available to the surgeons who wanted to study them. This was no longer an indignity set aside for murderers; now, any unclaimed body might be dissected, leaving the poor and those in workhouses and those who might die alone in a hospital to undergo what previously had been considered part of the punishment for committing murder. For those executed for murder, the law now states that they should be buried within the prison walls or gibbeted (until gibbetting was abolished in 1834),[51] meaning that those executed after 1832 are most likely still somewhere around the site of York Castle.

An example of this extended use of unclaimed bodies for anatomy can be found in the *Gaoler's Journal* for York Castle Prison:

March 30th 1834
Hannah Roberts, in custody for wilful murder departed this life in York Castle in the evening of Sunday the 30th March 1834, the usual notices given, Inquest held before Mr Wood the Coroner, Verdict died by the visitation of God. Her body given to the surgeons and removed to the anatomical school at Leeds for examination before burial.

Prisons Act 1835

It could be argued that the end of the era of prison reform coincided with the Prison Act 1835, which established regular prison inspections. There would be further changes throughout the Victorian period, but never on the scale of the changes seen during the latter part of the eighteenth century and the early nineteenth century. Furthermore, private citizens would no longer spend their time touring prisons in the UK to observe the conditions for prisoners.

Transportation: The Move Away from America

With the American War of Independence in 1776, Britain could no longer transport convicts to America. A temporary solution emerged when the idea of using old ships to house convicts for up to two years was proposed, pending the end of the war and the resumption of transportation.[52] The Hulks, as they were known, were old ships converted into temporary prisons; however, since they were no longer seaworthy, they were also unfit for human habitation. The conditions on board were terrible; it is estimated that one in four prisoners died on board the Hulks.[53] Hulks were privately run, just like the prisons of the period.[54] Located at Woolwich, Chatham, Portsmouth and Plymouth, these old ships would become familiar to anyone living in these areas. The punishment was essentially hard labour in the UK rather than being transported.

It is worth noting that the hulks were only used for male prisoners as it was seen that they were not suitable conditions for women to be held in, an opinion that speaks volumes about the conditions onboard. With the hulks and prisons filling up, some prisoners (especially women) were given pardons, and others were forced to join the armed forces.[55] While the Hulks were intended to be a temporary measure, the Hulk System would be utilised for many years. By 1778, it was becoming clear that transportation would never resume in America. The Penitentiary Act 1779 reduced the sentence on the hulks to a year. While never fully implemented, it also suggested a new type of prison to replace the Hulks – the penitentiary – a significant step on the road to our modern prison system.[56] The idea was that these new institutions would help Britain by 'reforming the prisoner for the benefit of the English, as opposed to a colonial society'.[57]

With this hiatus in the transportation system, the increasing use of hulks and the growing number of people held in prisons led to the apparent answer of resuming transportation, but the question remained: where? Africa had been considered but was ultimately deemed unsuitable.[58] In August 1786, it was decided that Botany Bay, part of modern-day Sydney, Australia, would be the new destination for those sentenced to transportation. The first convicts arrived at Botany Bay on 26 January 1788.

Yet this new transportation location did not mean the end of the Hulks, with men either dredging rivers or working in the naval dockyards. Why? The Napoleonic Wars increased transport costs to Australia due to the risk of capture along the way. Additionally, Britain's shipbuilding effort was focused on constructing ships for the war, not on transporting criminals. The success of the new prisoner-of-war camps, combined with the work that those imprisoned on the Hulks did, makes it unsurprising that Britain's first penitentiary would finally open at Millbank in London in 1816, just one year after the Battle of Waterloo.

It is important to note that this increase in incarceration in Britain should not be read as a decrease in transportation use. The number of people transported after the Napoleonic Wars increased from around 1,000 per year to a peak in the early 1830s of around 5,000 annually.[59] It is estimated that during this period (1788–1838), convicts (both current and released) made up approximately 40 per cent of Australia's population.[60] In part, this increase in the number of transportees was due to an increase in the pardon rate for capital crimes, which also rose after the Napoleonic Wars from a 50–60 per cent reprieve rate to as high as 90 per cent, with many now being reprieved after receiving a death sentence.[61]

The final change in transportation during this period occurred in 1834 when returning early from transportation sentences was no longer punishable by death; instead, it became a sentence of transportation for life.[62] Although

given that execution for returning from transportation early is not mentioned in the Offences Against the Person Act, it had effectively been abolished in 1828.

Life in York Castle Prison

While we have gained valuable insights into the lives of prisoners at York Castle Prison through the work of prison reformers, as well as the laws brought in during the early nineteenth century that impacted the lives of those who came to York Castle Prison, what we are missing is the voice of the prisoners themselves to help us understand their routine in prison and how they viewed the establishment where they were staying.

Thankfully, we have one person incarcerated at the end of the eighteenth century who left us a record of their time in York Castle Prison. James Montgomery was a newspaper editor and poet from Sheffield. He left us an invaluable account of his time at York Castle Prison during his two terms of imprisonment for seditious libel in 1795 and 1796. James spent a total of nine months at York Castle Prison and made the most of his time; he created a series of poems during his time there. The longest poem was called 'The Pleasures of Imprisonment' and was a tongue-in-cheek look at prison life.

There are two things to bear in mind while reading James Montgomery's poem. Firstly, it is a satirical look at his life; as such, we do have to read between the lines a little. Secondly, it must be remembered that James was sentenced to his time of imprisonment at the quarter sessions; as such, he was not a felon and was held away from the worst that York Castle Prison had to offer. His stay was more akin to that of a debtor, and as we will see, he shared some of his daily activities with the debtors.

Here are a few select snippets from James Montgomery's poem 'The Pleasures of Imprisonment',[63] offering a glimpse into life at York Castle Prison and the daily routine of a prisoner of his status. The whole poem is included in Appendix IV:

> Each morning, then, at five o'clock,
> The adamantine doors unlock;
> Bolts, bars, and portals crash and thunder;
> The gates of iron burst asunder;
> Hinges that creak, and keys that jingle,
> With clattering chains, in concert mingle:

Breakfast dispatched, I sometimes read,
To clear the cob-webs from my head:
For books, my friend, are charming brooms
To sweep the dust of upper rooms!

At half past ten, or there about,
My eyes are all upon the scout,
To see the lounging post-boy come,
With letters or with news from home.
Believe me, sir, upon my word,
Although the doctrine seem absurd,
The paper messengers of friends
For absence almost make amends:

The clock strikes one – I can't delay,
For dinner comes but once a day!

In this sweet place, where freedom reigns,
Secured by bolts and snug in chains;
Where innocence and guilt together
Roost like two turtles of a feather;
Where debtors safe at anchor lie,
From saucy duns and bailiffs fly;
Where highwaymen and robbers stout,
Would, rather than break in, break out;
Where all's so guarded and recluse,
That none his liberty can lose! –
Here each may, as his means afford,
Dine like a pauper or a lord;
And he who can't the cost defray,
Is welcome, sir, to fast and pray!

Now let us ramble o'er the green,
To see and hear, be heard and seen;
To breathe the air, enjoy the light,
And hail yon sun, who shines as bright

Upon the dungeon and the gallows,
As on York Minster or Kew Palace!
And here let us the scene review:
That's the old castle, this the new;
Yonder the felons walk, and there
The lady-prisoners take the air;
Behind are solitary cells,
Where hermits live like snails in shells;
There stands the chapel for good people,
And yon balcony is the steeple;

The days are only twelve hours long;
Though captives often reckon here,
Each day a month, each month a year!

But, lo! my frisking dog attends,
The kindest of four-footed friends;
Brim full of giddiness and mirth,
He is the prettiest fool on earth!
I call this fond companion Billy,
But wiser people call him Silly;
Because, in spite of rhyme and reason,
He chuses to reside in prison;
And, though his home is in the city,
He boards with me for bones – or pity!

But, lo! the evening shadows fall
Broader and browner from the wall;
A warning voice, like curfew bell,
Commands each captive to his cell;
My faithful dog and I retire,
To play and chatter by the fire:
Soon comes a turnkey with 'Good night, sir!'
And bolts the door with all his might, sir!
Then leisurely to bed I creep,
And sometimes wake – and sometimes sleep.

After James Montgomery's second release from York Castle Prison, he never found himself incarcerated again. He would champion political causes, such as the abolition of slavery, continue his role as an editor for the *Sheffield Iris* newspaper, and, of course, continue to write poetry. However, it is clear from his biography that he never forgot his time at York Castle Prison.[64]

James Montgomery's stay at York Castle Prison also shows us the beginning of a change in the use of prisons in the UK. While it would not be until the 1820s that imprisonment as a form of punishment began to become more common, we see that times were changing; by the turn of the nineteenth century, imprisonment was becoming the most common sentence in 'non-capital property cases',[65] as well as cases like that of James Montgomery, where loss of reputation through slander or libel were considered to be severe enough to warrant a prison sentence. You can argue that this saw crimes being punished more severely, as most offences now carried imprisonment or transportation rather than whipping and fining people. Women were also increasingly likely to be imprisoned rather than discharged or pardoned.

The Associated or Congregate System

A new era of prisons required a different type of system to run them. The first of these was the associated or congregate system. This system required separate cells for each prisoner with limited association during the day. This system was employed in most prisons until the 1840s. It was with this system in mind that the later buildings of York Castle Prison were designed.

Behaviour in Prison

The misbehaviour of people being held against their will, no matter how deserved, will always cause problems in prison. We have already seen examples of this, but with the introduction of the *Gaoler's Journals* in 1823, we started to get very specific details of some of the infractions. These notes give us insight into what the rebellious minority would attempt while incarcerated. Many of the infractions occurred again and again, fighting and attacking fellow prisoners (this was men, women and debtors alike). Cursing and swearing, getting drunk, bad behaviour in the chapel, destroying their clothing, refusing to clean their cell, passing into wards they don't belong, passing notes and refusing to obey orders all frequently appear in the *Gaoler's Journals*.[66] Others might include singing/whistling, impertinence to turnkeys, and not being dressed and ready to leave their cells at the usual time. Some of the more interesting prison infractions listed at York Castle Prison include (note the use of 'soly' as an abbreviation of solitary confinement):

> Edward Holden and Wm Walsh Soly two days for throwing Urine thro' their Cell window.[67]
>
> Stephen Jones Soly two days for breaking his Bedstead.[68]
>
> Benjamin Wiseman and Samuel Howard Soly two days each for refusing to empty & clean their chamber pott.[69]
>
> Stead and Pearson two felon prisoners Soly one day each for refusing to clean the day Room and Yard.[70]

It was not just the felons that could fall foul of the rules. Debtors could also get into trouble, like in this example from 1832:

> William Allisons, bread stoped until he cleaned his Lodging Room.[71]
>
> Richard Green a Debtor 1 day Solty for being drunk and breaking the door in his Room, to repair the same at his own expence.[72]

Finally, of course this kind of behaviour was not just confined to the male prisoners: 'Ruth Jubb and Mary Ann Forrest Soly one day for fighting &c.'[73]

Work in Prison

Employment was necessary to keep the prisoners busy while at York Castle Prison. Even with the removal of fees, more money could still make a difference to the quality of your stay within the confines of York Castle Prison. William Hargrove once again provides some details on what this might have been like around 1820:

> There is no employment provided by the county for persons in this prison; but Mr. Staveley is very active in procuring it for shoemakers, weavers, wool-combers, tailors, and other men accustomed to similar employments; and when work of this kind cannot be met with, the

> prisoners are taught to make laces, garters, purses, &c., which articles they expose for sale in the castle-yard, and there they render themselves more comfortable than they otherwise would be, under the unhappy circumstances of their confinement.[74]

Some of the women could be employed in the washhouse, washing for the debtors.[75]

However, as always, this was not an option for everyone, and Fry and Gurney note that some prisoners even resorted to selling or pawning their clothes to make money, which they describe as a 'prevalent custom' at York Castle Prison.[76] Fry and Gurney also clarify that while employment is available for most prisoners, this is not always the case. Instead, they are occupied 'by various devices for effecting their escape'.[77]

Visitors in Prison

Changes in the law and the end of the garnish system meant that visiting was no longer for anyone who could afford it. It was no longer a system where you could pay for access to whoever you wanted. In the nineteenth century, immediate relatives were the only ones permitted to visit prisoners. Then, they were still separated through a caged area with a guard between them to stop the passing of any contraband. This system of visitation stayed in place until the 1920s.[78] However, this only refers to official visitations. It is noted by Fry and Gurney on their visit that there are still problems with communication between the public in the castle yard and the felons in their exercise yard between the wings of the debtors' prison:

> Through this grating they keep up a free and easy communication, not only with the debtors, but with the public. At this very time a great number of persons were standing at the outside, holding conversation with the prisoners. Men and women, grown-up persons and children, have equal access to this scene of depravity and distress. It is evident that so free a communication must give every facility to the introduction of improper articles into the prison …[79]

Through this, the prisoners would pawn their shirts as described above, leading Fry and Gurney to observe that out of around forty felons held within the prison, two were without shirts. Again, there was still the problem of those who had and those who didn't. Fry and Gurney suggest that the lack of clothing provisions, especially the lack of a distinctive uniform at this time, made it surprisingly easy for felons to escape from York Castle Prison.[80]

Cleanliness in Prison

One thing that Fry and Gurney also hint at is the differing conditions regarding the prisoners' cleanliness and their environments. In theory, the unhealthy, dark, smelly, disease-ridden gaol of the Georgian period is now gone. They note that 'firing' is now allowed to keep warm, but this does not apply to the sleeping cells used at night. The cold would continue to be a problem into the Victorian era. Soap was now allowed, and every yard was supplied with water, as was the bathing facility. This would help control some of the diseases in the prison. This is further helped by the prison being white-washed twice per year.[81] The area for female prisoners is especially noted for being 'kept in a state of cleanliness and order'.[82] However, once again, we have a contrast where the felons' day room in the debtors' prison was described as being 'far from clean'.[83] Overall, these appear to be significantly better conditions than those in which the eighteenth-century prisoners found themselves, but they were still far removed from what we might consider a comfortable prison. The work of the reformers was paying off, albeit slowly.

Women in Prison

At York, the main changes we have seen for women were that they now had their own building away from the men, female staff were now looking after the female inmates, and the often female-biased crime of petty treason finally came to an end. As we have seen, the conditions were generally better for women than for their male counterparts at York Castle Prison for at least part of this reform period, especially after they were granted access to their newly built facilities, which would later become known as the female prison building.

As before, certain crimes disproportionately affected women. Until 1803, Infanticide was tried under a 1624 law that forced the accused to provide witnesses that proved the child was stillborn.[84] While this was changing in the late eighteenth century, it was not until 1803 that infanticide was treated like any other murder. Where the prosecution was required to prove guilt, a jury could also reduce this to 'concealment of birth' where necessary, with a maximum sentence of two years' imprisonment. This came too late for Martha Chapel, who in 1802 was hanged outside of York Castle for the murder of her just-born child. The 1803 Act also dealt with abortion. Previously, this was addressed through a fine or short-term imprisonment.[85] Interestingly, until 1861, it would be the abortionist and not the pregnant woman that would be prosecuted.[86]

In the early 1820s, regulations regarding the transportation of women also changed, allowing any children under the age of seven to accompany them. Similarly, a woman who has an 'infant at the breast' cannot be made to leave until the 'child is of proper age to be weaned'.[87] I will leave it to the reader to decide whether this was beneficial for the children. Women travelling for transportation are also 'not to be laden with heavy irons for their journey' although, as Elizabeth Fry notes, this rule was often infringed.[88] However, it should be noted that for the fortunate women on these voyages, who behave in an orderly manner while on their voyage, they would be, 'on their arrival at their place of destination, immediately hired as servants by the most respectable families in the colony'.[89]

Moving of the Gallows

As the population of York increased and more and more people came to witness the public executions, the act of moving the condemned 2 miles away to the gallows became a big problem. With large crowds lining the streets, there was always a danger of injury to the public and the chance of someone trying to free the condemned. An example of the problem can already be seen a century and a half earlier. In 1649, an execution of a husband and wife at Walmgate Without described difficulty passing down Castlegate because of the number of people, and when it came to Fossgate, 'the street was one mass of human beings. One woman had her leg broken in the crowd, and a young man had his thigh broken …'[90] The solution to this problem had already been seen in London, where the Tyburn Gallows had been moved to just outside the newly built Newgate Prison in 1783. York took the same approach as London and moved the gallows just outside of York Castle Prison.

> Near the grand Jury Room is the place for execution of criminals, where a temporary scaffolding is erected for the purpose … the present place of execution is called the New Drop. It was prepared in 1802 and on

> 28th August, that year, was first used for the awful sacrifice of human life to offended laws.[91]

The new gallows were not a permanent feature of the landscape as the three-legged mare had been. This new structure was designed to be disassembled and stored between uses. It would begin to be constructed between 4.00 and 5.00 am on the morning of the execution. One newspaper reports that

> the hollow sound of the booming timbers being audible as they were adjusted to their proper positions in this fearful machine of death, added no little, as may well be imagined, to the solemn awe which usually attaches to the environs of York Castle upon such occasions as the present.[92]

Some modifications were made to the new drop in 1813 for the execution of George Mellor and the Luddites, 'so that all the bodies were visible when they were suspended; in former executions, only the feet and head could be seen by the spectators'.[93]

The new drop also brought a new executioner, William 'Mutton' Curry, who would become the longest-serving executioner at York Castle Prison. Curry had himself been a convicted felon, twice sentenced to transportation, but he had been spared from this sentence by agreeing to become York's executioner.

Final Hours

A question that is always asked is what the final hours would have been like for prisoners who had been sentenced to death. In 1810, two debtors volunteered to act as 'wakers', those who would stay awake with the prisoners during their final hours and help them prepare for their fate.[94] One of them would write an account of their time with the condemned, giving us a window into the final hours of those preparing to be executed.

The act of two people being with the condemned prisoners was not uncommon. Two prisoners would be assigned to be with the prisoners through the night anyway. The two debtors who volunteered were in addition to the usual two prisoners. However, there was also a female prisoner condemned to death, and she would be attended by two women in the condemned cell in the female prison building. Regardless of the gender of the condemned, the structure of the evening would remain the same: prayer. These individuals were not concerned with getting a good night's sleep; likely, they would not be able to sleep knowing what was going to happen the next day. Instead, the night would be spent praying for forgiveness for themselves and the female condemned prisoner, in preparation for what was to come next.

But I am getting ahead of myself; this prayer would start at a special chapel service on that final day, which the friends and family of the condemned would be able to attend. 'The sorrow into which the prisoners relatives and friends were unavoidably plunged, was noticed'.[95] It was not until 9 pm that the two debtors were allowed into the condemned cell, and their observations started. They were escorted to the cell carrying a chair each and some ale and cheese:

> we entered one door, which was immediately locked; another door with many locks and bolts was then opened; we proceeded silently to the cell door … words equally expressive of mutual kindness were used by both keepers and prisoners.[96]

As already mentioned, the main activity of the night was prayer, and after a request was made, mats were brought in to make the prayer more comfortable on the wooden floor. What is striking about the recollection of these events is the resignation of the condemned prisoners towards their fate; after asking one of them how they felt, the debtor recalls, 'He had less terror on him than I had when I first entered the room'.[97] But this is probably a brave show as one of the prisoners had some bread and cheese 'thereby his poor body would be refreshed, and if not refreshed, he was afraid he would faint, and not be able to bear his approaching and present suffering …'[98] One prisoner ventured to get some sleep despite his fellow prisoner reminding them that this was the last night; the pressure of the situation was getting to him. 'He could bear no more, and laid himself down on the ground …'[99] We can see from this that the fear of the next day was present, but it varied greatly from prisoner to prisoner.

Aside from the emotions around the impending execution, there were other fears amongst them; for one, it was that 'his death would hasten his father's'.[100] One expressed shock that his irons had been left on for the last night. Another 'expressed a carelessness as to how their bodies were excited; but they were very careful of their souls, that it might please the Lord to prepare and receive them to life eternal'.[101] This brings us once again to the amount of prayer that was taking place in the cell, facilitated by both the wakers and the attendants. This was the role of the additional men in the cell: to help the condemned prepare for the next day's events as well as they could. Of course, this could only take away the thoughts of the next day for so long. When 4.00 am in the morning was reached, one of the men noted that 'By four in the afternoon I shall be in the earth'.[102]

Eventually, the time came for the prisoners to leave the condemned cell and the debtors to leave them:

> The prisoners waited with Christian fortitude their appointed time … 'They are coming.' I said, 'Let them find us as we are'. Mr. Wilson opened the door very softly, and his gentle carriage intimated, if a minute or two longer will be of any service, pray do take it.[103]

But this would only be a small delay before the inevitable:

> They went on the passage, some of the convicts stood ready to shake hands, and bid a last farewell to these men. We accompanied them to a small room, under the chapel; here was the poor woman and her female attendants. I never saw such sorrow before; she appeared terrified to death, with death's near approach. After the prisoners spoke to her … 'we have prayed for you as well as we were able.' For which she thanked them affectionately.[104]

Eventually, the debtors that had spent the night were taken up to the chapel before the prisoners were pinioned and led away.

Politics on the Eye of York

There is one tradition we have neglected to mention so far that came to an end towards the end of this period with the construction of the following prison facilities on the site. This was not a function of the prison but rather a function of the court. The Eye of the Ridings was used for county elections in Yorkshire, the proclamation of new monarchs following their accession and for announcing declarations of war or peace.[105] Courts were also used at this time as polling stations for elections. During the seventeenth century 'no less than twenty-nine elections for knights of the shire to serve in Parliament were held in the Castle yard'.[106] Another twenty-eight would be held in the eighteenth century. More would be held in the earlier parts of the nineteenth century, one of which was the county elections of 1807. A special court was established to elect the two knights of the shire, including William Wilberforce, the renowned slavery abolitionist. The election consisted of 13 polling booths in the castle yard, open for 15 days, with 23,000 freeholders travelling to York to record their votes.[107] Politics at the castle essentially came to an end in 1831, when the last election was held in the castle yard; however, the results of the North Riding elections continued to be declared in the castle yard until 1882.[108] However, one tradition persevered through all this change, and the area is still used to declare a new monarch to this day.

Although these events had no direct connection to the prisoners, we know that they affected those already residing at York Castle Prison. Hargrove tells us that the wealthier debtors held within the female prison were usually allowed to spend time on the castle yard. However, when the assizes, elections or other civic uses were around, these wealthy debtors were restricted to the central part of the female prison building and the exercise yards.[109]

Chapter 7

The Site of York Castle Prison, 1835–1877

The Prison

By the early 1800s, prison life in Britain was undergoing significant changes. Through the work of prison reformers, the nature of punishment and life inside prisons changed; prisoners were now being treated more humanely, and imprisonment as a form of punishment itself was becoming more common. This period in prison history is sometimes referred to as 'the great penitentiary experiment.'[1] However, after the initial surge in the 1780s and '90s, following John Howard's push for improved conditions, the construction of new prisons in Britain almost ceased. Large-scale prison building would not resume in Britain until after the revolutionary construction of Pentonville in 1842. It is somewhat surprising that in the early 1820s, York would begin constructing a new, purpose-built prison building. Elizabeth Fry and John Gurney's reports on the conditions showed that existing buildings were inadequate for their current purpose. However, there were three main influences on the decision to change, expand, or replace the buildings at York Castle Prison. Firstly, the number of prisoners was increasing; in 1802–1806, the average number of criminal inmates (convicted and remanded, i.e., not debtors) at York Castle Prison was 66; by 1819–1823, this average increased to 105.[2] The greater numbers of prisoners meant a decline in the conditions in which they were held. This was a challenge nationwide due to the expanding prison populations, which brings us to the second impetus, the facilitation of building new prisons allowed by the Gaol Act 1823. This Act required prisons to use a classification system, something York Castle Prison was not set up to do. At York Castle Prison, men, boys, hardened criminals, and first-time or minor offenders were all held together, and the old felons' cells on the ground floor of the debtors' prison could not be changed to accommodate these new classifications. The 1823 Act also allowed counties to raise money for any necessary improvements and permitted the compulsory purchase of land where deemed necessary. The third and final influence on the decision

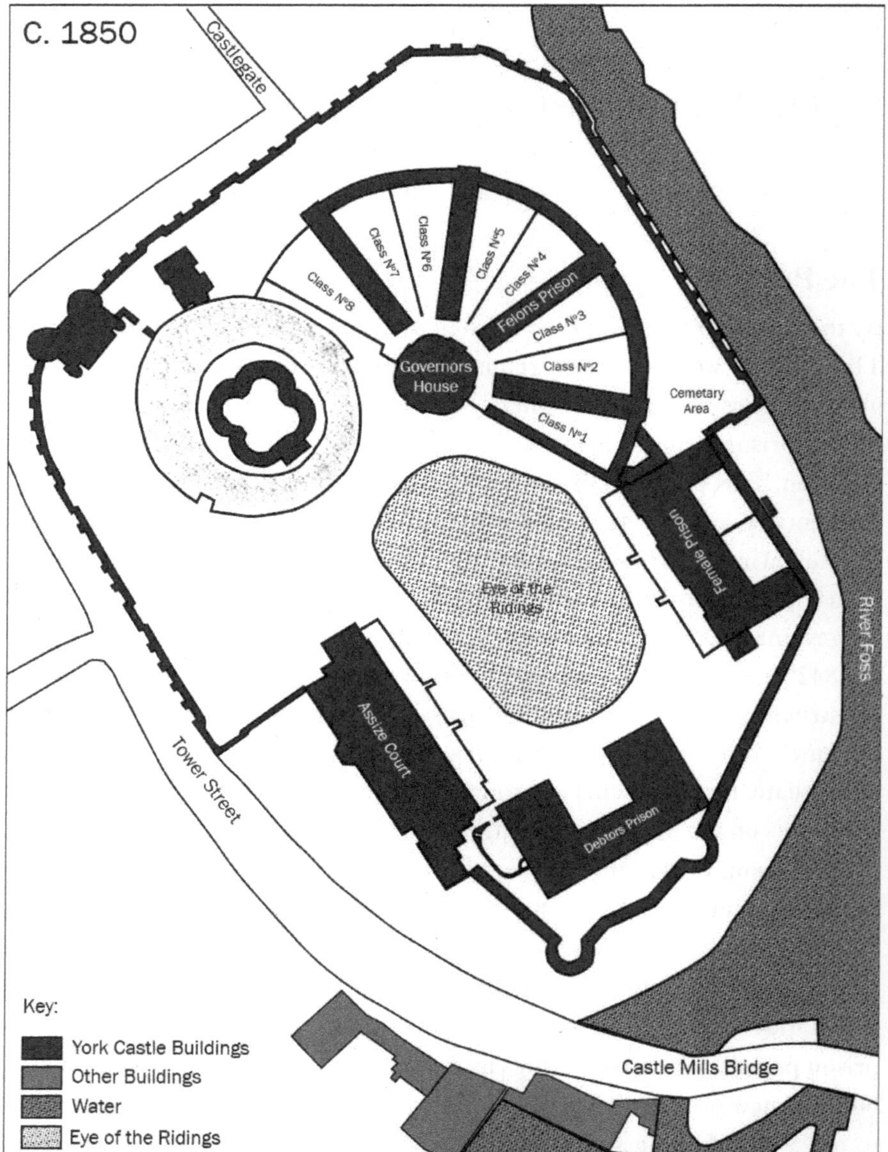

A plan of York Castle around 1850 showing the new buildings and surrounding wall.[3]

to rebuild was York wanting to maintain its position as 'the hub of Yorkshire affairs', with the West Riding becoming increasingly more influential.[4]

The process of expanding the prison was not easy. It would become a twelve-year ordeal involving the future of what remained of the original castle, a story of forced purchase, and the creation of an imposing landmark in the city centre. Behind all this was a clear recognition that York Castle Prison needed to expand to keep York a modern prison facility. The initial expansion was proposed in 1823, but the first meeting of the Yorkshire Court of Gaol Session in 1824 decided to push ahead.[5] The requirements of the new prison included not just a new prison building to house felons but also replacements for the gaoler's offices and a new chapel.

The debate over exactly what form this new construction should take was extensive. Do the magistrates demolish and rebuild the existing prison? Do they extend the current buildings or expand the prison through brand-new buildings? Would they even consider moving the prison elsewhere in York?[6] Several different designs were put forward:

> some individuals contending that a sufficient site can be found upon the very limited extent of ground already the property of the county; others, that the desired objects can be effected only by building a new prison, at a considerable distance, and at the opposite side of the river Foss; and others considering that Mr. Ward's ground is the best and most conveniently situated for the purpose.[7]

The merits of each of these choices was discussed at length. The idea of building a new prison further away appears to have fallen down because there were no plans to move the court with the prison. This would lead to problems when bringing prisoners to and from the courts, with possible delays noted.[8]

The big question became what to do with Clifford's Tower. Sydney Smithe proposed converting it into the prison chapel; Robert Wallace placed it at the centre of his designs.[9] Some of these proposed ideas even included the destruction of Clifford's Tower. The idea of pulling down Clifford's Tower might appear questionable today, but this was a serious debate within York, with substantial numbers of people on both sides. The main argument was that another prison further out or even on St George's Field, opposite the castle, was not a good option. The most sensible and cost-effective option was to acquire the land adjacent to the existing prison. However, this option raised the question of what to do with Clifford's Tower and its mound. Some argued that 'all agree that the ground is too limited, and therefore cannot be used for any effectual purpose, without pulling down that abominable incumbrance Clifford's Tower'.[10] It was quite a popular opinion in York that the tower was considered so 'highly offensive to the citizens of York that they commonly gave a toast to "the demolishing the mince pie",'[11] the 'Mince Pie' being a derogatory name given to the tower by the citizens of York at the time. However, the idea was not just to demolish the tower but 'that the stones it is composed of might be converted to fill up the foundations of the new buildings'.[12] Thankfully, as Strickland pointed out, removing the tower and making the ground right would be far more costly than leaving it be.[13] This might be one of the few occasions where the push of economics actually helped preserve the past.

The final plans for the new buildings, by architects P.F. Robinson and G.T. Andrews, were formally adopted in July 1825, with the first stone laid on 20 March 1826. However, the main building work would not be finally finished until 1835.[14]

Acquiring the land on which to build the prison was not straightforward. The land to the north of the castle's bailey belonged to Samuel Wilkes Waud; on it stood a mansion house and 'an ancient tower upon a mound called "Clifford's Tower".'[15] A compulsory purchase of the land for £8,800,[16] as stipulated in the Prison Act 1823, resulted in this area becoming part of the prison, thereby reuniting the keep and bailey areas of the old castle.

The accepted designs for the new buildings stopped any talk of demolishing Clifford's Tower, but saving Clifford's Tower did not necessarily mean saving all of the old castle. The last major demolition of part of the original castle comes with the construction of the new felons' prison building. The northern wall of the bailey area, from the assize court to the female prison building, including Castlegate Postern, the entrance into the prison complex, was demolished to provide room. The motte of Clifford's Tower was cut back and surrounded by a 20-foot-high retaining wall.[17] All that would now remain of the medieval castle structure was Clifford's Tower and part of the curtain wall at the south; this is largely what remains today.

The total cost of the building from 24 March 1825 to 26 June 1835 was £194,428 7s 6 ½p.[18] This was a huge amount of money; as one author points out, when Armley Prison, near Leeds, was constructed in 1847, it only cost £47,000 and had nearly twice the number of cells, 291, as opposed to York's 160.[19] Once again, a tax was raised to fund the new construction at York Castle.[20] Why did it take so long and cost so much? Part of the problem might have been that the architect was on an annual fee. It cost £500 for the first four years; £550 from October 1829 going down to £250 from April 1835. In hindsight, this was not the best motivation to finish things quickly.[21]

The Buildings

The building style chosen for this new part of York Castle Prison is quite interesting. It resembles a radial prison building with four wings emanating from a central tower. Yet the first radial prison building in the UK was Pentonville, completed in 1842. Why is this? When you look closely at the plans for the new felons' prison building, it is noticeable that the four wings are not connected to the central governor's tower; therefore, it was not technically a radial design.

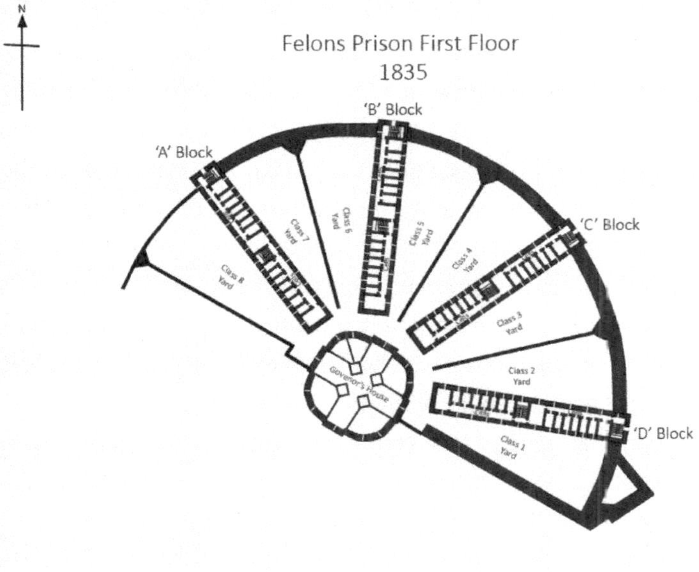

A Plan of the first floor of the new felon's prison building. Note how the two cell areas are easily separated, allowing for different classes of prisoners. The lower floor was a similar plan, just with a single large day room instead of each section of cells.[22]

The whole site was enclosed by a new 35-foot-high (10.6-metre-high) wall running from the assize court to the female prison building. Unlike the old bailey wall, the new wall would encompass Clifford's Tower rather than divide it from the prison. The new buildings stood just north of the female prison building on the site of Samuel Wilks Waud's old house.

The new entrance to York Castle Prison stood within this new curtain wall to the northwest of Clifford's Tower. The gatehouse was accessed by a pair of large black gates, above which was the crest of King George IV. These gates and crest can still be seen displayed in York Castle Museum. The idea of the prison gatehouse is summed up perfectly as follows:

> The gate marks the transition between the world outside and the world inside prison. It is usually the only part of the prison that the public sees and is designed with this in mind. It is also designed to be reassuringly secure, and in the 18th and early 19th centuries consciously resembled a robust Classical monument or a castle.[23]

The gatehouse served a more functional purpose than just an entrance. The inside of the new gatehouse has been described as housing a porters' lodge, committee rooms for the justices, and a muniments room, allegedly of fire-proof construction.[24] The porters' residence was located in the right-hand tower, with the left-hand tower and the area above the gate serving as record rooms and offices for the clerk of arraigns and assize. From 1836, the building also became home to the petty sessions for the City of York and East Ainsty.[25] Taking over from the guildhall after the Ainsty of York was split into two parts for trials, the western sessions were now taking place in Wetherby. These sessions would have been held in the larger apartments of the building, making it the most likely place for the trial of the Keithley Guardians in 1876. This new division also formally ended the medieval wapentake of York.

The new prison for felons consisted of two parts. At the centre was the governor's lodgings. Taking over from the functions that used to be contained in the east wing of the debtors' prison, this new building was now the administrative centre of the prison. The four cellblocks appeared from this central structure but were not connected. All the four new cell blocks appear to have been identical. The cell blocks were divided into two, with a stairway located halfway through the building separating the two. This allowed each cell block to accommodate two prisoner classes in the new classification system. Each half of the block had a day room on the ground floor with a corridor along one side. The two upper floors had a line of ten cells, each with a corridor on the other side.[26] Each of these new cell blocks was connected through a circular corridor that enclosed the exercise yards for the new cell blocks. This corridor, in turn, was attached to the female prison building through a passage that allowed, among other things, condemned prisoners to be moved to their designated cells. This corridor, connecting the female prison to the new felons' prison building, also allowed male felons to access the new chapel.[27]

The Rest of the Site

This project was the largest change to occur at the site in one go, not just because of the construction of the felons' prison building and the 35-foot-high wall and gatehouse surrounding it, but also because of the significant alterations made to the existing buildings. One of the key parts of the new building's design was that it should have a new chapel. The top floor of the central part of the female prison building was chosen to house this new chapel.

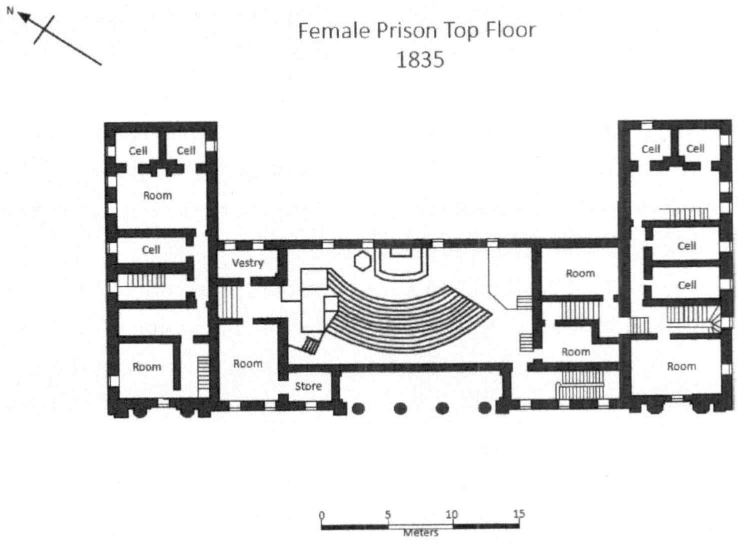

A plan of the top floor of the female prison after conversion to a chapel.[28]

This is likely the point in time when the roof of this central part of the building was raised, specifically to accommodate the new chapel and its organ.

Other changes are also taking place in the female prison building. It is already referred to as the female debtors' prison, indicating how the debtors were split up, a change since Hargrove's 1820 descriptions. However, one newspaper tells us that the work on the building consists of not just the new chapel but 'wards for the female felons, the condemned cell, the lunatic room, the kitchen, etc.'[29]

The debtors' prison building also underwent significant changes during this period of construction. With the former gaolers' offices and apartments, as well as the old chapel, both removed from the first floor of the two wings, there was now space for more cells to be placed in these areas. For the west wing, where the old chapel had been since 1705, adding cells to this area also meant adding a second floor. The weight of the additional floor and the supporting walls would add a significant amount of new weight to the ground floor's structure. As a result, the ground floor at the front of the west wing was completely modified to feature central walls supporting the new structure. However, the most striking visual change was the removal of the two staircases at the front of the debtors' prison building that used to lead up to the former gaoler's office and chapel.

The ground floor of the debtors' prison building no longer housed felons after they were moved to the new felons' prison building. Instead, now, poorer debtors would be held in the former felons' cells.[30] While we do not have an exact date, it was not long before the windows that had previously been only decorative outside the old felons' cells became actual windows for the first time; the walls were also plastered. While it was not as nice as the upper floors for the first and second-class debtors, these old cells were now much better than they had been for the felons in the 1700s.

The southern part of Half-Moon Court was also lowered in 1857, a few years after the introduction of third-class debtors.[31] This joined Half-Moon Court to the exercise yard behind the debtors' prison, providing the third-class debtors with a little more space, while the first and second-class debtors still exercised on the Eye of York.

In addition, we can see the courts got a small renovation in 1861:

> The courts, Judges, Jury and attornes & other apartments have been thoroughly cleaned painted and whitewashed, the Seats for Counsel

A plan of the old 'felons' apartments' after 1835. No longer housing the felons, they would become the third-class debtors' lodgings. Note that several walls have been knocked through, providing larger rooms for the debtors.[32]

> varnished; some of the pillars covered with new cloth and doors with green, some parts of the courts had not been painted for 20 years, the council tables have been covered with new cloth, the frost has caused us some damage by bursting water pipe.[33]

This kind of small renovation or housekeeping would have been quite common, although with twenty years between this and the last upkeep on the court, perhaps not as common as it should have been.

The Cemetery

Once again, the location of those prisoners buried on site is shrouded in mystery. We have been given some exact locations in the *Gaoler's Journals*, but they always refer to the site from the condemned cell. Unfortunately, we don't know the precise location of the condemned cell between 1835 and 1872. However, as we have previously done with the Hoppett, we can use some clues to determine a probable location of York Castle's cemetery and a probable location for the condemned cell itself.

On 7 August 1841, John Burlinson, Charles Gill and Henry Nuttal are all executed and buried 'in the corner near the circular passage'.[34] This likely refers to the passage or wall outside the new prison for felons enclosing the exercise yards. In 1853, Henry Dobson was buried 14 feet from the east wall and 12 feet from the north wall. The east wall is likely the easternmost wall of the prison that ran alongside the River Foss. The northern wall is a little harder to pinpoint, but it is plausible that this refers to the northern wall of the female prison building, as the north wall of the prison would make most locations inaccessible. With these assumptions, a familiar pattern begins to emerge. This location is north of the female prison, between the east wall and the circular outer passage. This area, which we previously suggested, was likely the location of the Hoppett burial ground after 1802. This same area likely continued to be used to bury those executed or those who died on-site, with no one to claim the body. With the removal of the wall around the Hoppett, there would also be an opportunity to expand north. This means that despite the recovery of some skeletons in 1998, there are still dozens of bodies in this general area today.

These descriptions perhaps give us an idea of the location of the condemned cell. Charles Normington was executed on 31 December 1859 and buried near the condemned cell, but also next to the boundary wall.[35] On 4 January 1862, James Waller was executed and buried 'in the usual ground' 13 yards from the condemned cell and 7 yards from the passage. These two suggest that the condemned cell is close to the boundary wall and is further away from the passage wall than the boundary wall. This last point rules out the 1835 building. This leaves the northern part of the female prison building as the most likely spot to house the condemned cell. We know that this was used as a condemned cell after 1868, but this evidence suggests that the condemned cell may have been relocated to this location after 1835, long before the gallows were added in 1868.

Problems

Having a brand-new building did not mean that York Castle Prison was immune to new problems, and they began to appear immediately. The material chosen for the outer wall was made from gritstone, which rapidly darkened in the smoke of an industrialising York,[36] creating an increasingly oppressive look for the buildings and their walls. However, the biggest problem was the time it took to construct the new buildings. Over a decade of changes had taken place in the prison system, meaning that by the time York Castle Prison was once again complete, the system was already starting to have different expectations of its prisons. Soon, silent and separate systems would become the more popular way of managing prisons, something that even the new architecture at York Castle was unsuitable for. Other new prisons would soon start to be built across the country. Many of these were of the new state-of-the-art radial design, which York Castle came so close to being, but the functionality of the prison was lacking. We can therefore say that the new buildings of York Castle Prison were outdated before they were ever completed.

Chapter 8

Life in York Castle Prison, 1835–1877

Victorian Prisons

As we have seen, before Queen Victoria ascended to the throne in 1837, significant changes had occurred in the ongoing reforms of British prisons and law enforcement. In 1829, the police force was established, which undoubtedly would have increased the number of people sent to prison. Most significantly, imprisonment had become an important form of punishment. This led to a significant increase in the number of people incarcerated in Britain. The focus of a prison also changed. The sentences now being handed out were intended to reform the prisoner's character,[1] sending a better person back into society than the one who came in. However, this philosophy primarily applied to large convict prisons, such as Pentonville or Millbank. For a county prison like the one at York Castle Prison, most sentences were relatively short; anyone serving six months or more would be transferred to the convict prisons. Many of these sentences at county prisons were often less than one month.[2] Those unfortunate enough to be held here were not intended to be reformed, as in a convict prison, but rather as a 'short, sharp shock' meant to deter future criminal activities.[3]

The focus of the prison system as a whole was now a battle of differing ideologies on how prisons should be run and how prisoners should be treated. However, we also began to see more and more standardisation over how prisons were run. The year 1835 did not just mark the end of construction at York Castle; it also saw the appointment of five HM inspectors of prisons to ensure that prisons were being run to the standards expected of them, with a surveyor general appointed in 1844.[4] Unlike the Gaol Act 1823, this one 'had teeth' and began to bring the prison system into line throughout the country. This Act can be seen as the end of the era of prison reformers, as their role of visiting prisons and reporting what they found had become an official part of the prison system.

Prisoner classification was now compulsory. There were nine classes of prisoners.

Class 1

1st – convicted prisoners not sentenced to hard labour, whose period of confinement does not exceed seven days.

Class 2

1st – convicted prisoners for any term exceeding seven days and not exceeding twenty-one days.

Class 3

1st – convicted prisoners employed at hard labour, for terms not exceeding twenty-one days but not more than six weeks and convicted prisoners not employed at hard labour for terms exceeding twenty-one days but not more than four months.

2nd – convicted prisoners sentenced to hard labour but disqualified for it by natural infirmity.

3rd – convicted prisoners sentenced to hard labour, whose period of confinement exceeds fourteen days, and does not exceed six weeks.

4th – convicted prisoners in close confinement for periods exceeding twenty-one days.

5th – convicted prisoners committed for trial or for further examination.

Class 4

Convicted prisoners sentenced to hard labour, for terms exceeding six weeks, but not more than four months.

Class 5

Convicted prisoners employed at hard labour for terms exceeding four calendar month.

Class 6

Prisoners sentenced by court to solitary confinement.

Class 7

Prisoners for examination before trial and misdemeanants of the first division who do not maintain themselves.

Class 8

Destitute debtors.

Class 9

Prisoners under punishment for prison offences for terms not exceeding three days and prisoners in close confinement for prison offences under the provision of the 42nd Section of the Gaol Act.[5]

Interestingly, no plans show any location for Class 9 prisoners at York Castle Prison, but it is likely that these were few and far between and could have been accommodated elsewhere.

The Silent System Versus the Separate System

When discussing Victorian prisons, a conversation typically focuses on the various systems employed during the period. From the late 1820s, two schools of thought dominated the British prison system. Firstly, there was the silent system, where prisoners were locked up on their own at night, and while allowed to mix during the day for work duties, this had to be done in silence. The idea was that the criminal classes were habitual criminals, and the silent system would scare the prisoners into not re-offending. The harsh punishments for talking included solitary confinement, three days of bread and water and even time added to their sentence in week increments.[6]

The second school of thought was the separate system. This American system gained significant support in Britain, particularly from Quaker reformers.[7] Here, prisoners were confined to their cells for most of the day, and when mixing was necessary, great lengths would be taken to strip prisoners of their individuality. For exercise, they wore masks that obscured their faces (a veil for women). This might extend even further in the chapel seating, a series of box stalls where prisoners would sit, separating them from other prisoners. Both systems had their advocates and opponents, and both could impact a prisoner's mental well-being, especially the silent system. The separate system was the more popular of the two, and between 1842 and 1877, nineteen radial prisons were constructed in Britain specifically to exemplify this system.

The debate between silent and separate systems continued for quite some time. The Prison Act 1835 strongly advocated for the separate system, and by 1856, approximately two-thirds of prisons in Britain had adopted this approach.[8] Many prisons would operate a hybrid of the two systems to suit their needs.[9] For York Castle Prison, however, the inadequate buildings stopped either system from ever being adopted. Instead, it appears that York continued to use the associated or congregate system, but with more modern prisoner classifications.

Work in Prison

Sitting idle in prison, waiting patiently for the end of your sentence, was certainly not the Victorian ideal for prisons. Prisoners were to be kept busy, working to pass the time. This could be hard labour or regular labour. Everything else in prison, including a prisoner's education, came second to their work. Often, a prisoner would prefer a longer sentence over hard labour in a county goal,[10] not least because they could earn time off their sentence for good behaviour at a convict prison. At a local or county prison, they would serve every day of their sentence.

There were three main schools of thought on what labour in a Victorian prison should be about: punitive, economic and reformative.[11] The punitive vision was work for the sake of work, solely for the prisoner's punishment. Economic punishment aimed to generate revenue from the prisoners' efforts to offset some of the costs of keeping them in the first place. Finally, reformative labour focused on teaching skills the prisoner might use after leaving prison.

While imprisonment was the primary form of punishment by the mid-nineteenth century, many of these sentences included hard labour, where it was expected that a prisoner would work for 'not more than ten or less than six hours (exclusive of meals), subject to the medical officer's approval'.[12] This was for the first three months of their sentence; after three months, they could be transferred to second-class labour. By 1877, hard labour had been reduced to a one-month maximum.[13]

The Prison Act 1865 states that

> the treadwheel, crank, capstan, shot-drill and stone breaking were listed as acceptable types of first-class hard labour, and such others as the justices wished to provide had to be approved by the secretary of state.[14]

For York Castle Prison, the punishment of choice would become the treadwheel. The treadwheel was a large cylinder with wooden 'treads' going around its circumference. As you and your fellow prisoners climbed up, your combined weight would move the wheel down. This forced the prisoners to constantly 'climb' the wheel. Created by William Cubitt in 1818, by 1824, some forty-one prisons had treadwheels.[15] However, they were not without controversy and were ultimately abolished in 1898, primarily because they were deemed unproductive.[16]

However, using the treadwheel was one of the areas where York Castle Prison could be considered a relatively good place to be imprisoned. At many prisons, prisoners were expected to climb 12,000 feet per day (just 8,640 from the 1860s);[17] at York, this was only 6,000 feet.[18] By 1880, work on the wheel had been standardised, requiring a 32 feet per minute ascent rate for a six-hour shift operated in a fifteen-minute work, five-minute rest pattern.[19]

However, the treadwheel should not be viewed as a simple task, and it is noted at the time that 'novice prisoners on the treadwheel or those incapacitated through drink found the wheel 'very trying, if not dangerous'.[20] As you are climbing, the treads are constantly moving down in sync with those of the other prisoners; if you cannot keep up, you could easily find yourself with a foot caught at the bottom and some serious injuries as a result.

At York Castle Prison, there are several references in the *Gaoler's Journals* to the treadwheel being used to saw marble. Presumably, this would then be sold on to fund the prison. This activity saw the worst accident involving the treadwheel at York Castle Prison. On 16 March 1853, Emmanuel Clough, sentenced to twelve months imprisonment for 'cutting and stabbing with intent to do grievous bodily harm', was attending the treadmill. He attempted to do something to the machinery while it was moving, when the flywheel struck him on the head. This left him with a fractured skull.[21] The injury was serious enough for the surgeon to contact Emmanuel's wife, asking her to come to the prison as Emmanuel was likely to die from his injuries. Luckily, by the time she arrived at the prison, Emmanuel was doing well.[22]

One exception to working on the treadwheel was the female prisoners. Instead, they essentially did the housework of the prison. One famous Victorian female prisoner, Mrs Florence Maybrick, held at Aylesbury, described her day as follows:

> To wash tencans, each holding four quarts; to scrub on table, twenty feet in length; two dressers, twelve feet in length; to wash a sack of potatoes; to assist in serving the dinners, and to scrub a piece of floor twenty by ten feet ... The work was hard and rough.[23]

There were other forms of hard labour throughout Britain, and while there is no evidence that they were used at York Castle Prison, it is interesting to examine the alternatives.

Oakum picking: how do you make money from old rope? To understand the phrase, you must look back at the Victorian prisons' most common form of labour. While in their cell, or a specially designed oakum shed or room, a prisoner would be given a set weight (varying from prison to prison) of old rope from ships. This could be covered in tar and have absorbed a significant amount of salt from the water during its use. The prisoner would be expected to undo this stiff rope, breaking it down, first into its smaller cords and then breaking them down into individual strands, forming a material called oakum. This could then be sold back to the navy or other shipbuilders as caulking to waterproof the ships by pushing it between the ship's planks, forming a watertight seal. This is how you can make money from old rope.

The task itself was hard. Picking the small parts of the rope apart with their fingers could leave a prisoner with very sore fingertips, and any small cut became very painful from the salt left in the rope. The old hands had a few tricks up their sleeves to make it easier. Beating the rope can make it easier to pick apart. However, the best solution was to acquire an old nail to pick the rope apart. Some prisoners recorded the placement of nails in specific locations within prisons, so that anyone who knew what they were looking for could locate them.[24] While not explicitly used at York Castle Prison, oakum picking would be used at York Castle Prison during its later life as a military prison.

Shot drill: here, a prisoner was expected to move a shot from one area of a prison yard to another. This repetitive motion with a heavy weight could be bad for a prisoner's health.

Crank: in some prisons, the alternative to the treadwheel was the crank. A box in the corner of the room, which had a handle that a prisoner had to turn or crank a set number of times per day.

Of course, refusing to work the wheel, do your laundry or pick the correct weight of oakum meant punishment, usually a dietary punishment, where your portions would be cut. As you can imagine, a task like the treadwheel leads to a vicious circle of refusing to work, undernourishment, and an inability to work, ultimately resulting in further dietary punishment.

There were some opportunities to escape the hard labour. If you had a skill the prison could use, the gaolers would likely take advantage of your presence. Two great examples of this are recorded in the York Castle Prison *Gaoler's Journal*:

> George Blakebouough a prisoner being a watchmaker, has repaired the Castle Clock, which was very much out of order and had gone very irregular for some time. It has now been finished a few weeks and seems to go very well, he says what he has done would have cost ten pounds had we employed any clock maker.[25]

> The pavement in the Entrance lodge is very much out of repair, having now some masons in custody I have set them to take up the floor and relay it.[26]

As well as hard labour as punishment, we also have the last remnants of the more medieval punishment of whipping in prison. With the public fear of garroters in the 1860s, that is, men who would attack people, choking them by the neck while either they or an accomplice went through the victim's pockets, taking anything of value, the Personal Violence Act 1863 brought back harsher punishment for those convicted of garrotting, including whipping, this was on top of the usual time in prison with hard labour. On 17 January 1867, two men convicted under this Act at York Prison faced their punishment:

> The prisoner was fastened to the triangle by straps at ankles, knees and hands and a leather band was placed around the neck to prevent the lash from hitting the victim in that part of the body. The 'operators' upon the occasion were two warders of the gaol, who administered in each instance a dozen strokes in succession.

Drawing of York Castle showing the south gate. It was behind these imposing walls that prisoners would have been held. (Image courtesy of York Museums Trust: https://yorkmuseumstrust.org.uk/)

Photograph of the ruins of the south gate today. (Author)

Drawing showing the Keep of Clifford's Tower and the drawbridge from the bailey area. (Image courtesy of York Museums Trust: https://yorkmuseumstrust.org.uk/)

Images of 'Irons' and 'Irons without Joints' on display at York Castle Museum. (Author)

Drawing of the ducking stool used in the ‘ditch’ of York Castle. The image suggests that this depicts an event in 1407. (Image courtesy of York Museums Trust: https://yorkmuseumstrust.org.uk/)

Drawing of ‘execution day at York’ by Thomas Rowlandson. Note the clear depiction of Micklegate bar and the crowds gathered to watch the procession. (Image courtesy of York Museums Trust: https://yorkmuseumstrust.org.uk/)

Image captioned 'the Knavesmire Gallows removed to the Castle 1802'. This image clearly shows the shape of the 'Three-legged Mare'. (Image courtesy of York Museums Trust: https://yorkmuseumstrust.org.uk/)

'A Perspective View of the Castle of York' showing the site about twenty years after the construction of the Debtor's Prison building. Note the court on the left, the jury house to the right and the stagecoach in the Castle Yard. (Image courtesy of York Museums Trust: https://yorkmuseumstrust.org.uk/)

‘A Perspective View of York Castle with part of the Court of Justice and Grand Jury House’. A detailed view of the Debtors’ Prison building as it was originally built. Note the Military presence and the public/ Debtors promenading in the Castle Yard. (Image courtesy of York Museums Trust: https://yorkmuseumstrust.org.uk/)

A photo of the Debtors’ Prison building today, showing the clear transition from the stone façade on the front of the building into the brick construction of the rest of the structure. (Author)

Drawing of the inside of the courthouse in 1813. This shows the lavish interior of the court, and indicates the control of the justice system by those of a higher class. (Image courtesy of York Museums Trust: https://yorkmuseumstrust.org.uk/)

The Courthouse as seen today. (Author)

The Female Prison Building as seen today. Note that the two ends of the building, with the round windows, were not added until 1802/3. (Author)

Graffiti from inside Half Moon Court by those awaiting transportation. (Author)

The Condemned cell (1778 to 1835), as it appears today, clearly shows the vaulted ceiling and the original window. Note that the iron bed is a later addition, dating to around 1820. The oven is also a later addition. Inset: a small opening in the room for airflow. (Author)

'An Execution at the New Drop' shows the gallows used just outside of the castle after 1802. (Image courtesy of York Museums Trust: https://yorkmuseumstrust.org.uk/)

Drawing of the old south entrance to the Castle, long after the gatehouse itself was demolished. This picture also shows the sallyport demolished in 1806. (Image courtesy of York Museums Trust: https://yorkmuseumstrust.org.uk/)

Drawing of the inside of York Castle after the construction of the new Felons Prison in 1835. You can clearly see the new Governor's House to the right, with 'A' Block running to the north of this. Trees now surround Clifford's Tower and it is difficult to access. The public still gathers at the Eye of the Ridings, awaiting the trials underway. (Image courtesy of York Museums Trust :: https://yorkmuseumstrust.org.uk/ :: Public Domain)

Another image of inside the prison was created not long after 1835. You can clearly make out the courthouse, the debtor's prison, and the female prison buildings, which are still visible today. However, you can also see part of the governor's house to the left of the image and what looks like two barristers viewing the public in the eye of York. You can also see that the steps on the front of the debtor's prison, present in earlier images, have now been removed. (Image courtesy of York Museums Trust: https://yorkmuseumstrust.org.uk/)

The outside view of York Castle in the 1800s, showing the immense scale of the gatehouse. (Image courtesy of Yorkshire Architectural and York Archaeological Society)

The Gatehouse from inside the prison. Here you can clearly see how it is designed to reflect the castle aesthetic. (Image courtesy of Yorkshire Architectural and York Archaeological Society)

A Photo of Tower Street looking north. Note the imposing nature of the western wall and how it restricts the width of the road. The back of the courthouse is visible to the far right of the image. (Image courtesy of Yorkshire Architectural and York Archaeological Society)

A drawing showing York Castle from St George's field. Once again, you can see the imposing wall of York Castle after 1835. The back of the courthouse, as it once appeared, is also visible. Not that this image also shows half-moon court extending to the very top of the debtor's prison building. (Image courtesy of York Museums Trust: https://yorkmuseumstrust.org.uk/)

The 'Last Drop', the last site used for executions within the City of York. Here you can clearly see the beam, the trapdoor and the drop itself. (Reproduced from an original held by City of York Council/Explore York Libraries and Archives Mutual Ltd., archive reference: HMU P 8 202)

A photograph of the reconstructed 'A' Block. To the left, you can see the smaller 'B' Block, illustrating how all four cell blocks looked until 1880. (Image courtesy of Yorkshire Architectural and York Archaeological Society)

Inside the reconstructed 'A' Block. This building now looks a lot closer to what many people might imagine a Victorian prison to look like. (Image courtesy of Yorkshire Architectural and York Archaeological Society)

Photo showing men on the treadwheel at York Castle. (Image courtesy of Yorkshire Architectural and York Archaeological Society)

Images from the Receiving book at York Castle Prison, unfortunately, only a couple of pages survive. These images also give a good idea of the uniforms worn by the men and women held at York Castle. (Image courtesy of York Museums Trust: https://yorkmuseumstrust.org.uk/, CC BY-SA 4.0)

Image of the demolition of the Felons Prison taken from the top of Clifford's Tower. Note the structures between 'C' Block and 'D' Block, where the military constructed workshops and a gymnasium. (Reproduced from an original held by City of York Council/Explore York Libraries and Archives Mutual Ltd., archive reference: HMU P 8 207)

The Felons Apartments on the ground floor of the Debtors' Prison Building, the best preserved part of York Castle Prison, as seen today in York Castle Museum. (Author)

The site of the 'New Drop' as seen today. Note the black door in the centre, where the condemned would be brought out to their fate. (Author)

The doors of the 'Last Drop', as they can be seen today. Note the damage to the wall to the right side of them where the 1835 building joined. (Author)

> The first descent of the whip made him cry 'Oh', in a piteous tone, and at the second he cried out 'Oh dear', after the fourth he begged for and was given a glass of water; and at the ninth he resisted so strongly, though without the least avail, that the framework to which he was bound was moved slightly from its original starting point. As the blows followed each other in quick succession his cries of suffering were louder and more frequent. It was in vain that he asked for mercy or, in a dreadful paroxysm of pain, promised that he would 'never do so again'.[27]

Food in Prison

'No other event in the prison day ... was so keenly anticipated ... as the arrival of food at the door of the cell.'[28]

Prison was supposed to be a deterrent. Some saw prison as a better alternative than other possibilities. The food in Victorian prisons was better than one could expect from other institutions, such as workhouses.[29] This incentivised criminals to end up in prison rather than the workhouse. A prison like York Castle Prison had to provide three meals a day, and that 'at least two of these be hot'.[30] That said, the idea was to feed the prisoners as cheaply as possible, so the food quality could often be questionable. Sometimes, it can include unpleasant things, such as beetles in soup, bread, or even tea.[31] Often, this can lead to dietary diseases such as diarrhoea or scurvy.[32] On average, some sources show that around 90 per cent of those sent to prison at this time would lose weight due to a poor diet.[33] Those undergoing extreme hunger might even eat weeds or any other source of nutrients, like the tallow candles provided in the prison. These candles, made from animal fat, provided a source of extra calories, albeit a smelly one. An offensive scent was added to these candles to deter consumption.[34]

However, the best way to ensure a better diet in prison was to find a way to access the hospital or infirmary. Nothing too serious, of course, but if it can get you a couple of days on a better diet, it is worth some minor injury or faking an illness. For example, a prisoner might swallow 'soap or soda' to bring on diarrhoea. Other strategies might involve faking easy symptoms such as 'paralysis, epilepsy, and insanity, spitting of blood, and vomiting of food'.[35]

However, by 1843, minimum food standards had been established. By 1864, a prisoner's diet had its own class system, which evolved as the prisoner spent longer at the prison. The following tables show the diet at York Castle Prison in August 1864. The information is taken from an original copy of the dietary requirements held by York Museums Trust.

These rules varied slightly, particularly for those awaiting trial, who would be in Class 3 for the first month, Class 4 for the second month, and Class 5 thereafter. Destitute debtors would also benefit from this dietary amendment. In addition, the gruel for classes 4 and 5, while still being 1 pint, now contains one ounce of molasses. Of course, the surgeon could modify this diet if necessary for the prisoner's health, thereby granting the surgeon considerable power.

Debtors, both male and female, who could not maintain themselves had their own diet consisting of the following each week:

- 7 pounds of wheaten bread
- 2½ pounds of oatmeal
- ½ pound of cheese
- 10 pounds of potatoes
- 4½ ounces of salt
- 4 red herrings
- 4 pounds of beef, without bone

York Castle Dietaries – August 2nd, 1864.

WITHOUT HARD LABOUR.

Meals	Days of the Week	Articles of Food	1st Class		2nd class		3rd Class		4th Class		5th Class	
			One Week or Less		After 1st Week and up to 1st Month inclusive		After 1st Month and up to 3rd month inclusive		After 3 months and up to six months inclusive		After six months	
			Men	Women	Men	Women	Men	Women	Men	Women	Men	Women
			Ounces	Ounces	Ounces	Ounces	Ounces	Ounces	Ounces	Ounces	Ounces	Ounces
Breakfast	Every Day	Bread	6	5	6	5	8	6	8	6	8	6
		Gruel	-	-	1 pint	1 pint	1 pint	1 pint	1 pint	1 pint	1 pint	1 pint
Supper	Every Day	Bread	6	5	6	5	6	6	8	6	8	6
		Gruel	-	-	-	-	1 pint	1 pint	1 pint	1 pint	1 pint	1 pint
Dinner	Sunday	Bread	8	6	8	6	10	8	10	8	12	10
		Cheese	-	-	1	1	2	2	3	2	3	2
	Monday, Wednesday, and Friday	Bread	6	5	6	5	4	4	4	4	4	4
		Potatoes	-	-	-	-	12	8	16	12	16	12
		Suet Pudding	-	-	-	-	8	6	12	8	12	8
		Indian Meal Pudding	6	4	8	6	-	-	-	-	-	-
	Tuesday, Thursday, & Saturday	Bread	6	5	6	5	8	6	8	6	8	8
		Potatoes	8	6	12	8	8	6	8	6	16	12
		Soup	-	-	-	-	1 pint	1 pint	1 pint	1 pint	1 pint	1 pint

WITH HARD LABOUR.

Meals	Days of the Week	Articles of Food	1st Class One Week or Less		2nd class After 1st Week and up to 1st Month inclusive		3rd Class After 1st Month and up to 3rd month inclusive		4th Class After 3 months and up to six months inclusive		5th Class After six months	
			Men	Women	Men	Women	Men	Women	Men	Women	Men	Women
			Ounces	Ounces	Ounces	Ounces	Ounces	Ounces	Ounces	Ounces	Ounces	Ounces
Breakfast	Every Day	Bread	6	5	6	5	8	6	8	6	8	6
		Gruel	-	-	1 pint	1 pint	1 pint	1 pint	1 pint	1 pint	1 pint	1 pint
Supper	Every Day	Bread	6	5	6	5	6	6	8	6	8	6
		Gruel	-	-	-	-	1 pint	1 pint	1 pint	1 pint	1 pint	1 pint
Dinner	Sunday	Bread	8	6	8	6	10	8	10	8	12	10
		Cheese	-	-	2	2	3	3	4	3	4	3
	Monday and Friday	Bread	6	5	6	5	4	4	4	4	4	4
		Potatoes	-	-	-	-	12	8	16	12	16	12
		Indian Meal Pudding	6	4	8	6	-	-	-	-	-	-
		Beef	-	-	-	-	3	2	4	3	4	3
	Wednesday	Bread	6	5	6	5	4	4	4	4	4	4
		Potatoes	-	-	-	-	12	8	16	12	16	12
		Suet Pudding	-	-	-	-	8	6	12	8	12	8
		Indian Meal	6	4	8	6	-	-	-	-	-	-
	Tuesday, Thursday, & Saturday	Bread	6	5	6	5	8	6	8	6	8	8
		Potatoes	8	6	12	8	8	6	8	6	16	12
		Soup	-	-	-	-	1 pint	1 pint	1 pint	1 pint	1 pint	1 pint

Of course, not everyone was happy with the diet. The *Gaoler's Journal* records that on 20 April 1853 at York Castle Prison:

> All the convicted prisoners refused the broth for dinner. The surgeon was here and said it was very good on seasoning. With some of the confines they agreed to take it as usual… they said they wanted something better. I told them it was the usual dish and if they would not take it they would get no other.[36]

Another example of poor food quality comes from Frederick Parker 1868, who petitioned for a better diet. However, after he was sentenced to death, it was decided that a better diet was not 'considered necessary for his health'.[37]

This system was changed in 1877, with the number of classes reduced to 4 and the final one reached after just four months.

Changes in the Law

These changes in prison design, life, sentencing, and conditions in the nineteenth century were not uniform and occurred over several decades. Significant laws passed and amended demonstrate progress towards a more standardised prison system. Three important changes in how prisons were run, especially county gaols like York Castle Prison, warrant closer examination.

The End of Transportation

Transportation underwent significant changes during the early nineteenth century. One of the most important was the opening of Millbank Prison in 1816, 'which acted as a holding point for those under the sentence of transportation'.[38] This results in a decline in the number of women and men being transported abroad. In 1837, a House of Commons select committee stipulated that anyone sentenced to seven years of transportation would serve their sentence in Britain (or occasionally Bermuda or Gibraltar) or be given the option, if physically fit, to join the armed forces.[39] These changes would be supplemented by the Penal Servitude Act 1853, marking the beginning of sentences designed to replace transportation. Instead, a new form of punishment, penal servitude, was introduced in Britain, where prisoners could perform tasks associated with colonial labour on British soil.[40] The Penal Servitude Act 1853 also introduced the ticket of leave to reward those transportees for good behaviour, allowing these convicts to reduce their sentence.

Public works prisons began replacing transportation in the 1850s with the construction of specialist new public works/convict prisons at Chatham (1856), Borstal (1874), Chattenden (1877) and Dover (1884).[41] New purpose-built prisons, such as Portland (1848) and Portsmouth (1852), replaced the last Hulks for prisoners awaiting transportation. The former prisoner-of-war camp at Dartmoor was reopened in 1850 to house convicts.[42] With the official end of transportation in 1868, penal servitude was the only long-term punishment available. From this point onwards, those convicted at York were transported to a convict prison for their sentence.

However, the push to stop transportation was not completely down to opinions within Britain. Many people at the transportation destinations in Australia did not always favour receiving convicts from Britain. As far back as the 1830s, efforts began to be made to abolish the sentence of transportation. As these Australian settlements grew, with many emigrants making up the population, it became increasingly difficult for the British government to compel them to accept the convicts Britain no longer wanted. These towns and cities were no longer backwaters where convicts could be forgotten, but thriving communities. These communities had their own criminal problems to deal with, without the burden of those from another country. The last prisoners were sent to New South Wales in 1841 and Van Diemen's Land in 1852. In January 1868, the last convict ship arrived in Western Australia.

Between 1788 and 1840, approximately 80,000 British and Irish convicts were transported from Britain to New South Wales. Between 1803 and 1853, a similar number were transported to Van Diemen's Land (now Tasmania), and from 1850 to 1868, 9,800 went to Western Australia.[43] Of the 169,800 estimated convicts sent to Australia, many would come from York Castle Prison.

The End of Public Execution

The execution had become a more uncommon sight throughout the country. After 1828, only six crimes could now carry a capital sentence. The 1841 Substitution of Punishments of Death Act removed rape from this list, and the Offence Against the Persons Act 1861 removed homosexuality. While this left murder, attempted murder, treason and piracy as capital crimes, in reality, execution for murderers was the only one that would be carried out with any regularity. However, it was not just the crimes that were changing. During this period, one of the most notable changes, especially to those outside the prison system, was the discussion around the abolition of public executions. The change was probably inevitable, given the passion for social reform in the mid- to late Victorian period and the shifting moral compass of what was considered acceptable and unacceptable during this time. Many social commentators at the time described the horrid spectacle of public execution. Charles Dickens wrote in *The Times* in 1849 about witnessing such a spectacle:

> I believe that a sight so inconceivably awful as the wickedness and levity of the immense crowd collected at that execution this morning could be imagined by no man …[44]

A local newspaper supported removing public executions, printing that 'Be determined and we shall soon hear no more of public slaughterings and legalised murder'.[45] However, it was not just the morals of public execution as a vile spectacle that was coming to a head, but feelings against the type of people attracted to the crowds. Once again, Dickens describes it:

> When the day dawned, thieves, low prostitutes, ruffians, and vagabonds of every kind, flocked to the ground, with every variety of offensive and foul behaviour. Fightings, faintings, whistlings, imitations of punch, brutal jokes, tumultuous demonstrations of indecent delight when swooning women were dragged out of the crowd by the police, with their dresses disordered ...[46]

Crime and social disorder, the problems that public execution had been designed to prevent, were now exemplified by the crowds that gathered to watch. As the population of Britain grew, so did the crowds that came to witness someone being hanged. A public execution was now an uncontrollable crowd with unseen danger all around. None of this even mentions the indignity of someone's final moments being so public. Their sentence is already the most severe that the law can offer. Must they also have the extra humiliation of spending their last moments being gawked at by the masses? Dickens wrote,

> When the two miserable creatures who attracted all this ghastly sight about them were turned quivering into the air, there was no more emotion, no more pity, no more thought that two immortal souls had gone to judgment ...[47]

It was hard to justify the public execution as a deterrent when those on the gallows were often not even seen as human by the crowd. The only way to control the situation was to remove the crowd. The 1868 Act mandated that future executions occur privately within the prison's confines. Michael Barrett became the last person to be publicly executed in Britain for a bombing of Clerkenwell Prison to aid the escape of Colonel Ricard Burke. On 26 May 1868, Barrett was executed outside Newgate Prison, three days before royal assent was given to the new regulations. For York Castle Prison, on 29 February 1868, Frederick Parker became the last person publicly hanged at the new drop outside the prison walls. It was not until 18 August 1874, that York Castle would again witness an execution, but this time it would take place within its walls.

York's last public execution, that of Frederick Parker, allows us to gain some idea of the last half an hour of a condemned prisoner's life. Preparations had already begun around 6.00 am. Frederick dressed in his own clothes and prayed for about fifteen minutes. He received 'the lord's supper' at 8.00 am – his last meal. At 10.00 am, he joined in with the morning service alongside the other prisoners; a requested hymn was sung during this service. At 11.30 am, half an hour before the allotted time of the execution, Parker was taken from the condemned cell across the courtyard to the pinioning room in the courthouse. He was reported to have walked firmly, but also 'cried repeatedly for Jesus to have mercy on his soul'. While in the pinioning room, Parker handed the governor, W.F. Lowrie, a letter that he had written and wanted to be published. This contained cases of him forgiving people he had met or transgressions against him, but interestingly, it also included a warning against drinking, 'which he said brought him to his present position.' He signed the letter 'unfortunate friend, F. Parker'. At 11.55 am, the under-sheriff, Mr Gray, came to the pinioning room and demanded the body of Parker. A procession to the scaffold was then formed consisting 'of four halbardmen, W. Gray, Esq., the Governor (W.F. Lowrie, Esq.), the Chaplain, (Reverend J.C. Thompson), the culprit, the Under Governor, (Mr Webster), three warders, and several of the Sheriff's attendants'. At 12.00 pm, 'the procession appeared on the scaffold when the murmur of the vast crowd immediately became hushed'. Parker turned his back on the crowd and shook hands with the governor, the under-governor and the warders. He then dropped to his knees in prayer with the chaplain, ending with the Lord's Prayer. Next, the executioner (Thomas Askern) placed the white cap over Parker's head, adjusted the noose and finally tied Parker's legs together. The bolt was then withdrawn, and 'the body fell with a loud thud which could be heard in the crowd and was lost to the sight of the spectators'.[48]

The End of Debtors' Prisons

Debtors still made up the majority of prisoners held at York Castle Prison in 1835. The way debt worked and the results of coming to a place like York Castle Prison were similar to how they had always been. Acts of benevolence could still help prisoners. One example is in 1840 when 'The Gentlemen of the Grand Jury' left in the hands of the keeper of York Castle the sum of £25 12s 6d, to be applied by him in obtaining the 'discharge of poor debtors'.[49] However, one significant change made imprisonment for debt far more of a problem and more of a stigma than it had previously been. The new Poor

Law 1834 had made the threat of the workhouse far more acute for many people. Previously, someone imprisoned for debt might rely on their family to help pay off the debt. Now, someone's financial stress, especially that of the primary worker and, therefore, the main source of income, could force unfortunate families into the workhouse.

There were also significant changes to how debtors' prisons worked. While the basic principle remained to remove freedom from people until they paid off their debt, the prison structure changed in 1843. Gone were the masters and common sides that separated those who could pay from those who would likely never get out. Now, the debtors' prison is separated into three classes. The first class and second class were made up of the existing master's side. They occupied the top two floors of the debtors' prison building and exercised on the Eye of York. The main distinction between the two was how well the debtor could 'maintain themselves', i.e. pay for their accommodation, food and other essentials while paying back their debt. The third class consisted of those who relied mainly on county subsidies to survive. They are defined in the rules of York Castle in 1843 as:

> Debtors remanded by the Commissioners of the Court for the Relief of Insolvent Debtors on the ground of fraud … debtors who neglect or refuse to file a schedule of their property … and bankrupts remanded by the court for not answering.[50]

First-class debtors were held in 20 rooms, capable of holding 100 debtors; they exercised on the Eye of the Ridings. Second-class debtors were held in eight rooms holding up to forty prisoners and exercised in Half-Moon Court. Third class were held 'in the 8 lower rooms of the building, also capable of holding 40 prisoners'.[51] This refers to the old felons' apartments on the ground floor of the debtors' prison building which had been modified to make them suitable for third-class debtors. Their exercise yard, located at the back of the debtors' prison building, was sometimes referred to as 'dog yard'.[52] Their life at York Castle Prison was now closer to imprisonment than the lives of previous debtors had been, and this caused some problems when the system first changed in 1843. George and William Bromitt were determined not to be moved out of their accommodation into the third-class area. The gaoler makes a note in the *Gaoler's Journal* stating that

> I have desired them to remove several times informing them that if they would not obey the rules, they must be punished, they still refuse, in consequence I have ordered them into solitary confinement for 2 days on bread and water.[53]

After their time in solitary, they were finally removed to the third-class debtors' area.

Third-class debtors would not have to fend for themselves like common-side debtors previously did. Now, there was an option to go through an insolvent court if you did not have enough to pay back your debt. It is important to note that this is not the same as bankruptcy, which would only come into force later in the century. If the debtor went through an insolvent court, they would serve a prison sentence in the third class rather than having to repay their debt. Of course, this system was open to interpretation, and in 1853, Matthew Blake, who was sentenced to four months imprisonment at an insolvent's court, was allowed to stay in first class because his attorney was hoping 'to make an arrangement for his discharge'.[54]

On some rare occasions, this hard barrier between the third-class debtors and the first two classes could be broken down, especially when it came to Britain's military success. In 1855, the gaoler notes that

> The Debtors being desirous to commemorate the victory of the Allies at Sebastopol, have requested me to allow the Debtors of the 3rd Class to dine with them … I have complied with their request.[55]

A proclamation of peace could benefit both the debtors and the criminals. In 1856:

> This day peace was proclaimed in the City of York. The High Sheriff gave the Debtors a treat of Roast Beef, plum pudding and a Quart of beer each. I gave permission for the 3rd class to associate with the first Class in the front yard a few hours in the afternoon – gave the Criminal prisoners Holyday in the afternoon.[56]

For a site like York Castle, where the main complement of those imprisoned were debtors, the decline and end of imprisonment for debt must have had a major impact. By the mid-nineteenth century, attitudes and laws regarding debt began to shift. Acts like the Bankruptcy Act 1861 removed the distinction between traders who could apply for bankruptcy to protect their enterprises and non-traders. This allowed most people to declare bankruptcy rather than face a debtors' prison. Bankruptcy had its own problems and lasting effects, so only some chose this path. Some were spared from going bankrupt, and in some cases, politics played a role in bringing them to places like York Castle Prison. A good example of this is the 'Railway King' George Hudson, whose name can still be seen in the street names of York. In the early eighteenth century, he had made a fortune as one of the men who defined Britain's railways during that period, but not every investment had worked out. He had also been an MP for Sunderland from 1845 to 1859. This position in Parliament protected him from being placed in a debtors' prison. With this protection removed, Hudson still had enough power to avoid facing his creditors. However, his political rivals saw an opportunity when Hudson tried to become MP for Whitby in 1865. On Sunday, 9 July 1865, just forty-eight hours before his seemingly inevitable re-election to Parliament, an officer for the sheriff came knocking on the door of George Hudson's lodgings in Whitby. Hudson was arrested for debt. He was put on the first train to York and brought to the debtors' prison at York Castle Prison. He would spend three months here until a colliery owner, George Elliot, paid for the release of 65-year-old Hudson. The idea of someone so old being incarcerated in a place like York Castle Prison was contrary to modern Victorian sensibilities.[57] Hudson would flee to France to avoid further arrest.[58] He returned in 1866 but was immediately arrested for debt again in London. He employed a clever legal tactic, enabling him to leave prison briefly to consult his solicitor. He fled abroad once again. On 1 January 1870, the Abolition of Imprisonment for Debt Act came into force. This meant that George Hudson could no longer be imprisoned for debt and could return to England safely.

Just as throughout the history of imprisonment for debt, the act of imprisonment did not carry the same stigma as those imprisoned for criminal offences. George Hudson welcomed himself back into society, becoming chairman of the Carlton Club smoking room, a position he had held before.[59] In April 1870, he took a 'tour of the North', visiting his friends and supporters who had helped him through his self-imposed exile.[60] In 1871, his tour brought him back to York, where he dined with the lord mayor at the Mansion

House.[61] However, on 14 December 1871, George Hudson succumbed to a heart attack at his home in London; he was 71.

The Abolition of Imprisonment for Debt Act prevented new debtors from being taken to York Castle Prison. However, there were still provisions in place to send someone to a debtors' prison if they had the means to pay a debt but refused to do so. It is also important to remember that the 1869 Act did not mean that debtors were released on 1 January 1870; many still had to serve their sentences, but no new debtors were coming to York Castle Prison.

Running the Prison

Governors and Matrons

> He shall exercise his authority with firmness, temper, and humility; abstain from all irritating language, and not strike a prisoner. He shall enforce similar conduct on the subordinate officers.[62]

As we have seen, the way prisons were run changed significantly from the 1820s to the 1830s. The system that emerged was a Victorian style of crime and punishment that differed significantly from the one that existed in the eighteenth century. Gaolers could be appointed as governors, although the term 'keeper of York Castle' appears to have been used most of the time at York Castle, and the term gaoler was still in use at York Castle until the 1870s. The idea behind this change was that the governors should move away from the

> men raised from the office of turnkey, often as ignorant and immoral as their very prisoners into something like 'Men of standing in society – men of education and ability – chiefly chosen from amongst naval and military officers.[63]

York had its share of men who fitted both these categories of gaoler well. Men such as Thomas Ward and Thomas Griffiths, who ran the prison in the 1700s, were now a memory of the past. Now, military men were a large part of York Castle life, with the appointments of Captain W.F. Lowrie in 1863 and his successor, Captain A.W. Twyford, in 1878.

The governor's duties involved visiting 'every ward, cell yard and division of the prison, and to see every prisoner once at least every twenty-four hours'.[64]

This made the position a seven-day-per-week role, and the governor was not allowed to be absent overnight at any point without written permission from the visiting justice. The governor would live on site, and this is evident in the layout of the Victorian prison, where the governor's house was the central feature of the newly built prison for felons. The governor was responsible for everything in the prison, from the prisoners to the buildings themselves, ensuring that escape was impossible, that fire was unlikely and that the bars, bolts, locks, doors and other pieces of prison equipment were in proper condition. Discipline was also part of the governor's remit and behaviour such as 'common assaults by one prisoner upon another; profane cursing and swearing; indecent behaviour, or any irreverent behaviour in chapel' would see the governor 'punish all such offences by ordering any offender to close confinement' and bread and water for up to three days.[65] If the prison governor was absent, their duties were assumed by the deputy governor.

Along with the role of the governor is the matron, who ran the female part of the prison. Her duties were essentially the same as the governor's to 'have the care and superintendence of the whole female department'.[66] Like a governor, she would inspect the prisoners daily and accompany the governor on weekly visits to the female prisoners. She was expected to live on site and, like the governor, could not be absent from the prison without the permission of the visiting justices. Not getting permission to leave could have serious consequences. In the *Gaoler's Journal* for York Castle Prison, there are the following entries:

> May 28th 1838
> I have this day suspended the Assistant Matron for absenting herself from the Castle without leave and Reported the event to B Hague Esqr one of the Visiting Magistrates.
>
> June 7th [1838]
> I have discharged Elizabeth Hutton Assistant Matron and given direction for the employment of Margaret Dunbar in her place.

While the job was essentially the same as that of the governor, it is worth noting that the matron's status differed; the matron had responsibility for 'the care and superintendence of the whole female department' but was still 'under the directions of the governor'.[67] Her position within the wider prison was equivalent to that of a turnkey.

Warders

The role of the warder (either male or female) was also becoming more specific in its requirements. From the 1870s, they had to be between the ages of 20 and 40, and pass an exam requiring reading, writing and arithmetic. Preference would be given to military personnel with a good record of conduct, and by 1893, some 66 per cent of appointments were from army or navy backgrounds.[68] Nevertheless, one contemporary describes ex-Royal Marines serving as warders elsewhere in the country as

> all the same foul-mouthed, bullying, completely uneducated man, and totally unfit for any position of trust, and, least of all, fitted for prison employment.[69]

It was a dichotomy of traits that meant that the prison warders could be far removed from each other depending on the environment in which they worked. These men and women were also required to work seven days per week, although two meals would be provided daily. They could live in apartments in most prisons or outside the prison in houses provided by the prison authorities; census records indicate that most lived on site at York Castle Prison. But the long hours and lack of free time for the warders meant this was a gruelling life, with many leaving after just a few days of service. It could also be a dangerous job; an entry in the York Castle Prison *Gaoler's Journal* on 9 August 1853 tells us:

> Elizabeth Graham, (Convicted of felony) this morning struck the matron with the sweeping brush and cut her head. This woman has frequent fits of insanity but I believe she knew very well what she was doing at the time. She has been very unruly and thinks she may do as she plans with impunity. I have ordered her hands to be bound from doing further mischief.[70]

Several factors influenced the control of prisoners by warders. There was a belief that a military background was a positive quality for a warder, but much more could influence the quality of a warder's work. It has been noted that 'female prisoners often like to be under the care of a good-looking officer, and will obey her and conduct themselves properly with her ...'[71] The female warders were very different from the males in that they 'were encouraged to form relationships with the prisoners based on trust and loyalty'.[72] It was generally believed that female warders possessed 'a greater moral force' over the prisoners than male warders, and 'their conduct was expected to be exemplary'.[73] One thing that was not different between the male and female warders, however, was the working conditions. The female warders were still expected to work the extremely long shifts, twelve or fifteen hours per day,[74] that their male counterparts were expected to. Due to this harsh working environment, some warders would bend or break the rules to earn a little extra income. While it is essential to note that most warders were honest, hardworking men and women, some were not. It was not uncommon for a symbiotic relationship to exist between prisoners and warders. The warders would receive payment for helping to smuggle contraband, such as tobacco, into the prison, and the prisoners would assist in ensuring that they were not caught, thereby receiving an easier time in prison.[75] This reliance on each other often allowed a small number of warders to control large prison populations. For the corrupt warder, 'he was able to double his salary at the very least'.[76]

The Surgeon

The surgeon's role gained significant importance following the introduction of journals in 1823. The surgeon's role, in addition to keeping inmates healthy, was to assess their fitness for hard labour. This was punishing work that could have had dangerous consequences for those who were not physically fit enough to endure it. The surgeon's job was a tough one. If an inmate died or committed suicide, questions would be asked of the surgeon, and they had to show that they had carried out the required steps to try and prevent the deaths. Any claims of criminal insanity would also go through the surgeon for a diagnosis. This could have serious consequences for trials and the life of a prisoner, including the outcome if they are found guilty. The surgeon would also perform an essential role in executions, being the first one into the pit after the drop to assess if the condemned had died and how quickly. The surgeon's responsibilities even extended to the staff of the prison and their families, as well as examining any potential employees for their well-being.

The ultimate power of the surgeon was to obtain, through an order from the Home Secretary, a medical release for prisoners who were too unwell to endure prison.[77] In York, the most prominent example of this was Chartist Samuel Holberry, who would be granted release by the Home Secretary, but unfortunately, only after his death.

To understand how the surgeon might handle certain situations, we can once again refer to *Gaoler's Journals*. Firstly, the surgeon could use his position to modify the standard diet of prisoners if he believed it would benefit their health.

> 16 September [1854]
> In consequence of a great number of prisoners affected with Bowel complaints the Surgeon has ordered that all the prisoners should have the same quantity of new milk in their Gruel as they have in the morning viz, one half penny worth each, to commence this evening, 16 criminals with bowel complaints and some debtors.[78]

Significant outbreaks of disease might not have been as prevalent as the almost endemic presence of gaol fever in the eighteenth century. Still, much of this was down to the surgeon using their discretion in separating those that potentially could help spread a disease from the rest of the prison population:

> 18 May [1857]
> The Surgeon informs me that the Schoolmaster's Wife is ill in the Small pox, and that it is requisite that he should not come into the prison for 14 days, I have therefore given him liberty for that time from this day.[79]

> 3 April [1860]
> I am informed by Mr Anderson the Surgeon, that Mr Thompson our Chaplain's Son is now very ill in Typhus fever, and being in the same house with his Father; to prevent Infection the Surgeon is of opinion that Mr Thompson's duties for the present should be suspended …[80]

The surgeon's primary duty was to care for those prisoners unlikely to recover from their illness in prison, as well as to inform their relatives and friends to come and say their goodbyes:

> 18 April [1856]
> Recd one male prisoner ... a Debtor in a very delicate state of health and requires some one to attend him, he has been removed into a room apart from the other debtors and his Wife allowed to remain with him night and day this has been recommended by the Surgeon who has also given him a medical Certificate to send to his friends in order that they may know the state of his health.[81]

Finally, it was the surgeon's unfortunate duty to inform the relevant authorities when a prisoner passed away while inside the walls of York Castle Prison:

> 25 January [1859]
> Mary Wragg convicted of misdemeanour Yorkshire Spring assizes 1857 and Sentenced to be Imprisoned 2 years has long been very ill of a cancer in her breast died this day at about 2 p.m. I have written to a magistrate and also the coroner to inform them.[82]

The Chaplain

One of the most fundamental aspects of the prison was the 'Christian Zeal' with which it was run and administered. For this purpose, in 1814, the role of prison chaplain was made compulsory. In addition to performing services on Sundays and special occasions, such as Christmas, they frequently visited the rooms and cells occupied by prisoners. They visited the infirmary and other sick prisoners daily. In addition, the chaplain would also visit those in solitary cells daily.[83] He would also see those spending their last days in the condemned cells if they were of the correct denomination. If these unfortunate prisoners were, for example, catholic, special arrangements would be made to bring someone in to tend to the condemned prisoner.

The role of chaplain can be seen as the most crucial role within the prison because it was the passion, enthusiasm and personality of the chaplain that could have a prisoner see their errors in life and reform themselves or, if these traits were lacking, could cause indifference in a prisoner that could keep them on the path that led them to prison in the first place. In addition, the chaplain was expected to exert control over what was being taught by the schoolmaster and monitor the progress of the prisoners' lessons. The chaplain might also censor letters the prisoner wrote to loved ones and those received, having to read them all before they made their way to the intended recipient. The letters were only to contain domestic and personal matters; any communication of current affairs, for example, would be censored. This role of censor would also extend to the prison library, where the chaplain would censor any books 'such as he may deem improper'.[84] However, the prisoners might not have seen the chaplain's intent the same way as it was viewed from the outside. Oscar Wilde wrote, 'The prison chaplains are entirely useless. They as a class, well-meaning, but foolish, indeed silly, men. They are of no help to the prisoner'.[85]

The role of the chaplain, like that of the surgeon, also extended to the staff. Many would consider the governor's and wardens' moral welfare their responsibility. As a moral man, the chaplain might help prisoners appeal for assistance for an impoverished family left behind or secure relief for debtors, thereby helping and serving his flock like a vicar or priest outside of a prison environment. However, life could be hard for the chaplain, even with the best intentions. As one commentator said, 'If he attempts … to win the hearts of prisoners, he finds the whole system of prison discipline arrayed against him.'[86]

For the prisoners, the one thing expected at York Castle Prison and every other prison in the UK was that they would attend compulsory chapel services once daily and twice on Sundays.[87] Britain was a Christian country. In the mid-nineteenth century, the only recognised religions were the Church of England, Judaism and Catholicism, which had recently been added.[88] This meant that you were required to attend either church or chapel during your time in prison. Atheism was not recognised, and other religions like Islam were not accepted. If you were in prison, you were de facto Christian or Jewish for your time there. After all,

> Chapel was just part of one's punishment. If one looked either to the right or the left or attempted to whisper to another fellow it meant three days' breads and water in close confinement.[89]

We have records, once again in the *Gaoler's Journal*, of many people getting into trouble through not attending or causing trouble while at service in York Castle Prison: Note the abbreviation of 'soly' used for solitary confinement.

September 12th [1824]
James Healey Soly two days for refusing to attend Chapel.

24 [August 1829]
Alexander Burn and Simon Hargreaves Soly three days for bad behaviour in Chapel during divine service.

July 6th 1837
Thomas Shaw Soly three days on bread and water for disorderly conduct in passing from his Ward to the Chapel.

This is only a tiny sample to give an idea of the different infractions being dealt with, but this is, in fact, a common listing in the *Gaoler's Journals*, giving us an idea of just how often this bad behaviour occurred.

The Schoolmaster/Schoolmistress

The final vital role in running the prison was the schoolmaster. These were usually warders who could read and write well and worked under the direction of the chaplain. Elizabeth Fry complained about the lack of education at York Castle Prison in 1819. However, York did appear to be educating its prisoners to some extent by 1835. This year, we have two references in the *Gaoler's Journal* referring to education for at least some prisoners.

November 1st [1835]
Nicholas Coyne Soly two days on bread & water for swearing and bad behaviour in the School Room.

November 9th 1835
John Coyne a convict boy Soly one and a half days for striking the assistant Schoolmaster.

Education was considered a crucial part of rehabilitating criminals during the Victorian period. York Castle Prison provided a schoolmaster and a schoolmistress for this purpose. However, as York was a county prison, the time spent there would have been less than six months, and hard labour as punishment would have been the norm rather than a primary focus on reform, as seen in convict prisons. In addition, in 1843, it was part of the prison regulations at York Castle Prison that 'No prisoner shall be compelled to attend school against his inclination'.[90]

It was not until the Prison Act 1865 formally allowed for the provision of education in reading, writing, and arithmetic in prisons that education became a major part of a prisoner's life. The prison would have had a schoolmaster, a classroom, and a library; every prison was required to allocate some time to educating prisoners.[91] It is worth noting that often, 'education' would be little more than teaching the prisoners to read and write. Education gained new importance throughout the country when the Education Acts came into force in the 1870s. After 1877, prospective schoolmasters and mistresses were tested by an inspector of the Education Department.[92] They were ensuring a minimum standard of education throughout the prison system. The education of female prisoners might fall to the matron or, more likely, the assistant matron.[93] However, we have a reference to a schoolmistress specifically employed at York Castle Prison later in the century.[94]

Other Roles: Porter and Night Watchman

Two other roles appear on the census records of York Castle Prison: the porter and the nightwatchman. The porter's role was to work in the newly constructed gatehouse, controlling who entered and left the prison. On the other hand, the night watchman patrolled the prison while the prisoners were locked in their cells, asleep. The watchman would look out for anything unusual and alert the rest of the staff if needed. These were the lowest-paid jobs at York Castle Prison, so it is unsurprising that they sought opportunities to earn a little more money. We are told that on 19 January 1842:

> Joseph Powell the night Watchman was detected in bringing into the Castle two Tin Bottles and one bladder containing nearly a Gallon of Spirits viz Rum & Gin, he was brought before Mr Hague the next day who fined him £10 and he was Discharged from his situation.[95]

This cost Joseph his job, but a good, respectable porter could spend an extended period in service. In fact, at York Castle Prison, three generations of the Pashley family held the position from 1777 to 1868.

Life in York Castle Prison

Leaving Prison and Discharged Prisoners Societies

With imprisonment being used more and more as punishment, the question of what happens to the prisoners after their sentence is completed becomes an important one. Prisons are no longer allowed to charge prisoners before they can be released; by the mid-nineteenth century, the opposite was happening. When a prisoner's sentence was over, they were given expenses to return home, enabling them to reintegrate into their community and start anew. There are several records of these in the *Gaoler's Journals*. Two examples are:

> December 10th [1853]
> Descharged Robert Roberts whose time expired this day gave him 8 shillings for his Expenses home to Sheffield.[96]

> 14 July [1855]
> Mary Elizabeth James convicted of Perjury at the assizes 7th March 1855 and sentenced to 4 years penal Servitude, was liberated this day on Ticket of leave paid her 6/6 for her Expenses home.[97]

While neither of these is exceptional, both demonstrate attitudes towards discharged prisoners and the increasing emphasis on helping them re-establish themselves within society.

Alongside the plethora of other social reforms of the Victorian period, we get the birth of discharged prisoner societies in 1857.[98] Essentially, it was a union for prisoners who had been through the system. The aim was to help prisoners reintegrate into society by facilitating employment and providing a supportive yet vigilant presence upon their release. York was no exception and had its own society. We know that 'At York Castle, a recommendation from the Chaplain and Governor was a prerequisite for an interview with the society's agent'.[99] In addition, at the very end of the century, the rectory of St Mary's Church, so long associated with prisoners who had died at York Castle Prison, was converted into a shelter for female prisoners who had been discharged.[100]

Unfortunately, these societies could not help everyone after leaving prison. Often, former inmates are left with few prospects after their release. The *Gaoler's Journal* tells us that on 20 June 1854:

> Martin …, the boy discharged on the 10th inst. And sent to Hull in hopes he might get a master to go to sea, has returned this day. Says he could not get any employment. I have got an order from the York Union Workhouse to receive him in that establishment and have sent him there.[101]

Sickness in Prison

Of course, making it to your release date was always the first concern. With the continued problems in the prison cells due to extreme cold during winter, as well as the presence of insects and vermin inside the prisons, it is not surprising that the health of the prisoners remained a major concern. Interestingly, during this period, we begin to see increased attention to the health of prisoners. Sometimes, it is for selfish reasons, as in the case of Mary Elders, who was imprisoned for stealing cheese in Whitby. Her original sentence was to be transported for seven years. However, while at York Castle Prison, she became very ill. The surgeon at the time, George Champney, describes her in a letter of 20 February 1839 to be 'confined to her bed … incurable if allowed to remain in prison'.[102] It is possible that it was some spinal disease, as indicated by Champney, but it was complicated further by severe diarrhoea. James Sheppard, keeper (gaoler) of York Castle Prison, describes the case as Mary Elders being coerced by her mother, 'an infirm old woman of bad character' who was also sentenced to 7 years transportation but was judged to be 'too old and infirm to be sent abroad'. For Mary, though, he states, 'Her husband and other relations are willing to take care of her if she be set at liberty'.[103]

This recommendation is taken in, and on 7 March 1839, Bernard Hague, the chairman of the visiting magistrates, requests 'with a view to avoiding the further expenditure to the county of a person to attend to and constantly wait upon her, her discharge is highly desirable …'[104] Therefore, Mary Elders was too expensive to keep in prison and was released. If it benefited the prison, a prisoner's health could be considered. This would be seen again with the chartist Samuel Holberry, who would be pardoned, albeit too late, for political reasons and poor health.

Women and Children in Prison

When people think of female prisoners during the Victorian period, many people think of the famous cases of female poisoners. This is not without reason, as many famous cases throughout the country at this period involved poisoners; for example, Florence Bravo, Adelaide Bartlett and Florence Maybrick were all accused of murdering their husbands in this way.[105] We see some examples of this in the prisoners convicted at York Castle Prison, with women like Ursula Lofthouse and Ann Gilmore. However, these highly publicised cases were rare and skewed in public perception. Instead, the story of female criminals in the Victorian period should be viewed in the context of other crimes.

In the second half of the nineteenth century, 17 per cent of prisoners were women, compared to approximately 4 per cent in the late twentieth century.[106] This significant statistic can be explained by the fact that 90 per cent of these women were in local prisons or houses of correction.[107]

While many of the crimes women were convicted of at this time were the same as those of men, pickpocketing and theft were common crimes for women to be charged with. Other crimes were far more common among women: infanticide, prostitution and an 'unlawful pledge' at a pawnbroker.[108] It was not unusual for women to either get themselves thrown into the local house of correction or permanently turn to prostitution to avoid the indignity of the workhouse.

Unlawful pledging involved taking something to a pawnbroker that did not belong to the individual in the first place. Prostitution was a common crime for women to be convicted of, although it was not unheard of for police officers to arrest drunken women as prostitutes.[109] However, drinking had more problems than just being mistaken for a prostitute. It is noted that on 16 February 1850, Richard Farrar, George Coates and James Oates were imprisoned at York Castle Prison for the manslaughter of Margaret Duggan on 6 February.[110] Margaret had just come out of the house of correction and had become intoxicated. The three accused played tricks and practical jokes on her, including carrying her out of the pub into a nearby field where she was 'heard to shriek out'.[111] She was found bruised and exposed. The three men would all be acquitted as

> these facts did not amount to the crime of manslaughter. The woman, being intoxicated, had voluntarily accompanied the prisoners; and she was not like an infant who, unable to take care of itself, had been left exposed to the cold and died in consequence.[112]

It should be remembered that it was not just the poor or unfortunate women who could find themselves in trouble. Even women of a higher standing sometimes found themselves on the wrong side of the law. While not exclusively a female crime, ill treatment of servants was common. It was also not uncommon for this ill treatment to escalate and result in the woman of the house being taken to court.[113]

Women were less likely to end up somewhere like York Castle Prison as they were less likely to commit felonies than men and would often be treated more leniently by judges and juries.[114] However, women still faced the problem of all-male judges and jurors, but it is notable that as the century progressed, there came a 'Great reluctance to hang women'.[115] That is not to say it did not happen, but the same judges and juries were more likely to find a reduced punishment if possible. It is for this reason that no woman was hanged in York after 1835.

For those women who committed serious crimes, life within York Castle Prison could be significantly different from that of a male prisoner. Within the prison, women were now held separately, attended to by an all-female staff, and interestingly, women were not allowed to work on the treadwheel.[116] Instead, their time in prison would be spent in the prison's laundry room. Within the legal system, as one author put it, 'Women in prison were seen as somehow anomalous: not foreseen and therefore not legislated for', being treated like 'difficult men or lunatics'.[117]

Having a child with you in prison might, on rare occasions, help reduce your sentence. A letter was written in 1836, in which Sarah Bready was fined £10 for selling unstamped newspapers. As she was

> utterly unable to pay the same [the magistrate] committed her to the Castle of York for three months ... having an infant child at the breast, for whom in consequence of her incarceration she is unable to provide with all the care and attention which its necessities demand.[118]

Her husband, Patrick Thomas Bready, was also incarcerated for the same offence, and it is inferred that he led her to commit the offence. As a result, the child's 'health has been serious, if not fatally affected in consequence'.[119] Demands were made for Sarah's immediate discharge; however, the records do not indicate whether this was the case.

This example does show that young children still 'at the breast' of their mother could still be admitted to prison alongside their mother if the magistrate had granted this. Only the medical officer could take the baby from the mother. Typically, a child in prison would be provided with the following:

- A crib, cot or cradle
- Binders, flannel
- Boots (when necessary)
- Flannels, head
- Frocks, flannelette
- Gowns, day, calico
- Gowns, day, flannelette
- Gowns, night
- Hoods (when necessary)
- Napkins
- Petticoats, flannel
- Pinafores
- Shawls
- Shirts, No.1
- Shirts, No.2
- Skirts, flannelette
- Socks[120]

The medical officer would assess if the child should stay in prison after reaching nine months, and it was extremely rare for a child to be kept in prison after reaching twelve months. If there were no suitable relative for the child to go live with, the unfortunate child would likely end up in the local workhouse, where the mother was arrested.

Children in Prison

Children themselves still end up in prison for the same two reasons that they always had. Firstly, they might have been born there or come in with their mother while she was still nursing. This was still fairly common, even in the early Victorian period, with many instances recorded in York Castle Prison's *Gaoler's Journals*. This would be an interesting place for a child to spend their first years in an all-female environment that could often become overcrowded. At the end of April 1856, the situation became so dire that the more well-behaved convicts were paired with those awaiting trial to alleviate overcrowding.[121] This overcrowding is understandable as the area of the female prison set aside for the women was relatively small. The life for those born in prison was probably not much better than it had been a century earlier. Yes, there was a chance that the mother would only be in for a short sentence, and the child would leave with a reformed mother, living a good life. However, for some, they never stand a chance. On 25 June 1856, we are informed that William Charlton Turner, the child of Mary Ann Williamson, then approximately 2 years old, is to be transferred to the union workhouse.[122] The prospects for William would not have been good.

Of course, children could find themselves imprisoned for a crime they had committed. They were subject to the same laws and, therefore, the same punishments as adults. This could include execution or transportation. It is not hard to imagine how brutal this could be on someone young, even sadder when descriptions of the time state things like 'as a rule within three days they have cried themselves quiet ...' or suggestions that the child's cries might be 'often suppressed by blows'.[123] The system as a whole was set up for adults, and this led to children becoming, as Oscar Wilde put it, 'utterly contaminated', not by the prisoners, but by 'the whole prison system – of the governor, the chaplain, the warders, the lonely cell, the isolation, the revolting food, the rules of the prison commissioners, the mode of discipline, as is termed, of the life'.[124]

However, this period also sees many of these long-standing problems begin to be addressed. The Juvenile Offenders Act 1847 and 1850 established minimum age limits of 14 and 16 for petty sessions, complemented by the Youthful Offenders Act 1854, which aimed to reform the system for those under 16. These acts establish that younger, less mature criminals should be treated differently from those with the age and maturity to understand the consequences of their actions. Young offenders could now only be sentenced to fourteen days in prison; the rest would be spent in the reformatory schools for two to five years. This was further enhanced in 1861 with the addition of different categories of child offenders.

Chapter 9

The Site of HM Prison York, 1877–1900

Later Changes

The final phase of York Castle Prison, serving as both a county gaol and a civilian prison, spanned the last twenty-three years of its existence. Several arguments can be made for when this phase of the prison began, as three significant changes in the prison occurred during the late Victorian period. Would the best point to define this change be from the creation of West Yorkshire's assize in 1863, the end of transportation, or the end of imprisonment for debt, all of which removed fundamental functions of the prison, resulting in a significant decline in the number of prisoners held at York Castle Prison? Since our previous compartmentalisations have all been defined by substantial building works at the prison, and further building would take place in 1881 with the redevelopment of the 1835 felons' prison, this could be another point where we could argue that York Castle Prison enters a new phase of its history. However, the way the prisons were run was also changing. The most significant change was undoubtedly the nationalisation of all prisons in Britain in 1877. This would forever standardise how prisons were run in Britain and also give a new name to the prison. Now, it would be known as Her Majesty's Prison York or simply HM Prison York.

Even before the transition to state ownership, the buildings of York Castle were still undergoing changes to meet the latest standards. The first of these changes was forced on York Castle in 1868. It was this year that public execution would disappear from Britain for good. After this time, all executions were to be private executions, carried out within prisons. The gallows had to be moved from their traditional location near the assize court. The location chosen was in the north wing of the female prison building. Next to the already existing condemned cell, another cell was converted into an execution room. The only visible changes to the outside of the building were two large doors that would be opened when required to complete the final act. For the public, all that

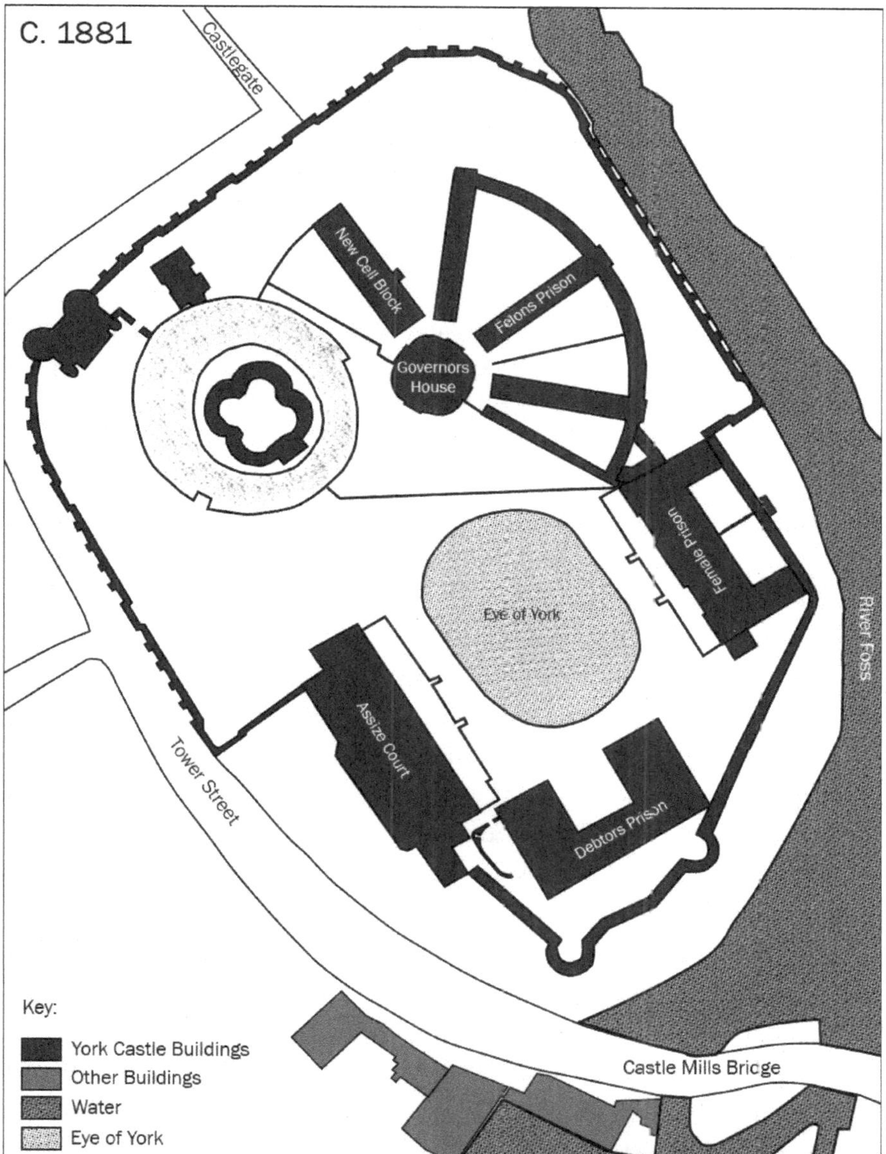

A plan of the site after reconstructing the northernmost 'A' block.[1]

would be known of an execution from now on would be a black flag hoisted above Clifford's Tower to signal a successful execution.[2]

Additional modifications to the prison were made during the later Victorian era, with a wall constructed in 1880 that divided the 1835 felons' prison from the rest of the site. Once part of the same institution, the prison was now run by the prison authorities, but the local magistrates still ran the court, causing great friction. In the end, it had to be declared that

> The Boundaries of the prison should be clearly defined and that such right of way should be granted to or retained by the Prison Commissioners ...[3]

The court authorities had their own modernisation programme at the same time, and they spent a significant amount of money, between £3,000 and £4,000, on it. The crown court itself was rearranged and enlarged, and an extension was constructed on the back of the court building, which was to be 'of classical design, and encased externally with Whitby stone'.[4]

However, neither of these changes addressed the issue of York Castle's unsuitable nature for a modern prison. With the prison authorities 'condemning York Castle for its insufficiencies as a prison ...'[5] York was once again in the firing line. By 1881, when the prison commissioners, chaired by Sir Edmund Frederick Du Cane, who had implemented the Prison Act 1877 and closed forty-four prisons, described York as having 'but little cell accommodation, and this of a very unsatisfactory kind – the place as it now stands can only be explicitly and conclusively condemned'.[6] It was evident that work would be needed to stop York Castle from potentially being closed. This resulted in the demolition of the most northern wing, 'A' block, of the 1835 felons' prison, replacing it with a modern-style cell block. A full-height hallway with four floors of cells. This was the last major building work on the site during its time as a prison. While it is impossible to say with certainty, this was likely the point at which the padded cell, which still exists in the female prison building, was added. We know that it does not appear on the 1852 plan of the site, and these changes provide a plausible impetus for its construction.

It is also worth noting that Clifford's Tower was saved for the nation at this time and became a national monument in 1880.[7] The tower was underpinned by the government in 1888 following the appearance of cracks.[8] However, the

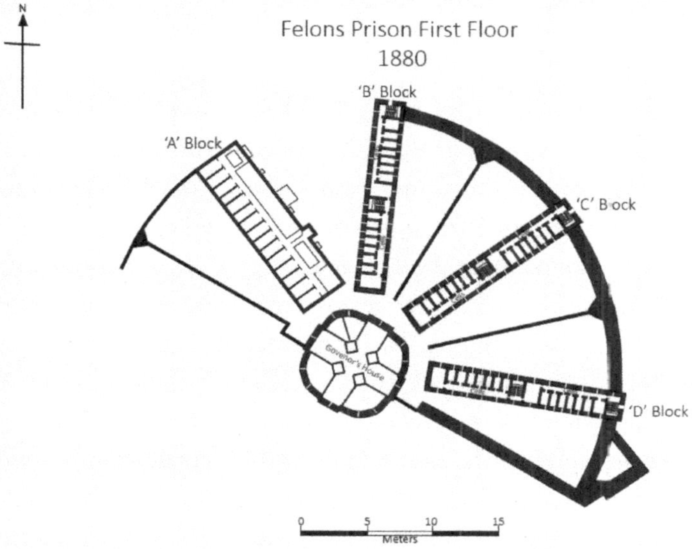

A plan showing the felons' prison after its reconstruction.[9]

A plan showing the female prison building, the new additions, including the padded cell and the new location of the execution room.[10]

idea of potentially destroying this monument would never again arise, and as a result, the tower remains accessible to visitors today.

Demise of York Castle Prison

Further attempts to modify parts of the buildings would follow, but these would not be pursued. Most notably, after the construction of Skeldergate Bridge in 1881, the council wanted to remove part of the 1835 curtain wall and widen Tower Street.[11] In 1890, a substitute wall and metal palisade were offered, but this did not happen. While it appears feasible, as this section was cut off from the rest of the prison, the fear of compromised security won.

However, times were changing, and many people were starting to feel uncomfortable having a prison in the city centre. Along with prisons constantly becoming more optimised for rehabilitation, the days of the nearly 200-year-old debtors' prison building, the over-a-century-old female prison building, and the half-a-century-plus Victorian prison building were all unsuitable for modern prisons. At this point, a somewhat surprising but very financially beneficial offer came from the military requesting that they take control of the prison for their own prisoners. The final prisoners at York Castle Prison were transferred to Wakefield Prison on 30 June 1900.[12]

Chapter 10

Life in HM Prison York, 1877–1900

> It was in the nineteenth century that prisons as we recognise them came into existence and were forced into a national system administered by the central government.[1]

The Consolidating Prisons Act 1877 was a pivotal moment in the history of prison reform. Several aspects of the act altered the perception of York Castle Prison. Firstly, there is the name itself. Under a standard nationwide prison system, all prisons are designated as Her Majesty's Prison. In this case, York Castle Prison officially became HM Prison York, although many newspapers still referred to it as York Castle Prison for many years. This change in semantics might appear purely superficial, but it signified a loss of individuality that many prisons, including York Castle Prison, had before the Act. Each prison had its own distinct character, shaped by the staff that ran it and the rules they enforced. York Castle Prison, for instance, was known for its relatively lenient treadwheel regime, enforcing only half the usual daily climb. However, with a standardised system, many prisons lost that unique character. York Castle Prison was now struggling to define its usefulness. No longer were there debtors or transportees being held here, nor were there public executions that brought a sense of fear to the institution. After the opening of Armley Prison and the movement of West Riding cases to Leeds Assize Court in 1863, even York Castle Prison's role as Yorkshire's county gaol had effectively ended, now only serving part of the area it was initially intended to.

The 1877 Act ushered in direct government control of Local Prisons, significantly altering the landscape of York Castle.[2] York's local prison had been moved to York Castle in 1838 after the change of York's New City Gaol into York House of Correction. The local house of correction then merged with the local prison in 1868,[3] following the passage of the Prison Act 1865, which resulted in all local and county prisoners being held at York Castle Prison.

The 1877 Act also distinguished between prisoners who were convicted and serving a sentence and those awaiting trial.

The Consolidating Prisons Act also standardised the terminology when referring to staff throughout the country. York Castle Prison is relatively late to the party when it comes to modernising prison staff roles. It was not until the 1871 Census that we first saw terms like governor and warder used at York Castle Prison. On the 1861 Census, the titles used were gaol keeper, deputy gaoler, turnkey, porter and matron. By 1871, the terminology had been modernised, and we now see a governor, deputy governor, warder, porter, matron and assistant matron. Some of these terms would change further, and by the 1881 Census, the assistant matrons had become standardised as warders to signify the similarities in their roles.

This standardisation led to improved prison conditions, with enhanced inspection and oversight of their operations. One newspaper report about HM Prison York in 1890 states that

> during the past year the discipline of the prison has been fully maintained, the cases of misconduct being few and the complaints none. The prisoner's food continues good under inspection, and the health of the prisoners generally satisfactory ...[4]

Of course, there were still unpredictable parts of a prisoner's life. Throughout the Victorian period, several outbreaks of flu and other diseases occurred. One particular outbreak, Typhoid in 1889, is particularly notable for 'The absence of sufficient facility for the isolation of infectious cases ...'[5] With a growing understanding of diseases, the recognition that slowing the spread in vulnerable places, such as prisons, was also becoming clearer and greater care was being taken. During this late period, concerns that we would now call health and safety were emerging, and mitigations were implemented to protect the prisoners. One of these was after a fire occurred in 1889, the

> Governor communicated with HM Prison Commissioners and expression of their opinion that further appliances for extinguishing fires should be obtained.[6]

The health and well-being of prisoners were now being treated with the respect that John Howard had suggested back in 1777.

We can see clearly how far the prison has moved on from the oppressive, unhygienic horror that was the Georgian prison. Now, barring the occasional outbreak of disease, the prison tries to care for the prisoners during their incarceration. It even examines fire provisions, an expense that would not have been incurred just a hundred years before.

However, it should be remembered that the 1877 Act was just one of several significant changes that affected York Castle Prison over a few short years. Firstly, the number of prisoners had been increasing. In 1843, the frequency of assize prisoner deliveries was increased from twice to three times per year, approximately twenty years after Reverend Sydney Smith had requested this change.[7] For those awaiting trial, this meant less time spent at York Castle Prison. This increase in the number of prisoners and, consequently, trials, led to the assize courts for Yorkshire being separated, with West Yorkshire having its own assize court in Leeds from July 1863.[8] This new court significantly reduced the prison population at York Castle Prison. When the removal of West Yorkshire prisoners is combined with the end of transportation and the imprisonment of debtors, the importance of York Castle faces its first challenge, eventually leading to its closure. These factors contributed to what was now a steadily decreasing prison population. The number of prisoners fell from 1,211 men and 314 women in 1888 to 1,008 men and 263 women in 1889, just one year.[9] Other ways had to be found to provide income for York Castle, such as filling the now-empty cells. This changed the makeup of prisoners held here compared to previous generations. Now, the prison would be supported by housing prisoners from elsewhere, for a fee, of course! In 1872, York took 81 prisoners from the County of Middlesex, and 1873 saw 202 from County Durham. In 1876, it is known that, on average, 171 prisoners were held at York, of whom only 62 were from Yorkshire. Fifty-two were from the City of York, i.e. local offenders convicted at petty sessions; two were from Carlisle, and fifty-five were military prisoners.[10] York Castle's primary role was no longer that of the county gaol for Yorkshire, but rather an overspill prison for other counties and, significantly, the military.

Of course, 1877 was not the last attempt at reforming the prison system. The final effort came with the Prison Act 1898. This ended unproductive labour in prisons, stipulating that prisoners should work together, learn trades, and have greater access to educational materials, including books. For York, however, this Act came too late to have any lasting impact. By the end of the century, prisons had evolved significantly, approaching what we might imagine today. A standard life sentence was typically twenty years, and finally, in 1898, someone on trial could give evidence on their own behalf.

Life in HM Prison York

The system itself became increasingly standardised as time passed. The new rules and regulations throughout the mid- and late 1800s meant even fewer differences from prison to prison. This means we can provide a general overview of a prisoner's experience at York Castle Prison. It is worth noting that many of the standard procedures we are about to examine emerged around 1835, and thus, most of this information also applies from the mid-1800s.

Arriving at York Castle Prison by the 'Black Maria', a common nickname for the prison system's transport vehicles, the prisoner would enter the gatehouse. Here, their names would be checked against those expected, and those convicted and those unconvicted, awaiting trial, would be separated.

The prison record book would then be filled out with the details from their paperwork. Their name, case, crime and, if appropriate, sentence would all be entered. The daily routine would be explained to the prisoners, as would the rules of conduct expected of them during their stay. The warders would ensure that the prisoners were aware of the rules regarding any disciplinary procedures that could be applied if the rules were broken. At this stage, the prisoners would also be required to surrender any property they might have on them, which would be logged and stored. The prison book would then be further filled in to include the prisoner's name, age, place of birth, occupation, marital status, number of children and the religion they observed.[11] Then, they were weighed, and this weight was also recorded. Subsequently, they would be weighed once per month. The final entry into the prison book would be a description that would 'include descriptions of features such as complexion, hair, eyes and any distinguishing marks such as scars, birth marks, tattoos or deformities'.[12]

Following the passage of the Prevention of Crime Act 1871, photographing prisoners as they entered prison became a widespread practice. This was to aid in recognising repeat offenders and possibly recording any distinguishing marks noted during their initial examination. This photo would then be added to the prison record book.

Up next was a visit to the bathhouse. This would become a daily part of the prisoner's routine, and the governor had the responsibility

> that every prisoner wash himself thoroughly, at least once every day, and his feet at least once each week; and he shall see that there is a sufficient supply of soap, towels, and combs.[13]

The exact nature of the bathhouse could vary from prison to prison. Even if you were lucky enough to have a bath to yourself, the water would no doubt have already been used by several prisoners, leaving it 'looking rather like mutton broth'.[14] Bathing for new prisoners was as much a ritual as it was practical. They were washing away, not just the dirt, but also the prisoner's old identity. This was accompanied by their hair being cropped to the scalp, at least for male prisoners; a style colloquially known as the 'county crop'.[15] Only three months before the end of a sentence were prisoners allowed to start to regrow their hair. Male prisoners also had to shave at least once per week. As for female prisoners, their hair could not be cut without their permission unless the governor deems it 'necessary on account of vermin or dirt, or when the medical officer deems it requisite on the grounds of health ...'[16]

Clothes were taken and stored, since most prisoners were at York for relatively short sentences of less than six months. These would have been fumigated before being stored. A prison uniform would be provided for the prisoners to wear for the rest of their stay at York Castle Prison. It is important to note that an unconvicted prisoner would be allowed to wear their own clothes until after the trial.

The clothing received at York in 1843 consisted of the following:

Male Prisoners

- Jacket
- Waistcoat
- Pair of pantaloons
- Stock or neckerchief
- Shirt
- Pair of stockings

- Pair of shoes
- Pocket handkerchief
- Cap
- Belt, when the prisoner has been in the habit of wearing one

Female Prisoners

- Dress or Jacket
- Petticoat
- Pair of stockings
- Shift
- Neckerchief
- Pocket handkerchief
- Cap
- Pair of shoes
- Other necessary articles
- Stays, when the prisoner has been in the habit of wearing them[17]

The medical officer would then undertake a medical examination of the prisoner. This would include their height, weight and physical description, as well as their hair colour, eye colour and distinguishing features, all of which would be noted. At this point, the medical officer would also determine if the prisoner was fit enough for hard labour.[18]

This would mark the first day of the prisoner's new life.

Living in York Castle Prison

Elizabeth Martin and Mary Green

We also have some great examples of what it was like to live at York Castle Prison, not just for the inmates, as we have already seen, but also for the staff and, importantly, their families who live on-site at HM Prison York. It is sometimes hard to remember when we talk about criminal history that the story of a prison is not just the inmates held within and the crimes they committed, but also those working in this dangerous place.

Life for those looking after prisoners was, for the most part, just a job; however, looking after a large group of prisoners who don't want to be in prison inevitably brings conflict and physical danger to the role. One of the best examples of this at York is the relationship between the matron and the assistant matron. We don't know the exact starting dates of either of these women at York, as neither appears on the 1871 Census; however, they were both in their positions by 1877. Mary Green was born in Bramham, Yorkshire, and is listed as a warder on the 1881 Census. However, it appears that initially, she was classified as the assistant matron, likely an indication of a name change to her role when York Castle Prison became HM Prison York in 1877. Elizabeth Martin was a local who was born and raised in York.[19] Her father passed away in February 1876, which may have been a motivating factor in her decision to take the position at York Castle Prison to help support her family.[20]

Margaret Barrett was serving a two-year sentence at York Castle Prison. In April 1877, she was brought to trial again at the petty sessions for assaulting the Matron Elizabeth Martin.[21] In addition, she was charged with 'willfully damaging the property of the country'.[22] On 19 April, Margaret Barret had refused to stop talking in the passage near her cell when asked to by the assistant matron, Mary Green. Consequently, the matron, Elizabeth Martin, ordered Margaret to be locked up.

> She resisted the attempt made to do this, and on the matron taking her by the shoulder, threw herself down on the floor and kicked her and the assistant matron violently several times.[23]

Margaret's violence then continued as she got up. She hit Elizabeth Martin in the face, cutting her lip and leaving it swollen for several days afterwards.[24] Eventually, Margaret was put in her cell, but she then broke the windows and damaged the cell door. It was estimated that Margaret did 20s worth of damage in her outburst.[25] Margaret would have to pay the 20s or have an additional month added to her sentence, and for the assault, she would have six months added to her existing sentence.[26]

Mary Green would later become the matron at Lincoln Castle. Elizabeth Martin continued as matron at York Castle Prison until 1881, when she married at St Mary's Church, just outside the castle walls, and appears to have left behind her life as a prison worker. However, this incident highlights the dangers that prison staff faced in the late Victorian period.

The Triffitt Family

Overall, it appears that working at York Castle Prison was not a particularly hazardous job despite the inherent dangers of the role. You got a good wage and accommodation for yourself and your family within the prison walls. That is probably why many staff stay for a long and successful career. The longest serving of these was Robert Triffitt. He started as a turnkey at some point before 1853; he worked his way up and became deputy governor by the 1871 Census. He would then take the top job as governor between 1883 and his death in 1885. He undoubtedly had a successful career, and he raised ten children within the grounds of York Castle.[27]

These children, born to staff at HM Prison York, would have spent much of their lives on the site, interacting with other children and staff. These bonds could become very strong. One example is Frances Triffitt. Frances would have known the young William Heald, whom we will meet next, who almost certainly played with her younger brothers, who were born in York Castle around the same time. She would have also considered many prison workers part of her extended family.

In 1882, Frances got married, and the officers of HM Prison York, who would have known Frances her whole life, bought her a clock as a wedding present. On it was a metal plate with the inscription:

> Presented By The Subordinate Officers Of HM Prison York To Miss Frances Triffitt On The Occasion Of Her Marriage York Castle 27th October 1882

W.L. Heald

Many children of staff would be born within the walls of York Castle, some would join their fathers in working for the prison service, and many would make a life away from what they knew as a child. However, one child from York Castle went on to lead an extraordinary life. Near the south-west corner of the roof of the debtors' prison, there is a piece of graffiti. It's small and easily missed if the light isn't favourable. It was carved with something softer than the lead it was carved into, and the writing becomes shallower as the message continues. It must have been done quickly, as no one ever returned to make it consistent. It reads: 'W L HEALD BORN IN YC 1875 DEC 25th'.

William Lofthouse Heald was born on Christmas Day 1875 to John Heald, a warder at York Castle Prison, and his wife Mary. We don't know much about his life growing up at York Castle, although the location of this graffiti indicates William's sense of adventure at an early age. We know he did not initially follow in his father's footsteps. William trained as a draper's apprentice, but this was not for him either. In 1892, he joined the Royal Navy, where he became an expert in explosives.[28] We know that the navy records him as having scars on his forehead, both knees and the left of his eye. We don't know how he acquired these, but misadventure is high on the list of likely causes. William became a leading seaman in 1899, and the navy notes his character as 'very good'. It was at this point that his life took an extraordinary turn. Between 1901 and 1904, he served on the voyage of the ship *Discovery* to the Antarctic. A voyage that would put him on the same ship as men who would become synonymous with Arctic exploration, notably Robert Falcon Scott and Ernest Shackleton. During this time, he would venture onto the ice with the expedition as they attempted to reach the South Pole. In something that must still be a somewhat exclusive club, William Heald would be one of the men who would man a reconnaissance balloon on the only day it could fly.[29] In 1902, William saved the life of the ship's geologist, Hartley Ferrar, who became exhausted while out on the ice, likely due to scurvy. Heald brought him back to base.[30] As a result, an island was named after him in Antarctica. Heald Island can still be found on maps (78°15'S 163°49'E). Heald was promoted to petty officer first class for his services during the discovery mission. William would leave the navy in 1908 and join the Royal Fleet Reserve.[31]

By 1909, he followed in his father's footsteps, briefly becoming a warder at Dartmoor Prison and joining the Freemasons.[32] However, his sense of adventure must have been itching, and he would return to Antarctica alongside Robert Falcon Scott in 1912 as part of the ill-fated Terra Nova expedition. He would not venture onto the ice this time to reach the South Pole; instead, he would stay with the ship throughout the expedition. Thus, he didn't have to face the fate of being trapped on the ice, which claimed the lives of many of the expedition's members.

After the Terra Nova, William married Agnes Gittins in 1913.[33] However, Agnes would die in 1917, and William would remarry in 1919, this time to Agnes Spilling.[34] William's career continued to evolve, with him switching roles and becoming a warder again, this time in London in 1913. During the First World War, William continued to serve in the Royal Fleet Reserve. His life appears to have been marked by fluctuations, with periods spent following his father's footsteps in the penal system and others at sea. By the time of the 1921 Census, he was a borstal officer at Feltham Young Offenders' Institute. William passed away at Feltham on 19 December 1929, aged 53, just a few days short of his birthday. He is buried near the chapel on the grounds of the Feltham Young Offenders' Institute.[35] He was a man who needed to be at sea and explore the world, a sense of adventure that possibly began on the roof of the debtors' prison.

Chapter 11

The Site of York Detention Barracks, 1900–1929

From the outside, the next phase of York Castle's life appears to be very similar to what had come before. York Castle was still a prison, just now exclusively for the military. However, the system that military prisons operated bore very little resemblance to the assize system that we have examined since the mid-twelfth century. There would be a lot to discuss on the nuances of military prison during this time, but this is not the place for such an in-depth discussion. The question we need to answer is why York Castle's function changed so much in 1900.

Following the establishment of an assize court in Leeds in 1863, the end of transportation and the closure of debtors' prisons, there was a significant shift in the importance of York Castle. The now-empty cells were being replenished by other prisons that paid York to house their prisoners, with the military also paying for the same service. It is against this background that it is not surprising that a letter arrived on 23 November 1899.

This letter from the undersecretary of state explains that holding military prisoners in local prisons is becoming increasingly common, as the military does not have a suitable location.[1] Another letter points out that this practice is 'unfair to the military offender, who … is treated as a criminal and thereby permanently disgraced'.[2] Another letter expresses concerns about military prisoners being sent to associate with the ordinary criminal prisoners in the civil prisons.[3] For the military, this practice of sending prisoners to state prisons was unsustainable. On the other hand, York Castle Prison only had an average of twenty-one prisoners from York City and thirteen from Scarborough. All of which could be accommodated at Wakefield and Hull, respectively. With the increasing frequency of imprisonment throughout Queen Victoria's reign, Yorkshire now had five major prisons. The number of cells available in each was:

York Castle … 155,
Wakefield … 927,

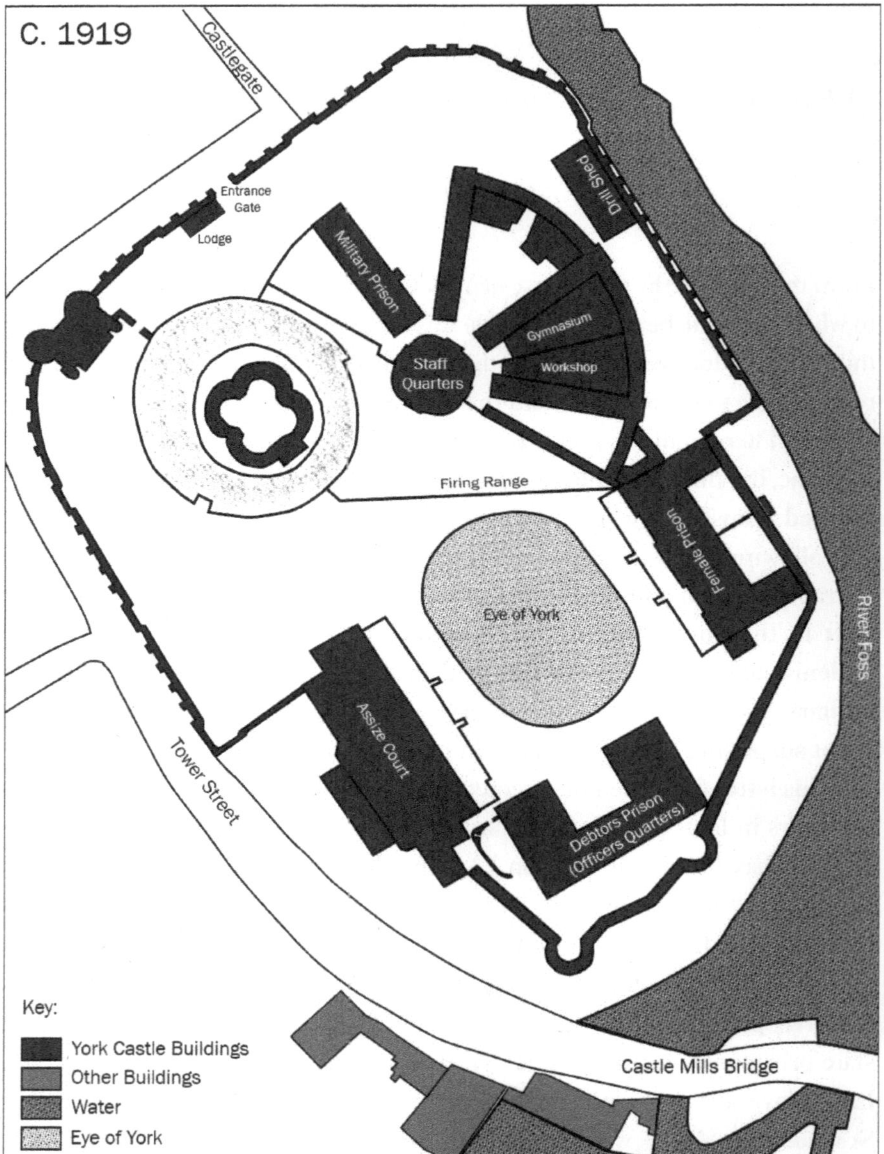

A plan of the site as used by the military, 1900–1929.[4]

Hull ... 333,
Leeds ... 437,
Northallerton ... 137.[5]

The military was seeking a location that could accommodate around 150 prisoners. With York Castle now being largely empty and plenty of spare accommodation available, especially in Wakefield and Hull, it is not hard to see what decision would be made. This decision was to hand over York Castle to the War Department in exchange for a small prison at Kendal that the military had used since 1894 and was 'found to be unsuitable'.[6]

> The County Prison would not cease entirely. The proposal was to retain the present female block of York Prison ... for the accommodation of prisoners who are brought up at York for Trial. The prison will not, therefore, be closed; but could be resumed at any time if required.[7]

This would mean that county trials would still happen at York Assize Court, and those on trial would still be held at York Castle, both before and during the trial. However, after the trial is over, any prison time that may result from the trial would now occur elsewhere.

While the final civil prisoners were transferred from York Castle Prison on 31 July 1900,[8] it was on 22 August 1900 that the secretary of state for war wrote a letter declaring, 'Under the power vested in me by section 133 of the Army Act I hereby declare York Castle to be a Military Prison under the said Act'.[9]

Refurbishing the Buildings for Their New Use

With the takeover of York Castle, the site's functionality needed to change to accommodate the military punishment system. The military prisoners would be housed entirely in the 1835 felons' prison building. This meant that there were no longer prisoners in or around the Eye of York. This allowed military parades to be started from the Eye every Sunday, processing through the streets of York to the Minster and back again. This tradition is still observed on a few select special occasions each year. The governor's tower in the 1835 complex was now home to the warrant officers.

Between blocks C and D, the military carried out additional building work. The exercise yard was rebuilt with two new structures, housing a workshop and a gymnasium. A firing range was established alongside the wall separating the Military prison from the Eye of York, and a stone-breaking shed was located along the east wall between 'A' block and the retaining wall around the base of Clifford's Tower. The military authorities invested substantially in this, with the gymnasium alone costing £5,000.[10]

The function of the debtors' prison changed a lot as well. It became the quarters for the Military Provost Staff Corps (MPSC), which ran the military prisons throughout Britain. The cells on the ground floor were used for storage. The two upper floors, which had historically housed debtors, now housed the officers running the military prison. As a result, there were some large-scale renovations within the building. The old day/night room sequence that had originally been put in place was altered for its new purpose. Newer fireplaces were installed, and the area was generally made a more amicable environment for those who lived and worked there. This is, in effect, the building that we still see today. During this period, additional small windows were installed in the corners of the debtors' prison to allow light into the water closet (WC) area. They were later covered up on the outside, but still survive on the inside today. The ranks of each officer and the area they occupied are clearly shown on the 1919 plans of the debtors' prison.

The female prison building appears to have been relatively unused by the military. The 1919 military prison plans show only two bedrooms and the chapel in use, with the rest of the building empty. As discussed earlier, the courts used the female prison building during trials. The courts kept a total of 23 cells for this purpose.[11] This area was not within the military's purview; therefore, they did not map its use.

Removing All Traces of the Former Prison

There was also a slow but systematic removal of anything linked to the prison that the military had no use for. One of the most interesting is the removal of the treadwheel around 1901. While its exact location within the prison is unclear, it gained new life as part of an exhibition at Madame Tussaud's in London after its removal. This was sold to Madame Tussaud's for £100.[12]

What Remained of the Castle

It was not long before the problems of inhabiting an old site started to appear for the military. By 24 January 1901, letters were being sent referring to

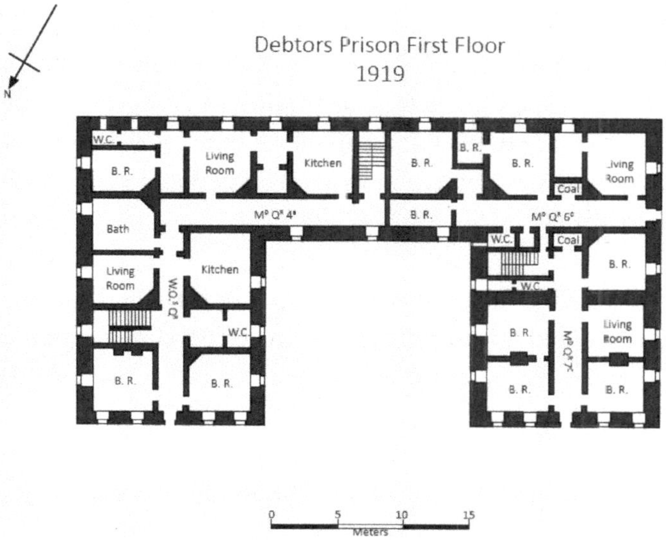

A plan of the first floor of the debtors' prison in 1919, showing the extensive renovations done by the military. This is essentially the floor plane that exists today.[13]

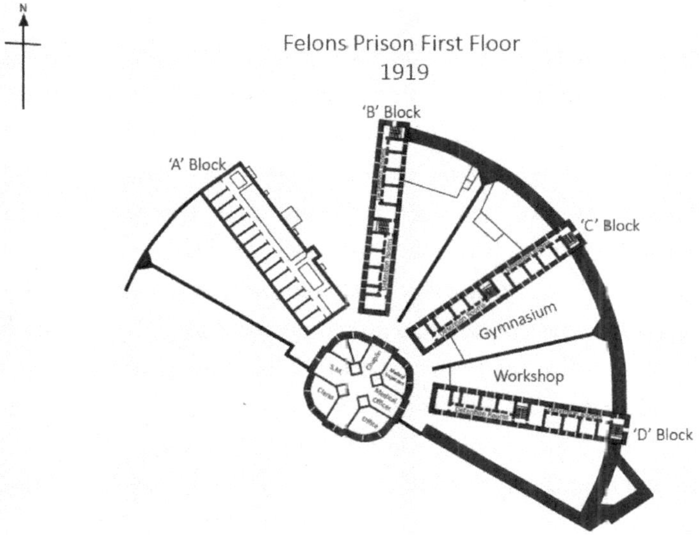

A plan of the felons' prison showing the modifications made. Note that the old cells in the original parts of the building have been knocked through to create more space.[14]

the 'dangerous condition of the portion of York Castle known as Clifford's Tower', with 'imminent risk that a part of the tower will collapse'.[15] The problem was the movement of the front part of the mound on which the tower stood. The issues appeared to have originated from the rebuilding of the mound in 1835. Cutting away the mound's outer edge and replacing it with a retaining wall was not as sound an engineering plan as might be imagined. In places, this

> revetment wall has given way and is broken up. The earth of the mound is moving forward and downward, and the corresponding portion of the old tower above has parted from the rest and is moving with the earth below it.[16]

Eventually, work was undertaken to underpin the mound. This was completed in 1903, costing £300 over the original estimate of £3,100. Luckily, the cost appears to have been borne by the Treasury.[17] This series of events also led to Clifford's Tower becoming the first historic building to be taken over by HM Office of Works in its role of preserving ancient buildings.[18] Commissioners of HM Office of Works again extensively repaired Clifford's Tower in 1920–1923.[19]

More historical problems were to come. On 12 December 1906, a letter was written by the undersecretary of state stating that a crack had appeared in one of the towers of what remained of the curtain wall at the south of the site.[20] This had already been growing for six or seven years. While not in immediate danger of collapse, suggestions were made that the tower might be demolished and rebuilt, or the hole in the wall could be filled in with stone from the demolition.[21] Luckily, this drastic option was not the one chosen. The problem was that the military had no money for the £340–£400 it would cost to repair or demolish the tower properly. Therefore, it was decided that the tower should be handed over to the Office of Works for maintenance.[22] This agreement was confirmed in a letter dated 23 February 1909. It must have taken a while for the Office of Works to complete the repairs, as there is a stone in that location of the tower today, marked 'O.W. 1911'. A final letter, dated 17 August 1911, confirms the transfer to the Office of Works with the proviso that the military can still use the passage through the tower to access the site.

Closure

By the 1920s, it was not just the castle's remaining structures that caused maintenance problems for the military. On 17 August 1928, a letter from the undersecretary of state stated that 'extensive repairs are now necessary to ensure the safety of the building known as the Old Debtors' Prison'.[23] This building, now home to the married quarters of the officers, had severe cracks in the walls of the Northwest wing, presumed to be caused by the subsidence of the foundations over the previous 220 years. According to the undersecretary of state, this would be expensive to fix and 'Cannot be justified at this period of financial stringency'.[24] Northern Command suggests in a letter received by the Home Office on 23 February 1929 that

> even if no special steps are taken, it is thought that the building will be inhabitable for 20 or 30 years. It is now 220 years old, and it is not considered that, in any case, it will be habitable for much longer.[25]

The suggestion appears to be that preserving the building was not worth the effort or cost. It would therefore not come as a shock to find that on 19 July 1929, a letter suggests that the Army Council would 'decide to discontinue the use of York Prison as a detention barracks in the autumn'.[26] With this abandonment, it was thought there would no longer be any need to repair the foundations of the debtors' prison. Therefore, the building and problems would be returned to the Home Department and the Secretary of State. The buildings were to be handed back on or after 10 October 1929. While the court functions of York Castle would continue, the use of the site as a prison would come to an end after nearly 800 years. Official information regarding the closure of York Castle Prison was received on 23 January 1932, marking this date as the official end of the prison's operation on site.

With a history of imprisonment dating back to 1166, the famous cases tried at the site, and its long history of a site of importance to the county and the Country, the end of York Castle Prison came on 23 January 1932, with a letter that simply read:

> In pursuance of the powers vested in me by the above act, I, the Right Honourable Sir Herbert Samuel, one of His Majesty's Principal Secretaries of State, do hereby order that the Prison at York shall be discontinued from this date.[27]

Chapter 12

Life in York Detention Barracks, 1900–1929

With the change in the type of prison at York Castle Prison, it becomes more difficult to track the changes in the lives and conditions for those held here without introducing a whole new history of military prisons. However, it's crucial to understand the major change in 1901, when the Military Provost Staff Corps was formed (officially, it was named the Military Prison Staff Corps 1901–1906). This resulted from an 1895 review of staffing, diet, and discipline within Britain's military prisons, and it can be seen as the most significant change in the history of military prisons in the UK. The prisons became known as 'detention barracks', and the prisoners were referred to as 'soldiers under sentence'.[1] This was a stark contrast to the system that had seen military prisoners sent to York Castle in the later Victorian period. Formerly staffed by the troops, discipline in a military prison could be unbearably harsh. Now, with the formation of the Military Provost Staff Corps, staff would be recruited for their qualities, those who 'possessed of the military spirit and thoroughly efficient as instructors'.[2]

Notably, the changes introduced through the 1901 Act also made York Castle the centre of discipline for the Northern Command. Comprising eighteen stations in northern England, York was the site used to house all who had received a sentence of more than seven days. For Barnard Castle, Bradford, and Strensall, which did not have detention facilities, all military prisoners would be housed at York Castle Prison.[3]

The work done by the military prisoners while at York Castle Prison was varied. Much of it would have involved drills and training so they could return to the unit as prepared as possible when released. This is why the firing range was constructed, despite it seeming like an unusual move to equip a prisoner with a firearm. Most prisoners were only there for minor infractions and would soon be released to return to their duties. York Castle and Dover Castle began operations in 1903 to produce and supply bread for consumption in military prisons throughout the UK.[4] As we will see, during the First World

War, tasks such as sewing sandbags for the front lines and the old Victorian task of picking oakum were employed to keep soldiers busy.

The First World War

The First World War was the most significant period in York Castle's history as a military prison. During this time, conscientious objectors were held at York Castle alongside the military prisoners. However, we also see one of the darkest times in the castle's history with the 'alien problem' of 1914.

'The Alien Problem': 1914

As a military prison, it appears reasonable that, early on in the war, York Castle would be prepared to accept prisoners of war; in fact, tents were added to the Eye of York to accommodate the influx of people into the castle.[5] Another inevitability was that the people living in York who were classed as German would end up paying the price for the ongoing war between Britain and Germany. With patriotic fervour running throughout the country, this was inevitable; however, what happened next was quite extreme. These tents on the Eye of York wouldn't initially house the prisoners they intended; rather, York Castle would become the temporary home for those Germans (and Austrians) living in Yorkshire. There was more patriotism than practicality around the decision, with the press proclaiming that York Castle could accommodate 40,000 people.[6] This was a clear exaggeration, and the report also misrepresented facts, such as the castle's origin, in a farcical manner.[7] However, the arrest and movement of Germans living in and around York started almost straight away.

Not every German would be brought here; instead, it was men of fighting age who were arrested to stop them from acting as enemy agents within Britain. Germans were required to report themselves under the 'Aliens Act'.[8] If they failed to do this or were suspected of espionage, they would also be sent to York Castle.[9] Soon, the newspapers would discuss 'Aliens in England'[10] or proclaim 'The Wholesale Arrests of Enemy Aliens'.[11] Soon, large numbers of prisoners would begin to arrive at York Castle. This was not unique to York Castle; other county gaols, such as Lancaster Castle, would also experience a similar phenomenon. Some would be brought to York Castle in small groups, but others were large, with fifty from Doncaster, fifty from Sheffield,[12] thirty-nine from Hartlepool, and another fifty from Bradford.[13] In Middlesbrough, they arrested

> all German subjects resident in the town who have previously served in the German Army or Navy, it being considered that all Germans not exempt from military service should be taken care of.[14]

They were all brought to York Castle, often arriving by train, and these prisoners would be marched across York from the train station under armed guard.[15] One paper describes them as 'to be of varying social station, some of them well-to-do persons in commercial life, while others were artisans, and some of them labourers'.[16] Officially, they were prisoners of war, but in reality, most were civilians. This was being viewed in the English papers even as an act of generosity, with one paper reporting 'the German band which has been staying in Whitby this season has taken up its winter abode at York Castle. Another example of English generosity'.[17] I'm not sure that the Germans would have considered this quite so generous.

In Hartlepool, *Herr* Emil Peter, the German Consul, was detained and brought to York Castle.[18] In York itself, Mr Schumacher was arrested, a man in his sixties who had served as a Prussian artilleryman and received the Iron Cross for valour in 1870 for 'continuing to serve a gun after all his comrades had been killed or disabled'.[19] Schumacher had an English wife and a son serving in the Royal Garrison Artillery.[20] These connections didn't matter, and he was arrested as he got onto a tram in Acomb and brought to York Castle. Others included employees of Selby's Olympia Oil and Cake Mills, the manager Julius Koch, and Herbert Lindenberg, who was a superintendent at the Ardol factory in Selby.[21] Eight coal miners were brought from Market Weighton, who were drilling for coal as part of the International Boring Company.[22] By 24 August 1914, 130 German civilians were living at York Castle.[23] By 27 August, this had increased to 160. The patriotic fervour was exemplified by the comments of the *York Herald*, which complained that these people were allowed to keep their property and were not given any labour to do while the British held abroad were treated in a 'shabby and almost brutal manner'.[24] However, these men and women were not being held in the buildings but in what can only be described as a makeshift internment camp on the Eye of York.

The *York Herald* continued to stir up tensions by denying that these interred received fuller rations than British soldiers and denying that prisoners had been shot for attempting to pollute the York water supply.[25] Both seem ridiculous, but denying them raised questions in the reader's mind.

We can learn about how these individuals spent their time at York Castle by consulting certain newspapers:

> Part of their recreation at York has been the privilege of playing football, but this has had to be forbidden owing to abuse. After a while, it was found that the ball was being purposely kicked over the fence, and a little over-fondness for fetching the ball was shown by the prisoners.[26]

The guards inform us that many of these men had no secret desire to join the fighting, and that there were 'strange stories' of attempts to escape custody.[27] These stories can be viewed as British propaganda to justify these imprisonments. Still, it is easy to see how people believed that many of these men would want to go and fight, especially against a country that had just imprisoned them.

The process of internment of Germans of fighting age had an impact that was far wider than the men themselves. We read in the *Yorkshire Post* and *Leeds Intelligencer* on 14 September 1914 that the families of three miners arrested in Featherstone had been sent to the local workhouse. The removal of the men left these families without any means of support. Unfortunately, it is unknown if the plea for the Pontefract Board of Guardians to be responsible for their maintenance was successful, although it is suggested that an 'Exchequer grant for alien inmates' might be available to these families in some form.[28]

Thankfully, this situation on the Eye of York would not last long. Some of them, mainly Austrians and Hungarians from York, were released by the end of October.[29] A new order had been announced for those still at York Castle in early September. The prisoners began to be moved to other locations like the 'concentration camps'[30] at Strensall and another hastily built on Leeman Road, which would house many prisoners of war, including a transfer of 300 prisoners from Edinburgh Castle at the end of September 1914.[31] However, there is a hint that nine Germans of military age were brought from Wakefield to York Castle as late as the end of October 1914.[32]

Conditions were as good as expected from an improvised tented village. One of those interred said that 'the authorities did all they could to make things as easy as possible for them'.[33] One of these measures was allowing Reverend Father Hawkswell to enter the prison on Sundays to celebrate Mass for the German Catholics held there.[34]

In addition to these civilians, there are examples of some prisoners of war being brought to York Castle. York was not an official prisoner-of-war camp, but as a military prison, it was occasionally used. One of these occasions would be to house two German sailors from *U-41*. Two incidents in August and September 1915 involving the Q-ship *Baralong* are infamous in both Britain and Germany, with some still considering them war crimes. In the second of these incidents, two of the German sailors from *U-41* managed to get to a lifeboat. As a result, Petty Officer Godan and Oberleutnant zur See Iwan Crompton, who was seriously injured, were rescued. Returning to land on 29 September, the two were brought to land 'in a quiet manner, wearing only shirts and underpants, and sent to hospital'.[35] On 6 October, the two prisoners were taken to Plymouth, and on 6 November, they were brought to York Castle as prisoners of war. Their stay was not very long, and by 13 December 1915, they were taken to Dyffryn near Cardiff.

Conscientious Objectors

> The most difficult job he had ever to do was to visit a certain class of prisoner in the detention Barracks at York Castle. They were conscientious objectors … One of them said quite frankly, 'I can't be a soldier: I'm a Christian'.[36]

By early 1916, it was becoming apparent that voluntary enlistment in the army was not bringing enough men into the fight. The Derby scheme, where men signed up to be called up when needed, was only a limited success. On 27 January 1916, the Military Service Act introduced conscription to the British Army. For those who had not volunteered because of anti-war beliefs, this brought a huge problem. What would you do if you were forced to enlist in a war you disagree with on moral grounds?

Approximately 6 million men enlisted and served in the British forces during the First World War. But others, especially those with Quaker backgrounds, objected to this new enforced service. They fell into two groups: firstly, alternativists, those who would work in the medical corps, factories or other work of national importance but refused to fight. Second, there were absolutists, those who refused to participate in the war effort. Today, both groups are remembered under the term conscientious objector.

To be exempt from service, the individual had to raise their objection to military service, and then a local tribunal would decide whether their claim for exemption was valid. There were around 16,000 conscientious objectors in Britain, but refusing to do their part was a crime, and for nine men, that led them to be imprisoned at York Castle. Five of these men would fall into a category with a history of being imprisoned at York Castle – they were Quakers.[37]

It is helpful to remember once again that Britain was swept up in patriotic fervour during this period, and those opposed to the war were definitely in the minority. Even those in power, like York Quaker MP Arnold Rowntree, were berated by the press as 'Friends of Germany', with others suggesting that they should be 'all either interred or deported'.[38] Those who were not in uniform, especially those from groups known to be against fighting like the Independent Labour Party (not to be confused with the entirely different party we now know as the Labour Party) or the Quakers, would be branded as 'pro-German cowards', handed white feathers to shame them, with people encouraged to walk on the other side of the road to them.[39] Those even more extreme said, 'If you see or know any of these conscientious objectors, go and shoot 'em'.[40] Therefore, it should be remembered that being an objector was not the easy way out. It could be dangerous, and at the very least, it could easily lead to being shunned by society for not doing your duty. It was a dangerous belief and took serious conviction to stand by it.

The Military Service Act provided some relief to those with conscientious objections to fighting. Known as the conscience clause, it recognised the right of certain groups to opt out of military service.[41] It was stated that this would

> take the form of an exemption from combatant service only, or may be conditional on the applicant being engaged in some work which, in the opinion of the tribunal dealing with the case, is of national importance.[42]

On the surface, this appears to allow those with anti-war beliefs to be exempt, but a careful look brings us to the tribunal, which decides if you genuinely are a conscientious objector and what your war would look like. These tribunals had nothing to do with York Castle, and no one was sent to York Castle as a direct result of these tribunals. However, in one case in Doncaster, one member of the Society of Friends was exempted because he could trace his Quaker heritage back to one of the Quakers imprisoned at York Castle in 1796.[43]

Ultimately, many conscientious objectors would be assigned to a unit. They would then refuse to follow orders and end up in a military prison, just like any other soldier would if they repeatedly refused to follow orders. At this point, York Castle becomes a home for nine conscientious objectors. The following is the story of two conscientious objectors who spent time at York Castle.

William Arthur Cooper, Ronald Edward Pond: 1916

A Cambridge graduate, William Arthur Cooper (1883–1943) was the first Quaker to be brought to York Castle as a conscientious objector. This made him the first Quaker imprisoned at York Castle since the 'Lotherside Quakers' were imprisoned for non-payment of tythes in 1795/1796.[44] William was appointed as a mathematics teacher at Bootham School in 1916. When he was conscripted, he refused and was taken to a tribunal. This tribunal exempted him from combatant service due to his long-standing Quaker heritage, but William also refused this exemption.[45] In April 1916, he was first sent to Litchfield and then to York Castle, where he spent two weeks in detention, as he was deemed to be a soldier.[46] Here, we get glimpses of his life at York Castle. William would wear his military uniform, 'regarding it as my prison uniform'.[47] However, he refused to do anything regarded as war or military related. William refused to participate in drills involving a rifle, for which he was put in irons for a day, which was still legal for the military at this time.[48] This did not stop him from refusing to take part in military drills. Part of Williams' labour was to sew sandbags, but again, he refused as they were seen as part of war work since these bags would be sent to the front to construct trenches. William would, however, agree to pick oakum, although he notes that he would 'not ask what it was used for!'[49]

William was asked to join the Friends Ambulance Unit, but as an absolutist, he refused. This would see him return once again to Litchfield. Later, he took part in work of national importance at Wakefield and then joined the Rowntree's confectionery company in York as a power plant assistant. After the war, he returned to teaching at Bootham School. He left in 1930 to go to the Quaker school at Ackworth.

Also a Cambridge graduate, Ronald Edward Pond was court-martialled on 2 May 1916, and sentenced to fifty-six days of detention. He was brought to York Castle, 'where he was forced with some unnecessary violence into kaki, which he had felt obliged conscientiously to refuse, and he had not been allowed to use his civilian clothes since'.[50]

After the First World War, York Castle would continue to operate as a detention barracks until 1929. However, none of the stories are as unique as those that occurred during the First World War.

Chapter 13

York Castle, 1929 and Beyond

The Prison Commission sold the site of York Castle to the Yorkshire County Committee for £4,000 on 29 September 1932.[1] This cost would not be paid until 20 May 1934, generating interest and an eventual payment of £4,224 14 shillings 8 pence. However, this was not the site's final sale. In 1934, it was once again sold, this time to York Corporation for £8,000.[2] As part of this, the corporation wanted to finally demolish the 1835 prison wall to allow for the widening of the road near Clifford's Tower.

However, certain considerations had to be taken into account, as the assize sessions were still to be held in the courthouse. The Yorkshire County Committee spent £6,000 providing cell accommodation in the assize court, allowing the assizes to remain on the site. The solution they came up with was to convert the ground floor level of the south portion of the courthouse to house prisoners brought to the assize trials at York. It can be considered that this was the last significant modification on the site that constitutes a change to York Castle Prison. It would consist of a male officers' room, six night cells, six separate cells, eight open compartments, one lavatory for prisoners and one for male officers. For the women, it would include one night cell, one separate cell, five open compartments, one women's officers' room and one lavatory.[3]

Trials of serious criminal cases continue in the 1777 courthouse to this day. However, these are not the assize courts discussed throughout this book. The Courts Act 1971 restructured the British court system, and in 1972, the assize courts and quarter sessions were replaced by the newly created crown court. This keeps the legacy of justice at the site of York Castle going into the twenty-first century, where, if you commit a serious crime, you could still end up on trial at York Crown Court.

Trials at the courthouse might be the most commonly occurring legacy of York Castle's history, but it is not the only one. On rare occasions, the site still sees the proclamation of a new monarch. Whenever a new monarch

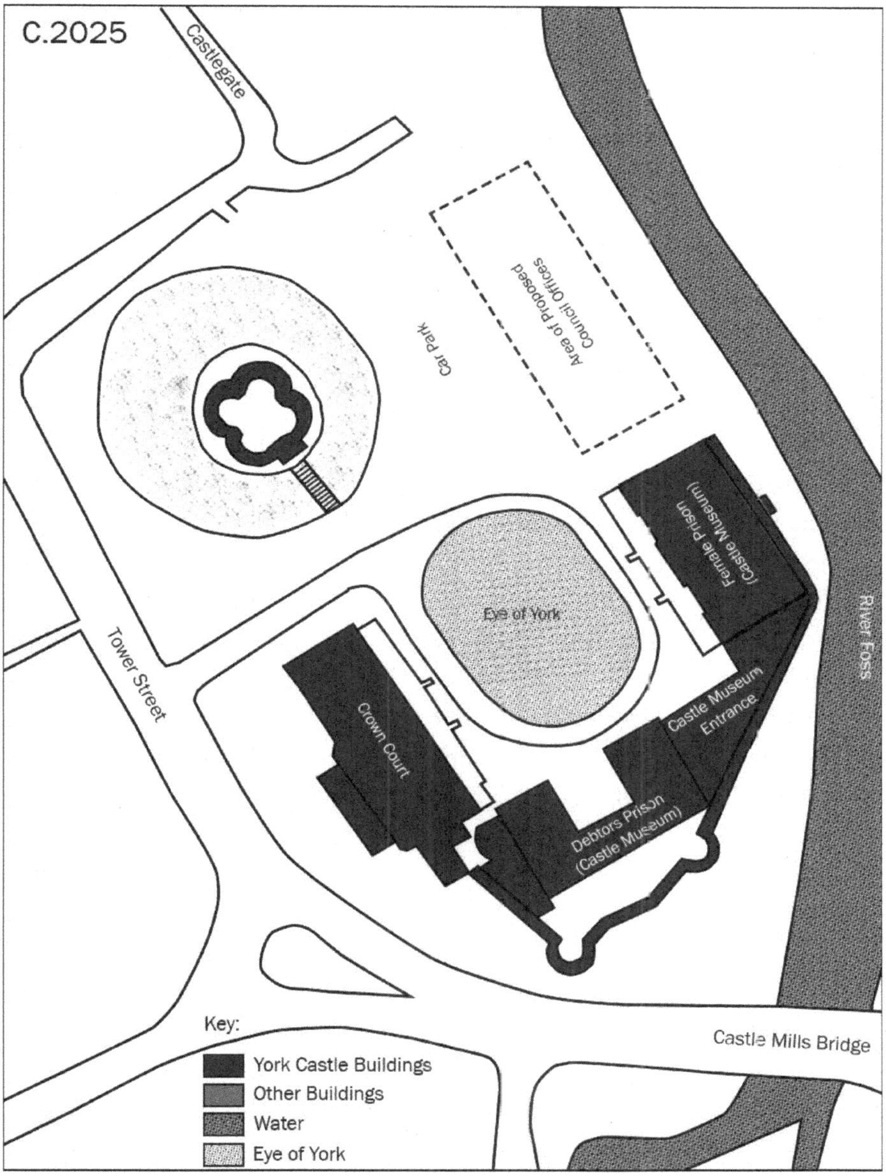

A plan of the site of York Castle as it stands today. Also note the area for the proposed council offices.[4]

came to the throne, they would be declared monarch on behalf of Yorkshire in the centre of the former castle, the political centre of the county. This tradition continued even when the site was within the prison; for example, King George V was declared on the site in 1910. Most recently, we saw the Proclamation of King Charles III on 11 September 2022 on the steps of the old female prison building. In a tradition that dates back to the ascension of King James I, the Eye of Ridings was where a new monarch would be proclaimed on behalf of Yorkshire; now, York Castle only holds this right for North Yorkshire. The other counties established under the 1972 Act, each have their own ceremonies on these rare occurrences.

Partial Demolition and the New Council Offices

The sale of the site, York Corporation's determination to widen Tower Street, and the financial burden placed on York Corporation by the forced purchase of the site led to an almost inevitable decision to demolish the parts of York Castle added in 1835. As a result, the demolition would open up the area around Clifford's Tower, once again allowing the public easy access to the Eye of York.

In April 1935, George Fort of Burnley won the tender to demolish the walls of York Castle and the felons' prison building. By December, he had the use of some land on Lower Dennis Street, opposite the castle, but on the other side of the river, to be used as a stone cutting yard for the next three years.[5]

The stone was used for several different projects. Some was used to strengthen the riverbank near Hungate, some was used to realign front garden walls when Stockton Lane was widened. Some was abandoned between Foss Islands Road and Navigation Road, and some was used to construct a pedestrian bridge on Landing Lane.[6] More was used to add new buildings to Leeds Grammar School.[7]

The question remained over what to do with the site after the demolition work had been completed. The plan was not always to keep the area around Clifford's Tower as open as it is today. By the 1930s, York Corporation now owned the land of the former castle, except for the court, which the Yorkshire committee managed, and Clifford's Tower, which HM Office of Works owned. The female prison building was to be retained, as it served as a counterpart to John Carr's courthouse.[8] The debtors' prison's future was less certain, but this would ultimately also be preserved. To the east of the tower, where the 1835 felons' prison once stood, York Corporation intended to build new council offices in keeping with the style of the existing prison buildings. The debtors' prison was being used temporarily for this purpose until the new construction was complete.

In 1935, an architectural competition was published to obtain potential designs for the new structure. It was to house the Education Department, the Public Health Department, the City Treasurer's Department, the City Engineer's Department and the Public Assistance Department, as well as Maternity and Child Welfare, School Clinics and a Tuberculosis Dispensary. Donald McMorran submitted the winning design, which consisted of two buildings.

Construction of the foundations for these new buildings began in 1939; however, the outbreak of the Second World War halted construction early. Unfortunately, the construction of these foundations likely destroyed any potential archaeology from the 1835 buildings and probably destroyed some of the graves of prisoners who had been buried in the area.

These foundations were roofed over and used by the Civil Defence League during the Second World War, a role they continued to play until October 1968.[9] Further discussions had involved turning the site into a cultural centre with an art gallery where the council offices were supposed to be located, a concert hall on Tower Street immediately north of Clifford's Tower, and municipal offices finally being built across the road to the west of Clifford's Tower.[10] However, these ideas never progressed beyond the discussion stage.

Creation of the Castle Museum

The most significant impact on the former site of York Castle Prison must be the creation of York Castle Museum, turning the remaining prison buildings into a tourist attraction. The opportunity for this change arose from an advertisement placed in the museum's *Journal* in 1932 by a local collector from Pickering, John Lamplugh Kirk. Kirk was a general practitioner in the Pickering area, but after witnessing the way of life he had grown up with in the 1870s beginning to disappear, he made it his life's work to collect and preserve objects from the late Victorian period. His collection had grown into a unique record of the period, filling his home. Dr Kirk had already begun a museum in Pickering. However, this building was not suitable for the long-term preservation of his collection, so he posted the advertisement to see if any town or city would take his collection to create a museum.

What resulted was a unique social history museum housed within the former female prison building of York Castle Prison. It included what Kirk termed the 'Museum of the Future', Britain's first recreated Victorian street, which he named 'Kirkgate'. However, 'recreated' is not quite the right word, as everything, including the buildings themselves, was saved from destruction by Dr Kirk's actions. This meant that the recreated street consisted of real buildings and shop fronts, filled with real objects from Dr Kirk's collection. This first-of-its-kind tourist attraction grew, and in the 1950s, it incorporated the debtors' prison building into its displays. Today, within the debtors' prison, housed in the old felons' cells on the ground floor, the museum has created a display commemorating the history of the site as York Castle Prison, ensuring that the stories of those who were held and worked here are not forgotten.

Sadly, though, for all the foresight Dr Kirk had in creating the Museum, this did not extend to preserving much of the female prison building. Along with the modifications to the debtors' building made by the military, there is very little to be seen of the prison once inside the Museum. However, if you know where to look, you can still see some small clues to the site's past as a prison. Amongst these, you can still see the graffiti left in the old felons' exercise yard of the debtors' prison. The original 1835 black gates and the coat of arms of King William IV were saved from demolition and placed on Kirkgate. Close by, you can see one of the chapel windows and the execution bell. A padded cell survives, looking conspicuously out of place along the Victorian street. On the outside of the building, you can find the large, now white, doors that created the 'last drop' where nine men were executed.

Who knows what the site's future will look like? Hopefully, York Castle Museum and Clifford's Tower will continue to thrive for many years to come, keeping the site's story alive. The courthouse appears to continue its centuries-old role as a centre of justice on the site for the foreseeable future. However, the former site of the 1835 buildings, currently used as a car park, is constantly being replanned to create a much more inviting space for people to enjoy. What form this will take is still uncertain, but hopefully, it will inspire people's interest in the stories of those who lived and died on the site throughout its history.

Appendix I

Other Prisons/Gaols in York

York Gaol

Not to be confused with the county gaol, York had its own gaol for local crimes and minor debtors, as well as several other small prisons or gaols for various other parts of the legal system. The most commonly referred to of these was on Ouse Bridge, often called 'Kidcots'.[1] This housed local criminals who were to appear at the Petty or Quarter sessions, usually held in the guildhall. It also housed some debtors, and in 1711, the former gaoler of York Castle, Edward Hinchcliffe, found himself imprisoned here for debt after granting bail to a pregnant woman because there was nowhere suitable for her to give birth within York Castle.[2] It was likely that this would have been the second prison building on Ouse Bridge, which was demolished and was described as 'A Shameful place, even in 1724 when it was taken down'.[3] After being sentenced to be pressed at the York Assizes, Margaret Clitherow spent her last days at Ouse Bridge Gaol.

The gaol on Ouse Bridge was notoriously bad, small and unhealthy, and when the River Ouse flooded, the lower parts of the gaol would also flood. The extent of Ouse Bridge Gaol's poor condition can be seen when John Howard, the renowned prison reformer, who consistently offered suggestions for improving prisons, stated, 'This Gaol cannot be made a good one'.[4]

However, it would not be until 1807 that York got a new local prison. This was constructed on the former bailey area of York's second castle, just across the River Ouse from York Castle. It was a much larger building and served York well until 1838, when local prisoners were moved to York Castle.

Houses of Correction/Bridewells

Houses of correction, sometimes called Bridewells, were often used to lock away people for misdemeanours. Houses of correction were established under the 1576 Poor Act,[5] but they took off with the Elizabethan Poor Law 1601.

They were designed to house people 'unwilling to work'. However, justices of the peace often used them to house petty offenders and vagrants. These were short-term facilities, and two-thirds of prisoners were released within two weeks.[6] Bridewells were employed as reformative corrective institutions and were sometimes mistaken for workhouses. However, it is important not to confuse houses of correction with the parish workhouses that began to appear all over the country from the early 1720s. These latter institutions were primarily for poor relief, with paupers usually applying to get into them rather than being committed there against their will.[7] The definition of those placed in a house of correction would be clarified again in 1823 as 'idle and disorderly Persons, Rogues and Vagabonds, incorrigible Rogues and other Vagrants'.[8]

There were three locations where the house of correction stood in York.

York City Bridewell, St Anthony's Hall, Peasholme Green (1665–1814)

Strangely, the only former house of correction that still survives today is the oldest. In 1665, York Corporation converted part of St Anthony's Hall on Peaseholme Green into a house of correction.[9]

In 1809, the prison reformer James Nield describes it as follows:

> Here are three spacious day-rooms; one for men and the other two for women-prisoners, with a fire-place in each. Over the women's room is the infirmary, which is light and well ventilated. Detached from this building are seven sleeping-cells, of about 6 feet square, and 7 feet high; two of which are totally dark, and the other five nearly so … The employment here is spinning, and making laces; and they receive all they earn: The men pound tile -shards, for which the Keeper pays them four pence per bushel, and then sells the dust at from ten-pence a bushel to one shilling …[10]

In 1705, York Corporation established the Blue Coat School on the first floor of the building directly above the house of correction. This was a charity school for poor and orphaned boys. After the house of correction was relocated, the Blue Coat School took over the entire building and expanded it to include all the buildings that still stand today.[11]

York City House of Correction, Toft Green (1814–1838)

In 1814, York House of Correction was moved to a purpose-built building on Toft Green. Little is known about this building apart from its octagonal plan. To the best of our knowledge, no pictures of the building have survived. It garnered praise from the prison reformer Elizabeth Fry, who described it as 'Conspicuously excellent'.[12] It was eventually removed for the construction of York's first railway station.

York New City House of Correction, Baile Hill (1838–1869)

In 1838, the York House of Correction moved again. It would take over the New City Gaol building on Baile Hill. Once again, few images of the building remain.

The building was demolished in 1878 as part of the project to construct Skeldergate Bridge, which opened in 1880.[13]

The Prison Act 1865 had amalgamated these houses of correction with county gaols to form 'an institution called a prison'.[14] This change resulted in the prisoners at the house of correction being transferred to York Castle Prison, where the city's prisoners had been held since 1838.[15] Due to this amalgamation, it can be argued that the houses of correction are the predecessors of today's prison system.[16]

These cover the main prisons in York outside of the York Castle Prison, but a few others are worth mentioning.

St Peter's and St Mary's

It should be remembered that the mayor or the sheriff did not control everything within the City of York. Important religious sites often held control over their land, and with that came the establishment of prisons. The Dean of York Minster had its own prison just near the minster. This was a relatively small facility, consisting of six rooms: four for debtors and two for prisoners.[17] It is described in 1777 by John Howard as 'All out of repair, dirty and offensive: no court-yard: no sewers. No allowance.'[18] The building was in use until 1837.[19] However, York Minster still has its own police force to this day, established by Jonathan Martin after a fire started in 1829.

Another prison associated with the church was St Mary's Lodge, located within the grounds of St Mary's Abbey, now home to the Museum Gardens.

The Abbot of St Mary's mainly used it for 'ill-disciplined or ill-conducted monks'.[20]

Monk Bar

Monk Bar was a prison from 1577, but relatively little is known about this, except that it was used to house freemen of the City of York.[21]

Forest Prison

Established to apply 'forest law' over the area of Galtres Forest, this would prohibit unauthorised hunting, felling trees or even collecting firewood from within the royal forest.[22] Those accused of these very specific crimes would be brought to a special prison at Davy Hall on Davygate in York. The back wall of this building still stands today.

There are undoubtedly other places or buildings within York that have held prisoners at one time or another; this is not intended to be an exhaustive list, but rather to provide some context for other prisons that may have been associated with the stories of York Castle Prison in some way.

Appendix II

Execution Sites in York

Execution is something that seems to fascinate most people when they think about it, either from morbid curiosity or the seemingly alien nature of the punishment in modern society. That fascination is something that has always occurred and often drew large crowds for public executions until 1868, where 'Crowds collected at the old bailey and elsewhere, as they had done from time immemorial, to see an unfortunate wretch turned off'. For York, like every historic city and town in the UK, the execution was part of the way of life, with some 564 people recorded to have been beheaded or hanged in York between 1370 and 1879.[1] This figure is likely higher, as records are only from the assize courts, excluding ecclesiastical records, and some of the records are undoubtedly lost to the mists of time.

Yet the locations of these execution sites were not always consistent and moved throughout history. The following is an account of the most important known locations.

Micklegate Without

'The Three-Legged Mare of York', as it became known, was the longest-serving and most widely used execution site in York. It had several names throughout the years, the Three-Legged Mare, Ainsty Gallows, York Tyburn or Micklegate Without, referring to its location just over a mile outside of York from Micklegate Bar.

Located on Tadcaster Road just opposite Little Hob Moor on the side of the Knavesmire, which is now York Racecourse, the site was first used for the execution of Edward Hewison in 1379. The decision to build the gallows here was also apparently made at York Castle.[2] However, it should be noted that the 'Ainsty Gallows' were probably located not too far from here, in Dringhouses, before the new construction.[3]

The design of the Three-Legged Mare was based on the design of the Tyburn Gallows in London, and therefore it was also referred to as York's

Tyburn. It comprised three thick pieces of wood, forming a triangular shape held about three metres off the ground by another thick piece of wood in each corner – hence the 'three-legged mare', or in London, the 'triple tree'. The size of the three-legged mare meant that multiple executions could take place at the same time. The bloodiest day in Yorkshire's history took place here on 30 April 1649, when twenty-one people were executed on the same day.[4] However, not all of these were hangings on the three-legged mare, as this was also the site of executions by burning until 1776.

In 1802, the site of York gallows would be moved: 'Thus will be removed from one of the principal roads leading to the city that disagreeable nuisance, the gallows'.[5] But the synergy of the first and last executions here is an interesting side note. The first execution was that of Edward Hewison in 1379, and the last was that of Edward Hughes in 1801; however, the similarities extend beyond similar-sounding names. Edward Hewison was aged 20, a private soldier in the Earl of Northumberland's Light Horse, and was executed for the rape of Louisa Bentley. Over 400 years later, Edward Hughes, aged 19, a private soldier of 18th Light Dragoons, was executed there for the rape of Mary Brown, bookending the use of the site with the same crime by men of the same occupation, of a similar age, with similar-sounding names. Sometimes, history is interesting in how it brings these little synergies to life.

Before moving on to the new gallows that replaced Micklegate Without, it is worth noting that there was a second, albeit less used, set of gallows located at what was known as Walmgate Without, also referred to as the Gallows of St Leonard, Green Dykes. It was located near the corner of Green Dykes Lane and Thief Lane on what is referred to as Garrow Hill, probably a corruption of Gallows Hill because of the site's history. This is very close to the modern-day site of the University of York.

The site was never utilised as extensively, and it is unclear what factors led to the decision to use a particular gallows at any given time. It was last used in 1676 to execute Rook and Gaskill, but stood unused for nearly a quarter of a century. It was not until 1700 that the grand jury finally decided to remove these gallows.[6] The structure was finally demolished on 3 June 1700.

The New Drop

By the late 1700s, York was already considering the impression it gave to visitors to the city, and it was perceived that the three-legged mare at the

Knavesmire was creating a bad impression.[7] Alongside this were the logistical and security problems posed by moving the condemned through the city to the place of execution. Consequently, the gallows moved to the 'new drop' just outside York Castle Prison, near the back of the court, after 1801. Without a long and potentially unruly procession, alongside the mechanised 'new drop' system, it was hoped that the execution process would become more regulated. This had already been successfully achieved in London, with the relocation from Tyburn to just outside Newgate Prison in 1783.

The new gallows were not a permanent landscape feature like the three-legged mare had been. This new structure was designed to be taken down and stored between uses. It would begin to be constructed between 4.00 and 5.00 am on the morning of the execution. One newspaper reports that

> the hollow sound of the booming timbers being audible as they were adjusted to their proper positions in this fearful machine of death, added no little, as may well be imagined, to the solemn awe which usually attaches to the environs of York Castle upon such occasions as the present.[8]

Between executions, it was stored in a room known as the lumber room.[9] However, it is unclear where this was within the castle buildings. This constant rebuilding meant that modifications occurred throughout the period during which these gallows were in use. For the executions of the Luddites, the scaffolding was modified 'so that all the body was visible when they were suspended; in former executions only the feet and head could be seen by the spectators'.[10] Later on, 'the gallows was draped round with black cloth, so that when the drop fell, not even the head of the culprit could be seen',[11] protecting the crowd from that same scene.

Joseph Halfpenny, a joiner from Blake Street in York, constructed the Gallows themselves. This was different from the three-legged mare used at previous execution sites. The new drop consisted of a raised platform with a trap door in it, and a wooden beam running above the trap door, held up by another timber at each end. This design allowed for a short drop, enabling the rope to tighten tightly around the condemned's neck, thereby speeding up their demise. With the older three-legged mare, the condemned would either be placed on a cart that would move away or led up a ladder that would be removed after the noose was placed around the neck of the condemned. Either way, this would usually lead to a prolonged death. The new 'short drop' method would reduce the torment of the condemned to just a few minutes.

The Last Drop

After public execution was abolished in 1868, the gallows had to be moved within the prison to allow a more private end for the condemned. The location chosen for this was the northern wing of the female prison building. This area was already being used to house the condemned before execution, and placing the gallows next door facilitated a swift and efficient execution process.

The gallows themselves were of a 'Balcony drop' design. The structure was stored in the execution room and installed into place as needed, a scenario that was less frequently happening by this period. The platform was over six feet off the ground, allowing for a longer drop than on the 'new drop', but this was not always a long drop hanging. The first execution to take place here in 1874 was carried out by York's last executioner, Thomas Askern, probably using the methods with which he was familiar. Long-drop hanging would be brought to York Castle in 1878 by the famous executioner William Marwood.

Long-drop hanging was very different from what came before. Now, the rope did not end with a traditional noose knot. Instead, it had a metal loop that the rope fed through to create the noose. This would be placed over the left shoulder so when the condemned fell; the rope would end under their chin, tightening rapidly while pushing their head back and breaking their neck in what was deemed to be instant death. A far cry from the prolonged public executions of the past.

It was here that the last nine executions in York took place. The doors where these executions took place can still be seen on the outside of the female prison building to this day.

Other Execution Sites

So far, we have covered the major execution sites in York, but some others were only rarely used, and are still worth mentioning.

After the construction of the New City Gaol for York, it appears those that committed crimes that carried the death penalty within the City of York would be executed, not at the 'new drop', but over the river at a gallows just outside of New City Gaol, sometimes referred to as Baile Hill, after the second Castle of York that once occupied the space. There are only two executions that are known to have happened here. David Anderson was executed here in 1809 for uttering bad notes, and William Brown, alias Morley Stubbs, was executed here in 1821 for robbery.[12]

Until the erection of York Tyburn in 1379, it appeared that the 'gallows of the abbot of St Marys', i.e. ecclesiastical law within York, was carried out on Clifton Ings.[13] There is also a reference to an Archiepiscopal Scaffold on Foss Bridge.[14] As previously mentioned, it was rare later on for an ecclesiastical court to sentence anyone to death, hence the wide abuse of the benefit of the clergy. Still, when someone was condemned to death by the church courts, these two sites appear to have been the ones used.

Finally, we have the only time that an execution took place on pavement outside of All Saints' Church. In 1572, Thomas Percy, the Earl of Northumberland, was beheaded at this location. The choice of this location was a combination of the unusual use of beheading as a form of execution and the desire for a very public spectacle because of his role in the Rising of the North.

There is a suggestion of Robert Aske being executed at York Castle itself, being hanged in chains from the front of Clifford's Tower. However, there is a question over whether he was executed like this or, as 'hung in chains' often refers to, his body was displayed here after execution.

Appendix III

Escape Attempts

No one wants to be incarcerated somewhere like York Castle Prison, and for some, the seemingly inevitable outcome of a trial outweighs any risks associated with escaping justice. As a result, escapes appear to have occurred frequently throughout York Castle Prison's history. What follows is the most complete list I can compile, but it is almost certain that other examples will come to light in the future.[1]

1292

Alan de Ellerbek was convicted, sentenced to hang, allowed to escape and sought sanctuary.[2]

1298

Twenty-six prisoners escaped from the castle, and John de Byroum, the sheriff, sought the King's Pardon, which was obtained because 'of his many cares and occupations at that time, and his diligent pursuit of the fugitives'.[3]

1304

Robert de cottingwyth, John Le Furbisour, Alexander Heroun, Henry Fairhert, William de Saxton and William de Fleccher escaped. Also escaped was the Scottish William de Vispont, who was taken prisoner at the battle of Dunbar (1296). The sheriff was once again pardoned as his pursuit 'caused some to be beheaded and others to be brought back to gaol'.[4]

1324

John de Castello, a rebel, escaped. The pursuit of the prisoner ended when he was beheaded at Kyngslane, Hereford, after pursuit by hue and cry.[5]

1570

Thomas Wilson, alias Mountain attempted an ultimately unsuccessful escape while awaiting execution. He

> made a hole through a brick-and-a-half partition, large enough for him to pass into the chapel gallery, from which he astonishingly ascended into another ten feet above, with fetters weighing nearly fifty pounds, and so formed as not to permit one foot to step six inches before the other. Here he broke through a plaster partition, and thus got over the brick ceiling of all the cells, and immediately under the roof of all the buildings, where he was overheard and soon secured.[6]

He was executed on 30 July 1570.

1586

Brian Stapleton, a Catholic School teacher, escaped. He was also present and escaped again during the raid on Margaret Clitherow's house.[7]

1726

Abraham Key was suspected, with Robert Bingley, of being a highwayman and not giving security for his appearance at the next assizes, committed to gaol 23 May 1724; reprieved in the summer of 1725. He escaped from York Castle in March 1726. The reward notice described him as

> a broad, well set Person, somewhat less than the middle Size, with a brown Coat, and a little stammering in his speech, flat Nos'd, the End of it turns up, in a light colour'd Wig, comes out of the Bishoprick of Durham.
>
> *London Gazette*, 6466,
> 5 April 1726

Presumably, he was recaptured as his name appeared on a bread petition at York Castle in 1728.

1726

Charles Walton was in gaol for stealing two cows: one belonging to Thomas Dobson and another belonging to Thomas Billings, both of Heighington, Durham. He was sentenced to transportation for seven years at the Lent assizes in 1725. He escaped while still at York Castle in March 1726. The reward notice described him as having

> black hair, pretty thick, a brown Coat, also a Drab-Coloured one along with him, he talks Devonshire Speech, his Eyes squinting a little, and of a dullish Complexion, going in a little with his Toes.

It is not known if he was ever recaptured.

1730

Joseph Askwith, Richard Freeman and John Freeman were on trial for the highway robbery of Matthew Wilks. They were tried at Yorkshire Assizes summer 1730 and marked in gaol book as reprieved. They may have been hanged the following December after an escape attempt.

1732

April 1732 saw what could be argued as the most significant escape in the history of York Castle Prison. Twenty-one felons escaped as the turnkey came to lock the door to those prisoners awaiting transportation, they rushed the turnkey, overpowering him, fleeing through the fence in the central courtyard and escaping. Although some seventeen of these prisoners were recaptured, it prompted significant changes to how the felons' cells were structured. Instead of the series of large rooms that had existed since the prison had been built, these were broken down into smaller sleeping cells. The idea was that it was easier for the turnkeys to manage smaller numbers of prisoners at a time. This escape also prompted the erection of a second fence at the front of the central exercise yard to make escape a little bit tougher.

This escape forced gaoler Richard Woodhouse to pay for their recapture, arousing suspicions that he might have been bribed to allow the escape.

One of those who escaped was James Willas/James Willis of Doncaster. He had been committed to gaol in September 1731 for breaking and entering the dwelling house of Lady Hustler of Acklam and stealing two purses full of gold, and into the dwelling house of John Adamson and Anne Adamson of Kirklevington and stealing a sum of money and household items with violence. He had previously escaped York Castle on 19 November 1731.

Of those recaptured, ten were hanged, including Willas. His wanted notice for the November 1731 escape describes him as 'James Willas, a Felon, late of Doncaster, a broad well-set Man, black down-looking Complexion, middle-siz'd, pock-ared, wears a black Wig'.

1746

The Jacobites, one of the largest groups of prisoners to be held at York Castle, also had two notable escapees:

> George Mills, who was ordered to be transported in 1748, escaped on 16 August 1747. This was during the Assizes, when the castle's outer gates were always kept open. The Turnkey allowed Mills to leave his place of confinement so that he could drink with a discharged fellow prisoner in the debtors' prison. However, instead of going there, he got behind a coach leaving the castle. Since he had recently acquired a new coat, he passed through the outer gates without being molested by the porter. A reward of ten guineas was offered, and adverts were placed in the York press, but to no avail. The Gaoler claimed he rode one hundred miles in a fruitless search for Mills.[8]

The second escape was by William Fraser (Farrier). However, the specifics of this escape are not clear.

1761

Prisoners of war: of the 121 prisoners of war held at York Castle Prison during the Seven Years' War, 20 would escape on 27 October 1761. William Hargrove describes it as follows:

> Some of them cut away the iron bars of the windows, during the night; and before any discovery, twenty of them escaped over the walls, by means of a rope, and though six were afterwards secured, the remaining fourteen were never more heard of.[9]

This raises significant questions, such as how they managed to cut through the bars and exactly where they obtained the rope. We may never know the answer to these questions, but this remains an intriguing story.

1761

George Harger: murder of John Moore at Southowram, near Halifax. In September 1761, Harger attempted to dig his way out of York Castle; he was found several yards underground, having dug so far with only a knife and a shoemaker's hammer; he was afterwards chained to a wall with his accomplices: John Wilson, William Andrews and George Cox. George Harger was executed on Thursday, 18 March 1762; his body was given to surgeons for dissection.[10]

1765

Thwarted by the debtors: perhaps the most fascinating escape attempt in the history of York Castle Prison is one that failed. On Tuesday, 9 April 1765, several felons attempted to get out of York Castle Prison only to be stopped by the debtors. Once again, William Hargrove gives us details on the events:

> About seven o'clock in the evening, whilst the under-jailer and turnkey were locking the felons in their cell, they were seized by the latter, and after much struggling, the felons succeeded in forcing them into a cell, in taking the keys from them, and in securing them there. They hastened to the porter's lodge, demanded the keys of the outer gates from the porter, and on his refusal, knocked him down, and treated him in a very brutal manner. Mr Wharton, the governor, was also secured by the felons; but an alarm being given to the debtors, they rescued him, and proceeded to the lodge, which had been entered by three of the felons, who had fastened the doors, and were scuffling with the porter and his wife for the keys. One of the debtors, however, entered by the window, and the felons then opened the doors, and retreated within the grates, where they were all secured. The under-jailer's leg was broken, and many of the parties were severely bruised. The debtors, who thus prevented the escape, were rewarded by a general subscription in the city.[11]

This escape attempt shows us the violence that some of these criminals were willing to inflict to avoid having to stand trial. They risked more serious punishment, and even death, for attempting to escape. However, it is difficult to trace these men as no names are given; nonetheless, no one is executed in relation to the escape, suggesting that these men appear to have gotten away lightly with this attempt. This case also shows us the dog-eat-dog world of the prison. The debtors' prospects improve dramatically if they help the gaoler and his men. Therefore, they put themselves in potential danger to stop the attempt. It also sounds like the porter's wife was not someone that you wanted to mess with, getting stuck into the fight with the felons.

1769

Some never even made it to York Castle Prison. Jonathan Catrill, who was being brought to York from Barnsley on suspicion of horse theft, escaped along with two others on Tadcaster Moor. He is described as

> about 27 years of age, has a black or swarthy complexion, and black short hair … is about 5 foot 5 inches high; had on when escaped, a little bound hat with a loop and button behind, a black neckcloth about his neck, a dark grey Frize Riding Coat, a blue grey Coat, with a green velvet neck, a red shag waistcoat with whitish buttons and red spots in the middle of 'em, a pair of dirty Leather Breeches with straps at the knees, but without Knee-buckles, a pair of dark-colour'd seamed stockings, and large silver or plated Buckles.[12]

It was advertised that anyone who apprehended them would be 'suitably rewarded for their trouble', but the lack of any evidence of a future trial suggests that they were never caught.

1785

John Edwards: in gaol for Highway robbery (along with John Beck) of William Sutherland of Rookby on 5 December 1784. He escaped from York Castle on 31 Jul 1785 along with Richard Crosby, another condemned prisoner, and was never heard of again.

1823

On the evening of Wednesday, 5 June 1822, Robert Gill, aged 55, James Ramsden, aged 26, and Joseph Fisher Brown, age not recorded, escaped:

'By forcibly breaking open the Doors of the Gaol by means of Iron Bars taken from a Fire Range ...'[13] The gaoler offered a reward of £15 for James Ramden and £10 was offered for the capture of the other two men. At least two of the men were recaptured. Ramsden and Gill were executed on 12 April 1823.[14]

17 August 1824

George Dickens and William Roberts Soly on bread & water 7 days each for attempting to Escape from York Castle.[15]

7 November 1824

'John Watson put in duble Irons for escaping from York Castle'.[16]

28 December 1824

'William Reed put in Irons for Escaping from Prison. Charles Holt put in Irons for Escaping from Prison.'[17]

February 1827

'William Atha and Benjamin Williamson Soly 2 days and Ironed for attempting to Esc from Prison The Revd. D.C. Currer order Irons to be continued'.[18]

1829

John Foulds, Alexander Burn, James Wood, Simon Hargreaves, John Mitchell, John Toppin, William Brewer, Edward Hamilton, George Cullingworth and William Parker, all awaiting transportation were put into close confinement for three days 'for attempting to make their escape from Gaol, by making a hole through the Wall of Half Moon Yard'.[19] Foulds, Hargreaves, Hamilton and Burn would additionally be put into irons because of the escape attempt.

Given that six of these convicts left graffiti carved into the wall of Half-Moon Court, which can still be seen today, it is possible that, in this case, 'making a hole', was in fact them carving their names and their punishment was the result of an overzealous gaoler punishing them in the most extreme way he could.

31 March 1832

'Thomas Hain a felon Soly three days for attempting to Escape from the New Prison'.[20]

27 July 1833

'John Fox Soly three days for attempting to escape from prison by undermining the boundary wall of the Large Room Day Yard'.[21]

9 January 1834

Margaret Peckett's escape in 1834 was unusual. First, we have her creative escape method:

> On Mrs. Holgate's [the matron] entering this cell on the morning in question, Margaret complained bitterly of having her rest destroyed by rats; and said, if a dog were brought, she would soon convince the matron that the cell swarmed with these vermin. After a short time, Mrs. H. returned with a dog and an assistant, and the task of rat-hunting was commenced. While they were thus engaged, Margaret contrived to lay her hands upon a shawl and bonnet which were in the room, and slipped out at the door, which she secured, making prisoners of the matron and her assistant. She then, habited in the bonnet and shawl, walked deliberately across the yard; and the porter, taking her for one of the debtor's wives, suffered her to pass without inquiry. She immediately proceeded to Hull ...[22]

A £10 reward was offered for her recapture, and soon she was back at York Castle Prison.

The second interesting part of this is that the entries on this list before and after Margaret Peckett's escape are listed in the *Gaoler's Journal*. Margaret Peckett is conspicuous in her absence from this official document. Her escape was possibly recorded in the *Matron's Journal* that has since disappeared, but other events regarding female prisoners are mentioned in the *Gaoler's Journal*, making this omission unusual. The careful reader might also notice that Margaret is the only woman on this list, suggesting that more female escapes might still be waiting to be uncovered.

27 November 1835

'John William Smith Soly three days on bread & water for assisting to make a rope and two keys for the purpose of effecting his escape from prison'.[23]

1 December 1835

'William Wilson and George Hainsworth Soly one day for making a rope and two keys for the purpose of effecting their escape from prison'.[24]

1839

James Coates was a resident of York Castle since 1835. He had avoided being transported to Australia by agreeing to become the executioner for York. However, on 27 November 1839 he made his escape from York Castle Prison alongside two other men. The other two men were recaptured, but Coates was never heard from again.

19 June 1854

'James Diggles, a debtor, made his escape. Supposed to have disguised himself and passed the porter. I have telegraphed to Hull and I sent a man to that place, also to Bradford, Leeds and Liverpool.'[25]

Appendix IV

Selected Works of James Montgomery While imprisoned at York Castle

The Pleasures of Imprisonment, James Montgomery, 1796

You ask, my friend, and well you may,
You ask me, how I spend the day;
I'll tell you, in unstudied rhyme,
How wisely I befool my time:
Expect not wit, nor fancy then,
In this effusion of my pen;
These idle lines – they might be worse –
Are simple prose, in simple verse.

Each morning, then, at five o'clock,
The adamantine doors unlock;
Bolts, bars, and portals crash and thunder;
The gates of iron burst asunder;
Hinges that creak, and keys that jingle,
With clattering chains, in concert mingle:
So sweet the din, your dainty ear,
For joy, would break its drum to hear;
While my dull organs, at the sound,
Rest in tranquillity profound!
Fantastic dreams amuse my brain,
And waft my spirit home again:
Though captive all day long, 'tis true,
At night I am as free as you;
Not ramparts high, nor dungeons deep,
Can hold me – when I'm fast asleep!

But every thing is good in season,
I dream at large – and wake in prison!
Yet think not, sir, I lie too late,
I rise as early even as eight:
Ten hours of drowsiness are plenty,
For any man, in four and twenty.
You smile – and yet 'tis nobly done,
I'm but five hours behind the sun!

When dressed, I to the yard repair,
And breakfast on the pure, fresh air;
But though this choice Castalian cheer
Keeps both the head and stomach clear,
For reasons strong enough with me
I mend the meal with toast and tea.
Now air and fame, as poets sing,
Are both the same, the self same thing;
Yet bards are not cameleons quite,
And heavenly food is very light:
Whoever dined or sapp'd on fame,
And went to bed upon a name?

Breakfast dispatched, I sometimes read,
To clear the vapours from my head:
For Books are magic charms, I ween,
Both for the crotchets and the spleen.
When genius, wisdom, wit abound,
Where sound is sense and sense is sound;
When art and nature both combine,
And live, and breathe, in every line;
The reader glows along the page,
With all the author's native rage!
But books there are with nothing fraught,
Ten thousand words and ne'er a thought!
Where periods without period crawl,
Like caterpillars on a wall,

That fall to climb, and climb to fall;
While still their efforts only tend
To keep them from their journey's end!
The readers yawn with pure vexation,
And nod – but not with approbation!
In such a fog of dulness lost,
Poor patience must give up the ghost;
Not Argus' eyes awake could keep;
Even Death might read himself to sleep!

At half past ten, or thereabout,
My eyes are all upon the scout,
To see the lounging post-boy come,
With letters or with news from home.
Believe it, on a captives word,
Although the doctrine seem absurd,
The paper messengers of friends
For absence almost make amends:
But if you think I jest or lie,
Come to York Castle, sir, and try.

Sometimes to fairy land I rove:
Those iron rails become a grove;
These stately buildings fall away
To moss-grown cottages of clay;
Debtors are changed to jolly swains,
Who pipe and whistle on the plains;
Yon felons grim, with fetters bound,
Are satyrs wild, with garlands crowned:
Their clanking chains are wreaths of flowers;
Their horrid cells ambrosial bowers;
The oaths, expiring on their tongues,
Are metamorphosed into songs;
While wretched female prisoners, lo!
Are Dian's nymphs of virgin snow!
Those hideous walls with verdure shoot;

These pillars bend with blushing fruit;
That dunghill swells into a mountain,
And, lo! the pump becomes a fountain;
The noisome smoke of yonder mills,
The circling air with fragrance fills;
Yon horse-pond spreads into a lake,
And swans of ducks and geese I make!
Sparrows are changed to turtle-doves,
That bill and coo their pretty loves;
Wagtails, turn'd thrushes, charm the vales,
And tomtits sing like nightingales!
No more the wind through key-holes whistles,
But sighs on beds of pinks and thistles;
The rattling rain, that beats without,
And gargles down the leaden spout,
In light, delicious dew distills,
And melts away in amber rills;
Elysium rises on the green,
And health and beauty crown the scene.

Then by th' enchantress Fancy led,
On violet banks I lay my head;
Legions of radiant forms arise,
In fair array, before mine eyes;
Poetic visions gild my brain,
Then melt in liquid air again!
As in a magic lantern clear,
Fantastic images appear,
That beaming from the spectred glass,
In beautiful succession pass;
Yet steal the luster of their light
From the deep shadow of the night:
Thus in the darkness of my head,
Ten thousand shining things are bred,
That borrow splendour from the gloom,
As glow-worms twinkle in a tomb!

But lest these glories should confound me,
Kind Dullness draws her curtain round me;
The visions vanish in a trice,
And I awake as cold as ice:
Nothing remains of all the vapour,
Save – what I send you – ink and paper!

Thus flow my morning hours along,
Smooth as the numbers of my song:
Yet let me ramble as I will,
I feel I am a prisoner still.
Thus Robin, with the blushing breast,
Is ravished from his little nest
By barbarous boys, who bind his leg,
To make him flutter round a peg:
See the glad captive spreads his wings,
Mounts, in a moment, mounts and sings,
When suddenly the cruel chain
Twitches him back to prison again.
– The clock strikes one – I can't delay,
For dinner comes but once a day;
At present, worthy friend, farewell;
But by to-morrow's post I'll tell,
How, during these half dozen moons,
I cheat the lazy afternoons.

EPISTLE II.

In this sweet place, where freedom reigns,
Secured by bolts and snug in chains;
Where innocence and guilt together
Roost like two turtles of a feather;
Where debtors safe at anchor lie,
From saucy duns and bailiffs fly;
Where highwaymen and robbers stout,
Would, rather than break in, break out;
Where all's so guarded and recluse,

That none his liberty can lose;
Here each may, as his means afford,
Dine like a pauper or a lord;
And he who can't the cost defray,
May live to dine another day.

Now let us ramble o'er the green,
To see and hear what's heard and seen;
To breathe the air, enjoy the light,
And hail yon sun, who shines as bright
Upon the dungeon and the gallows,
As on York Minster or Kew Palace.
And here let us the scene review:
That's the old castle, this the new;
Yonder the felons walk, and there
The lady-prisoners take the air;
Behind are solitary cells,
Where hermits live like snails in shells;
There stands the chapel for good people,
And yon balcony is the steeple;
How gayly spins the weather-cock!
How proudly shines the crazy clock!
A clock, whose wheels eccentric run,
More like my head than like the sun!
And yet it shews us, right or wrong,
The days are only twelve hours long;
Though captives often reckon here,
Each day a month, each month a year!
There honest William stands in state,
The porter, at the horrid gate;
Yet no ill-natured soul is he,
Entrance to all the world is free;
One thing, indeed, is rather hard,
Egress is frequently debarr'd;
Of all the joys in prison that reign,
There's none like – getting out again!

Across the green, behold the court,
Where jargon reigns and wigs resort;
Where bloody tongues fight bloodless battles,
For life and death, for straws and rattles;
Where juries yawn their patience out,
And judges dream in spite of gout.
There, on the outside of the door,
(As sang a wicked wag of yore)
Stands Mother Justice, tall and thin,
Who never yet hath ventured in.
The cause, my friend, may soon be Shown,
The lady was a stepping-stone,
Till – though the metamorphose odd is –
A chisel made the block a goddess:
– 'Odd!' did I say? – I'm wrong this time;
But I was hamper'd for a rhyme:
Justice at – I could tell you where –
Is just the same as justice there.

But, lo! my frisking dog attends,
The kindest of four-footed friends;
Brim full of giddiness and mirth,
He is the prettiest fool on earth.
The rogue's twice a squirrel's size,
With short snub nose and big black eyes;
A cloud of brown adorns his tail,
That curs and serves him for a sail;
The same deep auburn dyes his ears,
That never were abridged by shears;
While white around, as Lapland snows,
His hair, in soft profusion, flows;
Waves on his breast and plumes his feet,
With glossy fringe, like feathers fleet.
A thousand antic tricks he plays,
And looks, at once, a thousand ways;
His wit, if he has any, lies

Somewhere between his tail and eyes;
Sooner the light those eyes will fail,
Than Billy cease to wag that tail.

And yet the fellow ne'er is safe
From the tremendous beak of Ralph;
A raven grim, in black and blue,
As arch a knave as e'er you knew;
Who hops about with broken pinions,
And thinks these walls his own dominions!
This wag a mortal foe to Bill is,
They fight like Hector and Achilles,
Bold Billy runs with all his might,
And conquers, Parthian-like, in flight;
While Ralph his own importance feels,
And wages endless war with heels:
Horses and dogs, and geese and deer,
He slily pinches in the rear;
They start, surprised with sudden pain,
While honest Ralph sheers off again.

A melancholy stag appears,
With rueful look and flagging ears;
A feeble, lean, consumptive elf,
The very picture of myself!
My ghost-like form and new-moon phiz,
Are just the counter parts of his:
Blasted like me by fortune's frown,
Like me TWICE hunted, TWICE run down!
Like me pursued, almost to death,
He's come to gaol to save his breath!
Still, on his painful limbs, are seen
The scars where worrying dogs have been;
Still, in his woe-imprinted face,
I weep a broken heart to trace.
Daily the mournful wretch I feed,

With crumbs of comfort and of bread;
But man, false man! so well he knows,
He deems the species all his foes:
In vain I smile to soothe his fear,
He will not, dare not, come too near;
He lingers – looks – and fain he would –
Then strains his neck to reach the food.
Oft as his plaintive looks I see,
A brother's bowels yearn in me;
What rocks and tempests yet await
Both him and me, we leave to fate;
We know, by past experience taught,
That innocence availeth nought:
I know, and 'tis my proudest boast,
That conscience is itself an host;
While this inspires my swelling breast,
Let all forsake me – I'm at rest!
Ten thousand deaths, in every nerve,
I'd rather SUFFER than DESERVE!

But yonder comes the victim's wife,
A dappled doe, all fire and life;
She trips along with gallant pace,
Her limbs alert, her motion grace;
Soft as the moonlight fairies bound,
Her footsteps scarcely kiss the ground;
Gently she lifts her fair brown head,
And licks my hand, and begs for bread:
I pat her forehead, stroke her neck,
She starts and gives a timid squeak;
Then, while her eye with brilliance burns,
The fawning animal returns;
Pricks her bob-tail, and waves her ears,
And happier than a queen appears!
– Poor beast! from fierce ambition free,
And all the Woes of LIBERTY;

Born in a gaol, a prisoner bred,
No dreams of hunting rack thine head;
Ah! mayst thou never pass these bounds,
To see the world – and feel the hounds! –
Still all her beauty, all her art,
Have failed to win her husband's heart;
Her lambent eyes, and lovely chest;
Her swan-white neck, and ermine breast;
Her taper legs, and spotty hide,
So softly, delicately pied,
In vain their fond allurements spread.-
To love and joy her spouse is dead.

But, lo! the evening shadows fall
Broader and browner from the wall;
A warning voice, like curfew bell,
Commands each captive to his cell;
My faithful dog and I retire,
To play and chatter by the fire:
Soon comes a turnkey with 'Good night, sir!'
And bolts the door with all his might, sir!
Then leisurely to bed I creep,
And sometimes wake – and sometimes sleep.
These are the joys that reign in prison,
And if I'm happy, 'tis with reason:
Yet still this prospect, o'er the rest,
Makes every blessing doubly blest;
That soon these pleasures will be vanish'd,
And I, from all these comforts, banish'd!

Soliloquy of a Water Wagtail, on the Walls of York Castle.

I
ON the walls that guard my prison,
Swelling big with little pride,
Brisk and merry as the season,
I, a feathered Coxcomb, spied:
When the little, hopping elf
Gayly thus amused himself.

II
'Hear your sovereign's proclamation,
'All good subjects, young and old!
'I'm the Lord of the Creation;
'I – a Water Wagtail bold!
'All around, and all you see,
'All the world was made for ME!

III
'Yonder sun, so proudly shining,
'Rises – when I leave my nest;
'And, behind the hills declining,
'Sets – when I retire to rest:
'Morn and evening, thus you see,
'Day and night, were made for ME!

IV
'Vernal gales to love invite me;
'Summer sheds, for me, her beams;
'Autumn's jovial scenes delight me;
'Winter paves, with ice, my streams:
'All the year is mine, you see;
'Seasons change, like moons, for ME!

V
'On the giant heads of mountains,
'Or beneath the shady trees;
'By the banks of warbling fountains,

'I enjoy myself at ease:
'Hills and vallies, thus you see,
'Groves and rivers, made for ME!

VI
'Boundless are my vast dominions;
'I can hop, or swim, or fly;
'When I please, my towering pinions
'Trace mine empire through the sky;
'Air and elements, you see,
'Heaven and earth, were made for me!

VII
'Birds and insects, beasts and fishes,
'All their humble distance keep;
'Man, subservient to my wishes,
'Sows the harvest, which I reap:
'Mighty man himself, you see,
'All that breathe, were made for ME!

VIII
"Twas for my accommodation,
'Nature rose when I was born;
'Should I die – the whole creation
'Back to nothing would return:
'Sun, moon, stars, the world, you see,
'Sprung – exist – will fall with ME!'

IX
Here the pretty prattler ending,
Spread his wings to soar away;
But a cruel Hawk, descending,
Pounced him up – an helpless prey!
– Couldst thou not, poor Wagtail! see,
That the Hawk was made for THEE?

Castle of York, April 5, 1796.

VERSES TO

A Robin Redbreast,
Who visits the window of my prison every day.

I
WELCOME, pretty little Stranger!
Welcome to my lone retreat!
Here, secure from every danger,
Hop about, and chirp, and eat.
Robin! how I envy thee,
Happy Child of Liberty!

II
Now though tyrant Winter, howling,
Shakes the world with tempests round;
Heaven above with vapours scowling,
Frost imprisons all the ground; –
Robin! what are these to thee?
Thou art blest with Liberty.

III
Though yon fair majestic River
Mourns in solid icy chains;
Though yon flocks and cattle shiver,
On the desolated plains.
Robin! thou art gay and free,
Happy in thy Liberty.

IV
Hunger never shall distress thee,
While my cates one crum afford;
Colds nor cramps shall ne'er oppress thee;
Come and share my humble board.
Robin! come and live with me,
Live – yet still at Liberty.

V

Soon shall spring, in smiles and blushes,
Steal upon the blooming year;
Then, amid the enamoured bushes,
Thy sweet song shall warble clear; –
Then shall I too, joined with thee,
Swell the Hymn of Liberty.

VI

Should some rough unfeeling Dobbin,
In this iron-hearted age,
Seize thee on thy nest, my Robin!
And confine thee in a cage.
Then, poor Robin! think of me,
Think – and sigh for Liberty; –

VII

Liberty, the brightest jewel
In the crown of earthly joys!
All sensations else are cruel,
All delights beside are toys.
None but Captives – such as me –
Know the worth of Liberty.

York Castle, Feb. 2, 1795

Notes

Abbreviations

YCA York City Archive/ York Explore
PRO Public Records Office / National Archives
YMT York Museums Trust

Introduction

1. May, 2006, p.34.

Chapter 1: The Site of York Castle Prison, 1068–1705

1. 'York Castle' in *An Inventory of the Historical Monuments in City of York – Volume 2: The Defences*, London, 1972, British History Online https://www.british-history.ac.uk/rchme/york/vol2/pp57-86.
2. This is a conjectural plan with locations based on diagrams placed further into the book.
3. Cooper, T.P., *The History of the Castle of York*, Elliot Stock, London, 1911, p.8.
4. Ibid., p.14.
5. Rotherham, Ian D., *Yorks Military Legacy*, Pen & Sword Books, Barnsley, 2017, p.38.
6. Cooper, 1911, p.6.
7. https://www.british-history.ac.uk/rchme/york/vol2/pp57-86.
8. Rotherham, 2017, p.40.
9. Ibid., p.41.
10. Ibid., p.42.
11. Ibid., p.43.
12. Hargrove, William, *History and Description of the Ancient City of York: Comprising All the Most Interesting Information*, already published in Drake's Eboracum, York, William Alexander, 1818, p.226.
13. Higginbotham, Peter, *The Prison Cookbook*, The History Press, Stroud, 2010. p.10.
14. Ibid., p.27.
15. Pugh, R.B., *Imprisonment in Medieval England*, Cambridge U.P., London, 1968. pp.57–58.
16. Ibid., p.84.
17. Cooper, 1911, p.24.

18. Ibid., p.25.
19. B'nai B'rith Jewish Music Festival, Clifford's Tower commemoration, York, 15–18 March 1990: a programme and handbook of services, seminars and musical events in solemn commemoration of the 800th anniversary of the massacre in York Castle, York: 1190 Clifford's Tower 1990 Commemoration Committee, 1990, p.67.
20. Ibid., p.68.
21. Ibid., p.43.
22. Cooper, 1911, p.18.
23. Ibid., p.25.
24. Cooper, 1911, p.28.
25. Higginbotham, 2010, p.35.
26. Pugh,1968, p.333.
27. Based on information from https://www.british-history.ac.uk/rchme/york/vol2/pp57-86, and YCA: Asset ID: 1001508
28. Cooper, 1911, p.31.
29. Ibid., p.32.
30. Ibid., pp.34–35.
31. Ibid., p.48.
32. https://www.british-history.ac.uk/rchme/york/vol2/pp57-86.
33. https://www.british-history.ac.uk/rchme/york/vol2/pp57-86.
34. Cooper, 1911, pp.48–49.
35. Ibid., p.85.
36. Ibid., p.87.
37. https://www.british-history.ac.uk/rchme/york/vol2/pp57-86.
38. Cooper, 1911, p.63.
39. Ibid., p.81.
40. Ibid., p.76.
41. Ibid., p.77.
42. Pugh, 1968, p.308.
43. Cooper, 1911, p.143.
44. Ibid., p.148.
45. Ibid., p.149.
46. Ibid., p.157.
47. Ibid., p.84.
48. https://www.british-history.ac.uk/rchme/york/vol2/pp57-86.
49. Longley, Katharine, *Saint Margaret Clitherow*, Anthony Clarke, Wheathampstead, 1986, p.60.
50. Ibid., p.60–61.
51. Ibid., p.61.
52. Ibid., p.162.
53. Ibid., p.61.
54. Ibid., p.65.
55. Rotherham, 2017, p.66.

56. https://www.british-history.ac.uk/rchme/york/vol2/pp57-86.
57. https://www.british-history.ac.uk/rchme/york/vol2/pp57-86.
58. https://www.british-history.ac.uk/rchme/york/vol2/pp57-86.
59. Cooper, 1911, p.173.
60. Leeman, Stephanie Adele, 'Stone Walls Do Not a Prison Make: The Debtor's Prison', *York Historian 11*, York, 1994, p.24.
61. https://www.british-history.ac.uk/rchme/york/vol2/pp57-86.
62. Cooper, 1911, p.211.
63. https://www.british-history.ac.uk/rchme/york/vol2/pp57-86.
64. https://www.british-history.ac.uk/rchme/york/vol2/pp57-86.
65. https://www.british-history.ac.uk/rchme/york/vol2/pp57-86.
66. Cooper, 1911, p.183.
67. Hargrove, 1818, pp.252–253.
68. Ibid.
69. Ibid.
70. https://www.british-history.ac.uk/rchme/york/vol2/pp57-86.

Chapter 2: Life in York Castle Prison, 1068–1705

1. Mortimer, Ian, *The Time Traveller's Guide to Medieval England.* Vintage (Penguin Random House), Dublin, 2008. p.216.
2. Ibid.
3. Mortimer, Ian, *The Time Traveller's Guide to Elizabethan England*, Vintage (Penguin Random House), Dublin, 2012, p.301.
4. Emsley, Clive, *Crime and Society in England 1750–1900*, Longman, London, 1996, p.217.
5. Mortimer, 2008, p.216.
6. Sharpe, J.A., *Crime in Early Modern England 1550–1750*, Longman, London, 1999, p.49.
7. Ibid., p.46.
8. Mortimer, 2012, p.308.
9. Whittock, Martyn, *A Brief History of Life in the Middle Ages*, Robinson, London, 2009, pp.148–149.
10. Mortimer, 2008, p.239.
11. Sharpe, 1999, p.34.
12. Sharpe, 1999, p.39.
13. Mortimer, 2008, p.217.
14. Jones, Dan, *Magna Carta: The Making and Legacy of the Great Charter*, Head of Zeus Limited, London, 2014, p.17.
15. Ibid., p.18.
16. Webb, Simon, *A History of Torture in Britain*, Pen & Sword Books, Barnsley, 2018, p.1.
17. Jones, 2014, p.21.
18. Ibid.
19. Ibid., pp.21–22.

20. May, Trevor, *Victorian And Edwardian Prisons*, Shire Publications, Oxford, 2006, p.3.
21. Pugh, 1968, p.282.
22. Sharpe, 1999, p.33.
23. Sharpe, 1999, p.57.
24. Whittock, 2009, p.145, and Mortimer, 2012, p.302.
25. Mortimer, 2008, p.237.
26. Referenced on York Museums Trust image YORAG: R3811.
27. Webb, 2018, p.5.
28. Ibid., p.29.
29. Ibid., p.33.
30. Whittock, 2009, p.146.
31. Mortimer, 2012, p.314.
32. Mortimer, 2012, p.304.
33. Higgs, Michelle, *Prison Life in Victorian England*, Tempus Publishing, Stroud, 2007, p.9.
34. Emsley, 1996, p.188.
35. Ibid., p.193.
36. Ibid., pp.194–196.
37. McLynn, Frank, *Crime and Punishment in Eighteenth-Century England*, Oxford University Press, Oxford, 1991, p.121.
38. Jones, 2014, p.159.
39. Whittock, 2009, p.147.
40. Ibid., p.148.
41. Mortimer, 2012, p.300.
42. Ibid.
43. Whittock, 2009, p.150.
44. Knipe, William, *Tyburn Tales: The Criminal Chronology of York Castle*, Simkin, Marshall & Co., London, 1867 (2010 reprint), p.1.
45. Whittock, 2009, p.151.
46. Hawkins, David T., *Bound for Australia: A Guide to the Records of Transported Convicts and Early Settlers*, The History Press, Stroud, 2012., p.8.
47. Ibid.
48. McLynn, 1991, p.285.
49. Ibid., p.286.
50. Webb, 2018, p.40.
51. Day, Chris, *et al*, *A History of Treason*, John Blake, London, 2022, p.1.
52. Cooper, 1911, pp.94–95.
53. Day, 2022, pp.1–2.
54. Ibid., p.32.
55. Pugh, 1968, p.46.
56. Ibid., p.7.
57. Mortimer, 2008, p.224.
58. Pugh, 1968, p.150.

59. Ibid.
60. Ibid., p.151.
61. Ibid., p.152.
62. Ibid., p.161.
63. Ibid., p.165.
64. Ibid., p.180.
65. Ibid., p.181.
66. Ibid.
67. Ibid., p.183.
68. Webb, 2018, p.9.
69. Cooper, 1911, p.1.
70. Longley, 1986, p.61.
71. Pugh, 1968, p.179.
72. Cooper, 1911, pp.89–90.
73. Ibid., p.94.
74. Ibid., p.110.
75. Pugh, 1968, p.320.
76. Ibid., p.326.
77. Pugh, p.323.
78. Sharpe, 1999, p.46.
79. Sharpe, 1999, p.47.
80. Pugh, 1968, p.331.
81. Ibid.
82. Cooper, 1911, p.210.
83. Ibid., p.91.
84. Ibid., p.97.

Chapter 3: The Site of York Castle Prison, 1705–1777

1. Cooper, 1911, p.209.
2. Ibid., p.211.
3. Leeman, 1994, p.23.
4. Redington, Jospeh (ed.), *Calendar of Treasury Papers – Volume 2:1697–1702*, London, 1871, accessed via https://www.british-history.ac.uk/cal-treasury-papers/vol2/p473.
5. https://www.british-history.ac.uk/rchme/york/vol2/pp57-86.
6. Image based on information from: https://www.british-history.ac.uk/rchme/york/vol2/pp57-86, and Addyman, Peter, *British Historic Towns Atlas – Volume V: York*, York Archaeological Trust, York, 2015.
7. It was most likely designed by Wakefield although others have been argued, see Leeman, 1994.
8. Leeman, 1994, p.23.
9. Ibid., p.27.
10. Cooper, 1911, p.216.

11. Howard, John, *The State of the Prisons in England and Wales: With Preliminary Observations, and An Account of Some Foreign Prisons*, William Eyres, Warrington, 1777. p.15.
12. Cooper, 1911, p.212.
13. Ibid., p.214.
14. https://www.british-history.ac.uk/rchme/york/vol2/pp57-86.
15. Image based on Leeman, 1994, p.29, and https://www.british-history.ac.uk/rchme/york/vol2/pp57-86.
16. Howard,1777, pp.397– 398.
17. Leeman, 1994, p.28.
18. Ibid., p.38.
19. 'Register of York Castle, 1730–1743' in *Yorkshire Archaeological Journal: Volume 25*, John Whitehead & Son, Leeds, 1920, p.439.
20. Image based on Wakefield Archives: QSF 98/D/8 placed onto a general outline of the building.
21. Fawcett, Bill, 'The Nineteenth-Century Prison Buildings at York Castle', *York Historian 22*, York, 2005. p.3.
22. 'One Night Spent in the Condemned Hole, York Castle in April 1810', George Wilson, Leeds, 1815, p.26.
23. Howard, 1777, p.397.
24. Beverley Archives: DDGR/42/28/56.
25. Defoe, Daniel, *A Tour Thro' the Whole Island of Great Britain: Divided Into Circuites or Journeys – Giving a Particular and Entertaining Account of Whatever is Curious and Worth Observation – Volume 3*, S. Birt, London, 1748, p.167.
26. Smollett, Tobias, *The Expedition of Humphry Clinker*, Oxford University Press, Oxford, 2009 (reissue), p.180.
27. Leeman, 1994, p.36.
28. https://www.british-history.ac.uk/rchme/york/vol2/pp57-86.
29. https://www.british-history.ac.uk/rchme/york/vol2/pp57-86.
30. Cooper, 1911, p.214.
31. Ibid.
32. https://www.british-history.ac.uk/rchme/york/vol2/pp57-86.

Chapter 4: Life in York Castle Prison, 1705–1777

1. Leeman, 1994, p.25. Also Wakefield Archives: QS1/56/4.
2. Wakefield Archives: QS1/56/4.
3. Beverlly Archives: QSF 104/D13.
4. Beverlly Archives: QSF 104/D/14.
5. Beverlly Archives: QSF 104/D13.
6. Beverley Archives: QSF 88/D/5.
7. Brodie, Allan., *Crom, Jane, Davies, James O., Behind Bars: The Hidden Architecture of England's Prisons*, English Heritage, Swindon, 1999, p.6.
8. Twyford, A.W. and Griffiths, A., *Records of York Castle*, Griffith and Farran, London, 1880, p.155.

9. Ibid., p.157.
10. Ibid., p.158. Referencing Howard, 1777, p.399.
11. Higginbotham, 2010, p.29.
12. Wakefield Archives: QS1/48/6.
13. Wakefield Archives: QS1/54/4.
14. Wakefield Archives: QS1/67/4.
15. Beverley Archives: QSF 80/E/11.
16. Wakefield Archives: QS1/48/6.
17. Wakefield Archives: QS1/48/6.
18. Beverley Archives: QSF 48/D/9.
19. Beverley Archives: QSF 80/E/1.
20. Beverley Archives: QSP 157.
21. Wakefield Archives: QS1/57/8.
22. Pitofsky, Alex, *The Wardens Court Martial: James Oglethorpe and the Politics of Eighteenth-Century Prison Reform – Volume 24: Eighteenth-Century Life*, winter 2000, p.98.
23. Beverley Archives: QSF 15/D/4.
24. Wakefield Archives: QS1/47/1.
25. Cooper, 1911, p.310.
26. Howard, 1777, p.26.
27. Ibid.
28. Defoe, 1748, p.167.
29. Howard, 1777, p.401.
30. McLynn, 1991, p.243.
31. Ibid., p.244.
32. Ibid., p.ix. N.B. Some authors give different numbers, but they are always around 220 to 225.
33. Sharp, 1999, p.260.
34. McLynn, 1991, p.ix.
35. Ibid.
36. Ibid., p.xii.
37. Ibid., p.219.
38. Sharpe, 1999, p.253.
39. A good example can be found with the execution of Richard Clegg, 1799, Knipe, 1868, p.153.
40. Cooper, 1911, p.262.
41. Knipe, 1868, p.139.
42. Ibid., p.92.
43. McLynn, 1991, p.251.
44. Ibid., p.259.
45. *Derby Mercury*, Friday, 20 August 1756.
46. McLynn, 1991, p.280.
47. Ibid., p.279.
48. Ibid., p.253.

49. Ibid., p.258.
50. Ibid.
51. Higginbotham, 2010, p.8.
52. Howard, 1777, pp.397–398.
53. Woodfine, Philip, 'Debtors, Prisons, and Petitions in Eighteenth-Century England' *Eighteenth Century Life: Volume 30, Number 2*, 2006. p.174.
54. May, 2006, p.10.
55. Higginbotham, 2010, p.11.
56. McLynn, 1991, p.295.
57. Higgs, 2007, p.111.
58. Piotofsky, 2000, p.89.
59. Sheppard, Colin, 'Francis Drake and the Debtors' Prison', *York Historian 37*, York, 2020, p.18.
60. YCA: *Gaoler's Journal: Volume 3*, p.3.
61. Twyford, 1880, p.119.
62. Higginbotham, 2010, p.35.
63. Howard, 1777, p.10.
64. Siena, Kevin, *Prisons, Debtors, and Disease in the Early Eighteenth Century – Rotten Bodies: Class and Contagion in Eighteenth-Century Britain*, Yale University Press, London, 2019, pp.76–77.
65. Ibid., p.77.
66. McLynn, 1991, p.295.
67. Twyford, 1880, p.120.
68. Ibid., p.161. and Howard, 1777, p.401.
69. May, 2006, p.6.
70. https://yorkcastleprison.org.uk. This website cites *Public Advertiser*, 22 March 1771.
71. Twyford, 1880, p.149.
72. Higginbotham, 2010, p.10.
73. Ibid., p.11.
74. Ibid.
75. Twyford, 1880, p.120.
76. Howard, 1777, p.17.
77. 'Register of York Castle, 1730–1743' in *Yorkshire Archaeological Journal: Volume 25*, John Whitehead & Son, Leeds, 1920, p.439.
78. *Derby Mercury*, 10 November 1737
79. Siena, 2019, p.91.
80. Sharpe, 1999, p.97.
81. McLynn, 1991, p.xii.
82. Oates, Jonathan, 'York and the Rebel Prisoners, 1745–1752', *York Historian 17*, York, 2000, p.56.
83. McLynn, 1991, p.285.
84. Ibid., p.286.
85. Ibid., p.xii.

86. Sharpe, 1999, p.260.
87. McLynn, 1991, p.286.
88. *Stamford Mercury*, Thursday, 3 August 1732.
89. Beverley Archives: QSF 61/D/23 – the phrase used is 'indeaver for our selves'. In context, this clearly means escape.
90. McLynn, 1991, p.290.
91. PRO: ASSI 41/4.
92. Emsley, 1996, p.152.
93. McLynn, 1991, p.122.
94. Sharpe, 1999, p.158.
95. McLynn, 1991, p.117.
96. Ibid., p.119.
97. Rennison, 2012, p.71.
98. McLynn, 1991, p.129.
99. Wakefield Archives: QS1/57/8.
100. May, 2006, p.37.

Chapter 5: The Site of York Castle Prison, 1777–1835

1. Cooper, 1911, p.216.
2. Hargrove, 1818, p.231.
3. Image based on: https://www.british-history.ac.uk/rchme/york/vol2/pp57-86, Cooper, 1911, p.234, and Strickland, George, *Reasons for not Pulling Down Clifford's Tower, In Making the Proposed Enlargement of York Castle*, J. and G. Todd, York, 1825.
4. Cooper, 1911, p.218.
5. Ibid.
6. Cooper, 1911, p.218.
7. Image based on Cooper, 1911, p.217.
8. Chalkin, C.W., 'The Reconstruction of London's Prisons, 1770–1799: An Aspect of the Growth of Georgian London', *The London Journal*, 9:1, 21–34, 1983, p.30.
9. Twyford, 1880, p.146.
10. Ibid.
11. Beverley Archives: DDGR/42/28/56.
12. Nield, James, *State of the Prisons in England, Scotland, and Wales, Extending to Various Places Therin Assigned, Not for the Debtors Only, But for Felons Also, and Other Less Criminal Offenders*, John Nichols and Son, London, 1809, p.612.
13. Image based on https://www.british-history.ac.uk/rchme/york/vol2/pp57-86, Leeman, 1994, p.29, and Cooper, 1911, p.215.
14. Ibid., p.61.
15. Hargrove, 1818, p.237.
16. Nield, 1809, p.613.
17. Hargrove, 1818, p.237.
18. Nield, 1809, p.613.

19. Anonymous, 1815, p.6.
20. Ibid., p.7.
21. Hargrove, 1818, p.236.
22. Ibid., p.233.
23. Holland, John, *Memoirs of the Life and Writings of James Montgomery: Including Selection from His Correspondence, Remains in Prose and Verse, and Conversations on Various Subjects*, Longman, London, 1854, p.252.
24. Nield, 1809, p.614; also Hargrove, 1818, p.238.
25. Hargrove, 1818, p.242.
26. Nield, 1809, p.613.
27. Ibid.
28. Ibid.
29. Anonymous, 1815, p.5.
30. Nield, 1809, p.614.
31. Plan based on https://www.british-history.ac.uk/rchme/york/vol2/pp57-86, and Cooper, 1911, p.229.
32. Ibid.
33. Hargrove, 1818, p.242.
34. Gurney, Joseph John, *Notes on a Visit Made to some of the Prisons in Scotland and the North of England, in Company with Elizabeth Fry*, Archibald Constable & Co., Edinburgh, 1819, p.10.
35. Hoppet, quick search results, *Oxford English Dictionary*, https://oed.com.
36. Rimmer, Jayne, *Analysing the Skeletons Excavated at the Former Female Prison: An Insight Report*, 2016, https://research.yorkarchaeology.co.uk/wp-content/uploads/2023/08/AnalysingtheSkeletonsExcavatedattheformerFemalePrison-JayneRimmer.pdf.
37. Cooper, 1911, p.226.
38. Hargrove, 1818, p.250.
39. Ibid.
40. https://www.british-history.ac.uk/rchme/york/vol2/pp57-86.

Chapter 6: Life in York Castle Prison, 1777–1835

1. May, 2006, pp.7–8.
2. Howard, 1777, p.399.
3. Ibid., p.9 and p.11.
4. Ibid., p.12.
5. Ibid., p.21.
6. Ibid., p.2 and p.5.
7. Ibid., p.397.
8. Ibid., p.26.
9. Ibid., p.27.
10. Higginbotham, 2010, p.39.
11. McLynn, 1991, p.121.
12. Nield, 1809, p.612.

13. Ibid., p.612.
14. Ibid., p.613.
15. Ibid.
16. Ibid., p.614.
17. Gurney, 1819, p.101.
18. Ibid., p.102.
19. Ibid., p.133.
20. Ibid., p.112.
21. Ibid., p.121.
22. Fry, Elizabeth, *Observations on the Visiting, Superintendence, and Government of Female Prisoners by Elizabeth Fry*, John and Arthur Arch, London, 1827, pp.28–29.
23. Gurney, 1819, p.143.
24. Fry, 1827, pp.12–13.
25. Gurney, 1819, p.162.
26. Cooper, 1911, p.232.
27. Gurney, 1819, p.104.
28. Ibid., pp.13–14.
29. Ibid., pp.118.
30. Ibid., p.11.
31. Ibid., p.12.
32. Ibid., p.11.
33. Ibid., p.10.
34. Ibid.
35. Pitofsky, 2000, p.98.
36. Ibid., p.98.
37. YCA: *Gaoler's Journal: Volume 2*, various references.
38. Nield, 1809, p.611.
39. Hargrove, 1818, p.233.
40. Storey, Neil R., *Prisons & Prisoners in Victorian Britain*, The History Press, Stroud, 2010. p.67.
41. Priestly, 2020, p.10.
42. Higginbotham, 2010, p.68.
43. Storey, 2010, p.10.
44. May, 2006, p.17.
45. McLynn, 1991, p.259.
46. Opperman, Averil Douglas, *While It Is Yet Day: The Story of Elizabeth Fry*, Orphans Publishing, Herefordshire, 2015, p.208.
47. Emsley, 1996, p.197.
48. Ibid., p.235.
49. Ibid., p.225.
50. Ibid., p.216.
51. Priestley, 2020, pp.130–133.
52. Brodie et al, p.7.

53. Wade, Stephen, *Yorkshire Hangmen: The Lives and Careers of Hangmen Born or Working in Yorkshire from 1800 to the End of Hanging*, Wharncliffe Books/Pen & Sword Books, Barnsley, 2008, p.39.
54. McLynn, 1991, pp.292–293.
55. Ibid., p.291.
56. Ibid., p.292 and p.294.
57. Emsley, 1996, p.266.
58. Hawkings, 2012, p.8.
59. Emsley, 1996, p.271.
60. Hawkings, 2012, p.9.
61. Emsley, 1996, p.255.
62. Hawkings, 2012, p.9.
63. Montgomery, James, *The Poetical Works of James Montgomery: Volume 1*, Longman, London, 1841.
64. Holland, John, *Memoirs of the Life and Writings of James Montgomery: Including Selection from His Correspondence, Remains in Prose and Verse, and Conversations on Various Subjects*, Longman, London, 1854, pp.202–231.
65. McLynn, 1991, pp.310–11.
66. YCA: *Gaoler's Journal: Volume 1*, and *Gaoler's Journal: Volume 2.*
67. YCA: *Gaoler's Journal: Volume 1*, p.7.
68. Ibid., p.8.
69. Ibid., p.9.
70. Ibid., p.11.
71. Ibid., p.10.
72. YCA: *Gaoler's Journal: Volume 2*, p.9.
73. YCA: *Gaoler's Journal: Volume 1*, p.8.
74. Hargrove, 1818, p.244.
75. Gurney, 1819, p.11.
76. Ibid., p.12.
77. Ibid., p.14.
78. Brodie et al, p.88.
79. Gurney, 1819, p.11.
80. Ibid., p.114.
81. Ibid., p.11.
82. Ibid.
83. Ibid.
84. Emsley, 1996, p.156.
85. Ibid., p.157.
86. Ibid.
87. Fry, 1827, p.63.
88. Ibid.
89. Ibid., pp.64–65.
90. Knipe, 1868, p.27.
91. Hargrove, 1818, p.231.

92. *Yorkshire Gazette*, Saturday, 16 April 1853.
93. *Star* (London), Monday, 11 January 1813.
94. Anonymous, 1815, p.5.
95. Ibid., p.3.
96. Ibid., pp.5–6.
97. Ibid., pp.8–9.
98. Ibid., p.9.
99. Ibid.
100. Ibid., p.10.
101. Ibid., p.11.
102. Ibid., p.16.
103. Ibid., pp.21–22.
104. Ibid., p.22.
105. Leeman, 1994, p.37.
106. Cooper, 1911, p.280.
107. Ibid., p.283.
108. Ibid., p.287.
109. Hargrove, 1818, p.244.

Chapter 7: The Site of York Castle Prison, 1835–1877

1. Priestley, Philip, *Victorian Prison Lives: English Prison Biography 1830–1914*, Pimlico, London, 1999, p.x.
2. Fawcett, 2005, p.6.
3. Image based on: Cooper, 1911, p.247, https://interactivemaps.uk/york-1852/#17/53.955543/-1.079334, and Addyman, Peter, *British Historic Towns Atlas: Volume V – York*, York Archaeological Trust, York, 2015.
4. Ibid., p.2.
5. https://www.british-history.ac.uk/rchme/york/vol2/pp57-86
6. Fawcett, 2005, p.7.
7. Strickland, George, *Reasons for not Pulling Down Clifford's Tower, In Making the Proposed Enlargement of York Castle*, J. and G. Todd, York, 1825. p.6.
8. Ibid., p.14.
9. Fawcett, 2005, p.8.
10. Anonymous. A letter to George Strickland, Esq. In Reply to his *Reasons for Not Pulling Down Clifford's Tower, In Making the Proposed Enlargement of York Castle*, W. Storry, York, 1825, p.8.
11. Ibid., pp.5–6.
12. Strickland, 1825, p.17.
13. Ibid., p.21.
14. Cooper, 1911, pp.234–238.
15. Ibid., p.233.
16. Ibid., p.195.
17. https://www.british-history.ac.uk/rchme/york/vol2/pp57-86
18. Cooper, 1911, p.238.

19. Fawcett, 2005, p.7.
20. Cooper, 1911, p.238.
21. Fawcett, 2005, p.8.
22. Plan based on Fawcett, 2005, p.11
23. Brodie *et al*, p.54.
24. Fawcett, 2005, p.18.
25. *Yorkshire Gazette*, Saturday, 24 September 1836.
26. Fawcett, 2005, p.10.
27. Ibid.
28. Plan based on YCA: Y/PPT/6/1/5337.
29. *Leeds Intelligencer*, Saturday 12 April 1834
30. Twyford, 1880, p.149.
31. YCA: *Gaoler's Journal: Volume 4*, p.70.
32. Plan based on https://www.british-history.ac.uk/rchme/york/vol2/pp57-86, and https://interactivemaps.uk/york-1852/#17/53.955543/-1.079334.
33. Ibid., p.119.
34. Ibid., Vol 2, p.16.
35. Ibid., Vol 4, p.107.
36. Fawcett, 2005, p.21.

Chapter 8: Life in York Castle Prison, 1835–1877

1. Storey, 2010, p.9.
2. May, 2006, p.17.
3. Storey, 2010, p.9.
4. Ibid., p.10.
5. Ibid., p.68–70.
6. Storey, 2010, p.13.
7. Ibid., p.14.
8. Higgs, 2007, p.17.
9. Ibid., p.20.
10. Ibid., p.11.
11. Priestly, 1999, p.123.
12. Higgs, 2007, p.47.
13. Ibid.
14. Ibid.
15. May, 2006, p.28.
16. Ibid.
17. Storey, 2010, p.30.
18. Priestley, 1999, p.127.
19. Higgs, 2007, p.51.
20. Ibid., p.50.
21. YCA: *Gaoler's Journal: Volume 4*, p.38.
22. Ibid.
23. Priestly, 1999, p.142.

24. Ibid., p.123.
25. YCA: *Gaoler's Journal: Volume 4*, p.33.
26. Ibid., p.44.
27. Webb, 2018, pp.78–79.
28. Priestly, 1999, p.149.
29. Higgs, 2007, p.41.
30. YCM: Rules and regulations for governing York Castle, 1843, p.15.
31. Priestly, 1999, p.161.
32. Ibid., p.155.
33. Ibid., p.158.
34. Ibid., p.161.
35. Ibid., p.173.
36. YCA: *Gaoler's Journal: Volume 4*, pp.10–11.
37. *York Herald*, Saturday, 28 March 1868.
38. May, 2006, p.21.
39. Hawkings, 2012, p.9.
40. Priestley, 1999, p.5.
41. Brodie *et al*, p.20.
42. Ibid.
43. Hawkins, 2012, p.7.
44. Priestley, 2020, p.92.
45. *Leeds Intelligencer*, Saturday, 1 August 1846
46. Priestley, 2020, p.92.
47. Ibid.
48. *York Herald*, Saturday, 28 March 1868.
49. *Northern Star*, 21 March 1840.
50. YCM: Rules and regulations for the governance of York Castle, 1843, p.41.
51. Ibid.
52. Cooper, 1911, p.243.
53. YCA: *Gaoler's Journal: Volume 3*, p.19.
54. Ibid., p.18.
55. Ibid., p.45.
56. Ibid., p.53.
57. Beaumont, Robert, *The Railway King: Biography of George Hudson Railway Pioneer and Fraudster*, Headline Publishing, Chatham, 2002, p.192.
58. Ibid.
59. Ibid., p.199.
60. Ibid.
61. Ibid., p.203.
62. YCM: Rules and regulations for the government of York Castle, 1843, p.11
63. Storey, 2010, p.18, and Priestley, 1999, p.269.
64. YCM: Rules and regulations for the government of York Castle, 1843, p.12.
65. Ibid., p.17.
66. Higgs, 2007, p.129.

67. YCM: Rules and Regulations for the governance of York Castle, 1843, p.23.
68. May, 2006, p.32.
69. Priestley, 1999, p.255.
70. YCA: *Gaoler's Journal: Volume 4*, YCA, p.15.
71. Higgs, 2007, p.129 and Priestley, 1999, p.266.
72. Higgs, 2007, p.129.
73. May, 2006, p.35.
74. Higgs, 2007, p.130.
75. May, 2006, p.33. and Priestley, 1999, p.260.
76. Priestley, 1999, p.261.
77. Ibid., p.189.
78. YCA: *Gaoler's Journal: Volume 4*, p.30.
79. Ibid., p.71.
80. Ibid., p.109.
81. Ibid., p.52.
82. Ibid., p.95.
83. Storey, 2010, pp.25–26.
84. Ibid., p.26.
85. Higgs, 2007, p.136.
86. Priestley, 1999, p.115.
87. Higgs, 2007, p.54.
88. Priestly, 1999, p.91.
89. Ibid., p.93.
90. YCM: Rules and regulations for the governance of York Castle, 1843. p.29.
91. Storey, 2010, p.33.
92. Higgs, 2007, p.144.
93. Storey, 2010, p.34.
94. YCA: *Gaoler's Journal: Volume 4*, p.52.
95. Ibid., Vol 2. p.17.
96. Ibid., Vol 4, p.19.
97. Ibid., p.42.
98. Priestly, 1999, p.283.
99. Higgs, 2007, p.65.
100. *York Herald*, Saturday, 13 January 1900.
101. YCA: *Gaoler's Journal: Volume 4*, p.26.
102. PRO: HO 17/75/172.
103. Ibid.
104. Ibid.
105. Emsley, 1996, p.156.
106. May, 2006, p.34.
107. Ibid.
108. Emsley, 1996, p.155.
109. Ibid., p.154.
110. *Yorkshire Gazette*, Saturday, 16 February 1850.

111. *Halifax Guardian*, Saturday, 16 March 1850.
112. Emsley, 1996, p.162.
113. Ibid., p.155.
114. McLynn, 1991, p.128.
115. Emsley, 1996, p.157.
116. Higgs, 2007, p.99.
117. Priestley, 1999, p.69.
118. PRO: HO 17/33/18.
119. Ibid.
120. Storey, 2010, p.58.
121. YCA: *Gaoler's Journal: Volume 4*, p.53.
122. Ibid., p.55.
123. Priestley, 1999, p.56.
124. Ibid., p.57.

Chapter 9: The Site of HM Prison York, 1877–1900

1. Image Based on: Fawcett, Bill, 'The Nineteenth-Century Prison Buildings at York Castle', *York Historian 22*, York, 2005, p.25, and YCA: Y/PPT/6/1/5337.
2. *Yorkshire Gazette*, Saturday, 17 August 1895.
3. Cooper, 1911, pp.330–334.
4. *Sheffield Daily Telegraph*, Friday, 3 December 1880.
5. Ibid.
6. Fawcett, 2005, p.22.
7. Ibid., p.24.
8. Cooper, 1911, p.242.
9. Plan based on Fawcett, 2005, p.11.
10. Plan based on https://www.british-history.ac.uk/rchme/york/vol2/pp57-86, Cooper, 1911, p.229, and YCA: Y/PPT/6/1/5337.
11. Fawcett, 2005, p.24.
12. Cooper, 1911, p.242.

Chapter 10: Life in HM Prison York 1877– 1900

1. May, 2006, p.3.
2. Priestly, 1999, p.6.
3. https://www.prisonhistory.org/prison/yorkcity-gaol/
4. *Yorkshire Gazette*, Saturday, 18 January 1890.
5. Ibid.
6. Ibid.
7. Cooper, 1911, pp.241–242.
8. Ibid., p.242.
9. *Yorkshire Gazette*, Saturday, 18 January 1890
10. Fawcett, 2005, p.21.
11. Storey, 2010, p.47.

12. Ibid.
13. YCM: Rules and regulations for the governing York Castle, 1843, p.13.
14. Storey, 2010, p.51.
15. Priestley, 1999, p.278.
16. YCM: Rules and Regulations for governing York Castle, p.13.
17. Ibid., p.46.
18. Higgs, 2007, p.23.
19. 1881 Census, accessed via ancestry.com
20. England & Wales, Civil Registration Death Index, 1837–1915, 1876 Q1-Jan-Feb-Mar, accessed via ancestry.com.
21. *York Herald*, Monday, 30 April 1877.
22. Ibid.
23. Ibid.
24. Ibid.
25. Ibid.
26. Ibid.
27. Cooper, 1911, p.313.
28. Baughman, T.H., *Pilgrims on the Ice: Robert Falcon Scott's First Antartic Expedition*, University of Nebraska Press, London, 1999 (2008 new edition), p.68.
29. Ibid., p.106.
30. Ibid., p.165.
31. https://www.spri.cam.ac.uk/museum/shackleton/biographies/Heald,_William_Lofthouse/
32. Library and Museum of Freemasonry; London, England; Freemasonry Membership Registers; Description: Membership Registers: Country I 602–702 to Country J 703–815; Reel Number: 12.
33. London Metropolitan Archives; London, England, UK; London Church of England Parish Registers.
34. Ibid.
35. *Middlesex Chronicle*, 16 January 1997

Chapter 11: The Site of York Detention Barracks, 1900–1929

1. PRO: HO 45/15499
2. Ibid.
3. Ibid.
4. Image Based on: Fawcett, Bill, 'The Nineteenth-Century Prison Buildings at York Castle', *York Historian 22*, York, 2005, p.25, and YCA: Y/PPT/6/1/5337.
5. Ibid.
6. Ibid.
7. Ibid.
8. Cooper, 1911, p.244.
9. PRO: HO 45/15499.
10. *Yorkshire Post* and *Leeds Intelligencer*, Wednesday, 19 March 1902.
11. Ibid.

12. *Lloyd's Weekly Newspaper*, Sunday, 13 January 1901 and *Jersey Evening Post*, Monday, 24 February 1902.
13. Plan based on YCA: Y/PPT/6/1/5337.
14. Plan based on YCA: Y/PPT/6/1/5337.
15. PRO: HO 45/10047 – A62358.
16. Ibid.
17. Ibid.
18. PRO: PCOM 9–78.
19. https://www.british-history.ac.uk/rchme/york/vol2/pp57-86.
20. PRO: HO 45/15500.
21. Ibid.
22. Ibid.
23. Ibid.
24. Ibid.
25. Ibid.
26. Ibid.
27. PRO: PCOM 9–78.

Chapter 12: Life in York Detention Barracks, 1900–1929

1. https://www.nam.ac.uk/explore/military-provost-staff-corps
2. https://www.britishmilitaryhistory.co.uk/military-provost-staff-corps/
3. https://www.longlongtrail.co.uk/soldiers/a-soldiers-life-1914-1918/military-crimes-1914-1918-british-army/british-army-military-prisons-detention-barracks-1914/
4. *Manchester Evening News*, Wednesday, 8 April 1903.
5. *Leeds Mercury*, Friday, 7 August 1914.
6. Rubinstein, David. *War Comes to York: Summer 1914*. York: Quack Books. 2010, pp.23–24.
7. *Yorkshire Evening Post*, Monday, 10 August 1914.
8. *Wakefield Advertiser & Gazette*, Tuesday, 11 August 1914.
9. *Yorkshire Post* and *Leeds Intelligencer*, Monday, 10 August 1914.
10. *Yorkshire Post* and *Leeds Intelligencer*, Thursday, 22 October 1914.
11. *Yorkshire Post* and *Leeds Intelligencer*, Friday, 11 September 1914.
12. Ibid.
13. *Bradford Daily Telegraph*, Thursday, 22 October 1914.
14. *Daily Gazette for Middlesbrough*, Thursday, 10 September 1914.
15. *Yorkshire Post* and *Leeds Intelligencer*, Monday, 10 August 1914.
16. Ibid.
17. *Cleveland Standard*, Saturday, 12 September 1914.
18. *Yorkshire Post* and *Leeds Intelligencer*, Monday, 10 August 1914.
19. Ibid.
20. Peacock, A.J., *York in the Great War 1914–1918*, York: York Settlement Trust, 1993, p.299.
21. *Hull Daily Mail*, Friday, 7 August 1914.

22. Peacock, 1993, p.300.
23. Rubinstien, 2010, p.34.
24. Ibid.
25. Ibid.
26. *Bradford Daily Telegraph*, Thursday, 22 October 1914.
27. Ibid.
28. *Yorkshire Post* and *Leeds Intelligencer*, Monday, 14 September 1914.
29. *Yorkshire Evening Post*, Thursday, 22 October 1914.
30. Ibid.
31. *Leeds Mercury*, Thursday, 24 September 1914.
32. *Yorkshire Post* and *Leeds Intelligencer*, Thursday, 22 October 1914.
33. *Todmorden Advertiser* and *Hebden Bridge Newsletter*, Friday, 2 October 1914.
34. *Weekly Freeman's Journal*, Saturday, 31 October 1914.
35. *Sheffield Daily Telegraph*, Tuesday, 7 November 1916.
36. *Skyrack Courier*, Friday, 6 April 1917.
37. Patmore, Charles, A *Missing Chapter from the History of York Castle: The Imprisonment of Quakers,* accessed via https://ffhyork.weebly.com/york-castle.html
38. Peacock, 1993, p.376.
39. Peacock, A.J., 'Conscience and Politics in York, 1914–1918', *York Historian 5*, York, 1984, pp.39-40.
40. Ibid., p.43.
41. Peacock, 1993, p.376.
42. Ibid.
43. *Sheffield Independent*, Thursday, 6 July 1916.
44. Rubinstein, David, *Faithful to Ourselves and the Outside World: York Quakers During the Twentieth Century*, William Sessions, York, 2001, p.41.
45. Ibid., pp.40–41.
46. Ibid., p.41.
47. Ibid.
48. Ibid.
49. Ibid.
50. *Yorkshire Post and Leeds Intelligencer*, Saturday, 1 July 1916.

Chapter 13: York Castle, 1929 and Beyond

1. PRO: PCOM 9/78.
2. Ibid.
3. Ibid.
4. Image based on previous plans and modern satellite images. Proposed office locations based on Fawcett, Bill, 'The Municipal Offices at York Castle', *York Historian 23*, 2006, p.23.
5. *York Press*, Tuesday, 30 April 2002.
6. *York Press*, Tuesday, 30 April 2002.
7. *Yorkshire Evening Post*, Wednesday, 4 November 1936.

8. Fawcett, Bill, 'The Municipal Offices at York Castle', *York Historian 23*, York, 2006, p.21.
9. Ibid., pp.37–38.
10. Ibid., p.37.

Appendix I: Other Prisons/Gaols in York

1. Howard, 1777, p.404.
2. Beverley Archive: QSF 15/D/4
3. Twyford, 1880, p.136.
4. Howard, 1777, p.405.
5. Higginbotham, 2010. p.26.
6. https://www.londonlives.org/static/HousesOfCorrection.jsp.
7. Siena, p.75.
8. Higginbotham, 2010, p.68.
9. Morgan, 2022, p.115.
10. Nield, 1809, pp.605–606.
11. https://www.york.ac.uk/borthwick/history/borthwick-unboxed/st-anthonys-hall/
12. Gurney, 1818, pp.94–97, and p.117.
13. *Yorkshire Gazette*, Saturday, 22 February 1890, and Cooper, 1911, p.267.
14. Higgs, 2007, p.14.
15. https://www.prisonhistory.org/prison/york-city-gaol/
16. McLynn,1991, p.296.
17. Howard, 1777, p.407.
18. Ibid.
19. http://www.historyofyork.org.uk/themes/the-liberty-of-st-peter
20. Twyford, 1880, p.132.
21. Ibid.
22. Higginbotham, 2010, p.11.

Appendix II: Execution sites in York

1. This is an estimate based on Knipe, 1868. However, it is obvious that this is not a comprehensive list, especially for the earlier years, so in reality, the total is far higher than this.
2. Twyford, 1880, p.92.
3. Cooper, 1911, p.251.
4. Ibid., p.259.
5. Ibid., p.266.
6. Ibid., p.257.
7. Priestley, 2020, p.11.
8. *Yorkshire Gazette*, Saturday, 16 April 1853.
9. *Leeds Mercury*, Monday, 6 April 1868.
10. *Star* (London), Monday, 11 January 1813.

11. *Leeds Mercury*, Monday, 6 April 1868.
12. Knipe, 1867, p.165 and p.174.
13. Twyford, 1880, p.132.
14. Cooper, 1911, p.256.

Appendix III: Escape Attempts

1. Many of these are taken from www.yorkcastleprison.org.uk and are searchable there. References are included for all others.
2. Cooper, 1911, p.95.
3. Ibid., p.98.
4. Ibid.
5. Ibid.
6. Knipe, 1868, p.5.
7. Morgan, 2022, p.126.
8. Oates, 2000, p.57.
9. Hargrove, 1818, p.235.
10. Knipe, 1868, p.82.
11. Hargrove, 1818, pp.235-237.
12. *Leeds Intelligencer*, Tuesday, 14 February 1769.
13. *Yorkshire Gazette*, Saturday, 22 June 1822.
14. Knipe, 1868. p.186.
15. YCA: *Gaoler's Journal: Volume 1*, p.1.
16. Ibid.
17. Ibid., p.2.
18. Ibid., p.4.
19. Ibid., p.6–7
20. Ibid., p.10.
21. Ibid., p.11.
22. *Hull Packet*, Friday, 17 January 1834.
23. YCA: *Gaoler's Journal: Volume 1*, p.15.
24. Ibid.
25. YCA: *Gaoler's Journal: Volume 4*, p.26.

Bibliography

Books

Addyman, Peter, *British Historic Towns Atlas – Volume V: York*, York Archaeological Trust, York, 2015
Anonymous, A letter to George Strickland, Esq in Reply to His Reasons for Not Pulling Down Clifford's Tower, in Making the Proposed Enlargement of York Castle, W. Storry, York, 1825
Anonymous, One night spent in the Condemned Hole, York Castle, in April, 1810, George Wilson, Leeds, 1815
B'nai B'rith Jewish Music Festival, Clifford's Tower commemoration, York, 15–18 March 1990: a programme and handbook of services, seminars and musical events in solemn commemoration of the 800th anniversary of the massacre in York Castle, York: 1190 Clifford's Tower 1990 Commemoration Committee, 1990
Baughman, T.H., *Pilgrims on the Ice: Robert Falcon Scott's First Antarctic Expedition*, University of Nebraska Press, London, 1999 (2008 new edition)
Beaumont, Robert, *The Railway King: Biography of George Hudson Railway Pioneer and Fraudster*, Headline Publishing, Chatham, 2002
Brodie, Allan, Crom, Jane., Davies, James O., *Behind Bars: The Hidden Architecture of England's Prisons*, English Heritage, Swindon, 1999
Cooper, T.P., *The History of the Castle of York*, Elliot Stock, London, 1911
Day, Chris, et al, *A History of Treason*, John Blake, London, 2022
Defoe, Daniel, *A Tour Thro' the Whole Island of Great Britain: Divided Into Circuites or Journeys – Giving a Particular and Entertaining Account of Whatever is Curious and Worth Observation – Volume 3*, S. Birt, London, 1748
Emsley, Clive, *Crime and Society in England 1750–1900*, Longman, London, 1996
Fry, Elizabeth, *Observations on the Visiting, Superintendence, and Government of Female Prisoners, John and Arthur Arch*, London, 1827
Gurney, Joseph John, *Notes on a Visit Made to Some of the Prisons in Scotland and the North of England, in Company with Elizabeth Fry*, Archibald Constable & Co., Edinburgh, 1819
Hargrove, William, *History and Description of the Ancient City of York: Comprising All the Most Interesting Information*, already published in Drake's Eboracum, William Alexander, York, 1818.
Hawkins, David T., *Bound For Australia: A Guide to the Records of Transported Convicts and Early Settlers*, The History Press, Stroud, 2012
Higginbotham, Peter, *The Prison Cookbook*, The History Press, Stroud, 2010
Higgs, Michelle, *Prison Life in Victorian England*, Tempus Publishing, Stroud, 2007

Holland, John, *Memoirs of the Life and Writings of James Montgomery: Including Selection from His Correspondence, Remains in Prose and Verse, and Conversations on Various Subjects*, Longman, London, 1854
Howard, John, *The State of the Prisons in England and Wales: With Preliminary Observations, and an Account of Some Foreign Prisons*, William Eyres, Warrington, 1777
Jones, Dan, *Magna Carta: The Making and Legacy of the Great Charter*, Head of Zeus Limited, London, 2014
Knipe, William, *Tyburn Tales: The Criminal Chronology of York Castle*, Simkin, Marshall, & Co., London, 1867 (2010 reprint)
Longley, Katharine, *Saint Margaret Clitherow*, Anthony Clarke, Wheathampstead, 1986
May, Trevor, *Victorian And Edwardian Prisons*, Shire Publications, Oxford, 2006
McLynn, Frank, *Crime and Punishment in Eighteenth-Century England*, Oxford, Oxford University Press, 1991
Montgomery, James, *The Poetical Works of James Montgomery: Volume 1*, Longman, London, 1841
Morgan, Tony, *Power, Treason and Plot in Tudor England: Margaret Clitherow an Elizabethan Saint*, Pen & Sword Books, Barnsley, 2022
Mortimer, Ian, *The Time Traveller's Guide to Medieval England*, Vintage (Penguin Random House), Dublin, 2008
Mortimer, Ian, *The Time Traveller's Guide to Elizabethan England*, Vintage (Penguin Random House), Dublin, 2012
Nield, James, *State of the Prisons in England, Scotland, and Wales, Extending to Various Places Therin Assigned, Not for the Debtors Only, But for Felons Also, and Other Less Criminal Offenders*, John Nichols and Son, London, 1809
Opperman, Averil Douglas, *While It Is Yet Day: The Story of Elizabeth Fry*, Orphans Publishing, Herefordshire, 2015
Peacock, A.J., *York in the Great War 1914–1918*, York Settlement Trust, York, 1993
Pugh, R.B., *Imprisonment in Medieval England*, Cambridge University Press, Cambridge, 1968
Priestley, Philip, *Victorian Prison Lives: English Prison Biography 1830–1914*, Pimlico, London, 1999
Priestley, Samantha, *The History of Gibbeting: Britain's Most Brutal Punishment*, Pen & Sword Books, Barnsley, 2020
Rennison, Eileen, Yorkshire Witches, Amberley, Stroud, 2012
Rotherham, Ian D., *Yorks Military Legacy*, Pen & Sword Books, Barnsley, 2017
Rubinstein, David, *Faithful to Ourselves and the Outside World: York Quakers During the Twentieth Century*, William Sessions, York, 2001
Rubinstein, David, *War Comes to York: Summer 1914*, Quack Books, York, 2010
Sharpe, J. A., *Crime in Early Modern England 1550–1750*, Longman, London, 1999
Siena, Kevin. *Prisons, Debtors, and Disease in the Early Eighteenth Century – Rotten Bodies: Class and Contagion in Eighteenth-Century Britain*, Yale University Press. London, 2019

Smollett, Tobias, *The Expedition of Humphry Clinker*, Oxford University Press, Oxford, 2009 (reissue)

Strickland, *George, Reasons for Not Pulling Down Clifford's Tower, In Making the Proposed Enlargement of York Castle*, J. and G. Todd, York, 1825

Storey, Neil R. *Prisons & Prisoners in Victorian Britain*, The History Press, Stroud, 2010

Twyford, A.W. and Griffiths, A., *Records of York Castle*, Griffith and Farran, London, 1880

Wade, Stephen, *Yorkshire Hangmen: The Lives and Careers of Hangmen Born or Working in Yorkshire from 1800 to the End of Hanging*, Wharncliffe Books/Pen & Sword Books, Barnsley, 2008

Webb, Simon, *A History of Torture in Britain*, Pen & Sword Books, Barnsley, 2018

Whittock, Martyn, *A Brief History of Life in the Middle Ages*, Robinson, London, 2009

Poems

Montgomery, James, *Poetical Works*, Longman, London, 1858

Articles in Periodicals

Chalkin, C.W., 'The Reconstruction of London's Prisons, 1770–1799: An Aspect of the Growth of Georgian London', *The London Journal*, 9:1, 21–34, 1983

Fawcett, Bill, 'The Nineteenth-Century Prison Buildings at York Castle', *York Historian 22*, York, 2005

Fawcett, Bill, 'The Municipal Offices at York Castle', *York Historian 23*, York, 2006

Leeman, Stephanie Adele, 'Stone Walls Do Not a Prison Make: The Debtor's Prison, York', *York Historian 11*, York, 1994

Oates, Jonathan, 'York and the Rebel Prisoners, 1745–1752', *York Historian 17*, York, 2000

Peacock, A.J., 'Conscience and Politics in York, 1914–1918', *York Historian 5*, York, 1984

Pitofsky, Alex, 'The Wardens Court Martial: James Oglethorpe and the Politics of Eighteenth-Century Prison Reform', *Eighteenth-Century Life: Volume 24*, winter 2000

Sheppard, Colin, 'Francis Drake and the Debtors' Prison', *York Historian 37*, York, 2020

Woodfine, Philip, 'Debtors, Prisons, and Petitions in Eighteenth-Century England', *Eighteenth Century Life: Volume 30, Number 2*, 2006

'Register of York Castle, 1730–1743', *Yorkshire Archaeological Journal: Volume, 25*, John Whitehead & Son, Leeds, 1920

Online

Patmore, Charles, A Missing Chapter from the History of York Castle: The Imprisonment of Quakers, accessed via https://ffhyork.weebly.com/york-castle.html

Rimmer, Jayne, Analysing the Skeletons Excavated at the former Female Prison: An Insight Report, 2016, https://research.yorkarchaeology.co.uk/wp-content/uploads/2023/08/AnalysingtheSkeletonsExcavatedattheformerFemalePrison-JayneRimmer.pdf https://archive.org

'York Castle', *An Inventory of the Historical Monuments in City of York – Volume 2: The Defences*, London, 1972, British History Online: https://www.british-history.ac.uk/rchme/york/vol2/pp57-86

https://www.britishmilitaryhistory.co.uk/military-provost-staff-corps/

https://www.longlongtrail.co.uk/soldiers/a-soldiers-life-1914-1918/military-crimes-1914-1918-british-army/british-army-military-prisons-detention-barracks-1914/

https://www.nam.ac.uk/explore/military-provost-staff-corps

https://www.spri.cam.ac.uk/museum/shackleton/biographies/Heald,_Willia
m_Lofthouse/https://www.yorkcastleprison.org.uk/visiting-the-prison.html

https://www.prisonhistory.org/prison/york-city-gaol/

Newspapers

Bradford Daily Telegraph
Derby Mercury
Halifax Guardian
Hull Daily Mail
Hull Packet
Leeds Intelligencer
Leeds Mercury
Northern Star
Sheffield Daily Telegraph
Stamford Mercury
Star (London)
Wakefield Advertiser & Gazette
Yorkshire Evening Post
Yorkshire Gazette
Yorkshire Post and *Leeds Intelligencer*
York Herald

Index

Acknowledgments

There isn't enough room to thank everyone who has helped me create this book individually; you all know who you are, so thank you.

I do need to thank the staff at all the archives that I have visited during my research for their help, for putting up with my questions, and for finding missing items for me. Especially those at the National Archives and York Explore.

Most of all, I need to thank the staff of York Museums Trust who, at all levels, have supported me, inspired me, challenged me and generally discussed things with me, without which this book would not have been anywhere near what it has become.